LIVING CORALS

LIVING CORALS

Photographs and Commentary
DOUGLAS FAULKNER

with text by

RICHARD CHESHER

Clarkson N. Potter, Inc. / Publishers New York
DISTRIBUTED BY CROWN PUBLISHERS, INC.

Library of Congress Cataloging in Publication Data
Faulkner, Douglas
Living Corals. Includes bibliographical references.
1. Corals. I. Chester, Richard H. II. Title.
QL377.C5C44 593'.6 79-14618 ISBN 0-517-53854-7

THIS IS A RUGGLES DE LATOUR, INC., BOOK • NEW YORK

CONTENTS

4

"The thing that is important is the thing that is not seen..."

 "Yes, I know..."

"It is just as it is with the flower. If you love a flower
that lives on a star, it is sweet to look at the sky
at night. All the stars are a-bloom with flowers..."

 "Yes, I know..."

"It is just as it is with the water. Because of the
pulley, and the rope, what you gave me to drink
was like music. You remember—how good it was."

 "Yes, I know..."

"And at night you will look up at the stars.
Where I live everything is so small that I cannot
show you where my star is to be found. It is better,
like that. My star will just be one of the stars, for you.
And so you will love to watch all the stars
in the heavens...They will all be your friends.
And, besides, I am going to make you a present..."

FOR SALLY
WILD FLOWERS

Juliet *I have forgot why I did call thee back*

Romeo *Let me stand here till thou remember it.*

Juliet *I shall forget, to have thee still stand there,*
Remembering how I love thy company.

Romeo *And I'll still stay, to have thee still forget,*
Forgetting any other home but this.

More than fifty millions of years ago, long, long, long before man built his first crude hut, a bizarre, intricate form of life began construction of the world's greatest edifices. Time passed and Earth was transformed. Battling against wind and wave, thwarted and harassed by the icy breath of a planet in the throes of the ice ages, this pulsing mass worked on and on and on. While mountains lifted and seas drained and continents floated over the face of the Earth, the diaphanous creatures perfected their craft. Half plant, half animal, the blind, unthinking workers toiled to the rhythms of the oceans, steadily building up and out. From ions dissolved in the sea, they shaped delicate microscopic crystals that were wedded to older tissues—day after day, millenium after millenium. The accretions grew into massive boulders, and slowly, very slowly, into giant walls and buttresses that could withstand the mighty poundings of the ocean.

I have lived on the largest of these structures, the Great Barrier Reef of Australia, 2300 kilometers long, one of the Earth's natural wonders. I have held my breath and slid down the underwater flanks of a beautiful Pacific atoll knowing it was only the exposed portion of a limestone monolith nearly two kilometers thick, its base resting on the peak of a long-submerged volcano.

Even as I write this, the keel of my 14-meter fiberglass cutter floats above the panorama of the reef. My vessel is a self-contained field laboratory outfitted with a full complement of diving equipment, electronic instrumentation—including a small computer, photographic gear, and a scientific library on microfilm. Modern technology has given us the means to reach those inaccessible and hazardous places where these coral megalopolises thrive. Today we can utilize aerial photography, satellite sensors, aqualungs, wet suits, underwater habitats, and deep submersibles. Finally, scientists have begun their explorations of the living world of coral in earnest.

This book comes at a time when mankind is awakening to a fearful realization of its own impact on the living Earth. In the crowded coral complex we discover how a galaxy of creatures have evolved intimate, indispensable, and thoroughly interdependent bonds.

And it is my earnest conviction that we may well discover that what is true for the coral community applies also to the community of man—if only we probe deeply enough.

The individual coral animal, the polyp, begins life as a tiny mass of cells called a planula larva that is ejected from the parent body and swept along by ocean currents until it reaches a suitable site where it can anchor itself permanently. In stony coral the skeleton begins to form soon after the larva is attached to a firm bottom. The larval cells flatten and the top forms into a dome with six or twelve—in some species as many as 24—tentacles sprouting from the body wall around a central disc and mouth. Soft coral polyps are equipped with eight feathery tentacles.

The polyp's sac-like body consists of an inside layer called the gastrodermis and an outside epidermis. The stomach is divided into pie-shaped sections by vertical sheets of tissue called mesenteries. These will later increase the stomach surface areas, house the reproductive organs, and support special tentacles. The coral secretes its skeleton from the lower portion of its body and lives within the little cup-shaped structure it manufactures. Stony corals produce a hard skeleton of calcium carbonate in the form of aragonite; soft corals make several different kinds of skeletons, some with horny stalks and others with fleshy lobes supported by needle-like spicules of calcium carbonate.

When the young polyp grows to a critical body mass, depending on the species involved, special cells accumulate in the disc and begin growing another polyp. It may first appear as a new mouth within the tentacles of the original polyp and then divide into look-alike twins. Or the polyp may appear outside the tentacles and organize its body parts from new growth. In any case, there are soon two polyps taking in sea water and converting it to crystals of calcium carbonate. Except for the unusual solitary corals such as the genus *Fungia*, corals do not move from place to place. They cement themselves onto the bottom and build from that spot. The layers of calcium carbonate are deposited one on top of the other, forming raised ridges, or septa, that grow in the spaces between the mesenteries. These raised partitions subdivide the gut and may increase its digestive surface area. In addition, when the coral polyp is disturbed, it can pull back into its stony cup or calice and the raised septa can prevent small animals from eating or crushing the polyp. Sometimes the stony septa ridges are topped with sharp spines and thorns that can poke through the retracted polyp's tissues to give bristly reception to a potential predator.

Soon, the two polyps become four, the four eight, and so on. The polyps remain connected with each other by a common skin that covers the whole group now called a colony. Together they produce a common skeleton, forming calices where the polyps live and bare spaces where connecting skeletal material spans the distance between the calices. In some species polyps are crowded together, each individual almost tentacle-to-tentacle with its neighbors. In other species the polyps are separated by broad spaces, the individuals living in raised calices on a broad plain of calcium carbonate. In brain corals, the polyps never really separate. Each one simply buds off a new mouth and oral disc and adds tentacles without partitioning itself from its neighbor. This forms long snake-like rows of polyps with the mouths alined in the bottom of valleys that form over the surface of the coral head in twisted convolutions that resemble a brain.

The rate of budding new polyps and thus expanding the size of the colony and its skeleton varies, depending on environmental conditions. For one thing, reef corals grow best when irradiated with sunlight. Their normally slow skeletal growth is cut in half on a cloudy day. And at night growth stops almost entirely. As a result, microscopic analysis of the skeleton shows daytime accumulations of rather porous limestone, and bands of denser areas where growth slowed in the dark.

Monthly and annual bands also appear in many corals, and biologists have been able to learn the age of many species of corals by studying thin sections of the skeleton and simply counting the bands like annular rings of a tree.

Our most definitive information on growth, however, comes from specimens of corals tagged in the water by diving scientists and then later, measured again. Massive domed heads, we have learned, can take a whole year to grow to millimeters in diameter. Branching corals are the most prolific growers, and tips of staghorn coral sprout 100 millimeters per year, with the fastest growth in the warm summer months.

Some corals never grow very large while others produce vast thickets or massive boulders. The golf-ball sized *Favia fragum*, for example, is a colony of polyps that never seems to get much bigger than 3 or 4 centimeters in diameter and often dies out seasonally. The Caribbean rose coral, *Manicina areolata*, seems limited to smaller than 20 centimeters and its growth rate, as in many animals, slows as it gets older.

Larger, more massive corals may live for hundreds of years forming colonies—called coral heads—reaching 3 or 4 meters in diameter. But even they seem to have a maximum age limit and eventually they slide into senescence and death. Fossil remains of corals and even a casual survey of any modern reef disclose that really large coral colonies are scarce and that almost all corals have a "typical" size that differs from one species to the next.

The classification of stony corals is, to a large extent, based on their complex skeletons. Scientists consider the shape and size of the colony, the size of the individual calices and the distance between them, the arrangement of the septa and the tiny, twisted rods of calcium carbonate crystal in the bottom of the calices, the density and fashion in which the crystals are laid down, and the kinds of ridges, spines and so on. Unfortunately, many of these characteristics are subject to variation, depending on environmental conditions.

Branching stony corals from a quiet lagoon, for example, tend to have longer, thinner, more delicate branches than those that are exposed to heavy wave action. And these differ in shape from colonies of the same species that grow in swift tidal currents. Sometimes a coral will form branches and other times, due to lack of sunlight or rough water, the same species may just expand over a substrate and form no branches at all.

The amount of silt in the water also can change the form of the colony as can the depth where it grows. Even the relative position of other life forms helps to mold the shape of the colony. Where leafy algae are abundant on reefs, for example, the corals may be forced to grow into pillars instead of domes. As a result, the classification of corals can be confusing, even for the expert.

Soft corals also begin life as a swimming larvae but, with few exceptions, they do not secrete massive calcium carbonate skeletons. These fleshy and tree-like corals can therefore grow more rapidly than the stony corals. Many of the Alcyonaria or octocorals are supported only by small needle-like spicules of calcium carbonate and hydraulic pressure within the fleshy tissues of the colony. Others, like the gorgonians or sea fans, have the polyps embedded in a soft layer of tissue that surrounds an internal, wood-like stalk. This stalk contains gorgonin, a protein resembling keratin which is used in the biological production of fingernails, hair, and hooves.

Zooxanthellae are plant-like in form, but animal in nature, and I sometimes facetiously think of them as "plantimals." When they are inside coral tissues they are in a cyst-like stage of their life cycle and measure some ten microns in diameter. Which means you could lay some 8000 or 9000 of them on the period at the end of this sentence. Under certain conditions, these cysts sprout whip-like flagella and flick off into the sea as dinoflagellates called *Gymnodinium microadriaticum.*

Corals, as animals, can survive without these tiny partners. In fact, hundreds of species do, especially those living in the deep parts of the sea where no light penetrates. Even corals that normally have zooxanthellae can survive without them, at least for a time, and specimens of reef corals kept in the dark for a month or so eject the zooxanthellae into the sea, probably to reduce the metabolic load imposed by plant cells in darkness. Once returned to sunlight, the corals become reinfested by zooxanthellae cells, perhaps by regrowing them from a few that were not ejected, or perhaps from dinoflagellates in the sea water.

Without zooxanthellae, corals do not build the huge tropical reefs. It is the zooxanthellae that contain the chlorophyll without which corals can neither secrete adequate amounts of calcium carbonate, nor live in such close proximity to one another.

The partnership between coral and zooxanthellae does not end with skeleton production. The coral provides a home for the tiny cysts, even arranges them within its own tissues so they receive the proper amount of sunlight. Also, corals provide carbon dioxide, nitrogenous ammonia, phosphates and trace minerals needed for the chlorophyll-producing zooxanthellae. These are poisonous byproducts of the coral's own metabolism and ridding fleshy tissues of these toxic substances is a major problem for all animals. But animal waste toxins can be the breath of life for plants. And, in exchange for coral fumes and ashes, zooxanthellae provide the coral with food and fuel. Within the zooxanthella's microscopic body are chloroplasts containing thousands of coin-shaped grana, each with tens of thousands of quantasome spheres, each made up of some 200 chlorophyll molecules. Each molecule is a daisy-shaped chain of atoms with a core of one magnesium atom and 136 associated carbon, hydrogen, oxygen, and nitrogen atoms that transform sunlight, carbon dioxide, and water into sugars and oxygen.

Coral colors are due more to plant pigments than to animal tissues. On a mass to mass ratio, corals are more plant than animal (sometimes as much as 3 to 1) with zooxanthellae packed into every nook and cranny among the coral cells. As a result, biologists who measure metabolism of reef corals during the day find that oxygen production (from the chloroplasts) outraces the oxygen consumption (of both coral and zooxanthellae), and coral heads actually release oxygen that may be used by small animals living in the crevices of the reef.

During the day the coral polyps rest quietly in their limestone calices while the zooxanthellae busily swap chemicals with them. At night, with the photosynthetic oxygen supply cut off by darkness, the polyp unfolds into the sea, inflates its tissues with water in a hydraulic yawn that plumps up the body wall and pops out tentacles. Its respiratory surface area is increased hundreds of times as it shifts from sleeping to hunting. Meanwhile, great clouds of zooplankton swim up from deep water to graze on the algal pastures of the shallows. The coral, like the animal it is, begins to feed. This is the same system that supports all life on the planet. For oxygen and sugars made by plants are the building blocks upon which the pyramid of Earth life is built. In corals, things are just a bit more compact.

How did the partnership of coral and zooxanthellae begin? In the case of every modern reef building coral the answer is simple. They inherited it. The young coral or planula larva, or in some cases, the egg, is furnished with zooxanthellae before leaving home. It is a kind of metabolic legacy from mother to child which capitalizes itself with compound interest as the polyp matures.

Planula larvae, according to C. M. Yonge, come swimming out of their mother's mouth with up to 7400 zooxanthellae cysts tucked here and there in their still somewhat unorganized bodies. These, no doubt, provide some sustenance on the journey to a new growing site, and they will form the basis for the population of plant cells that will be cultivated within the coral colony as it grows larger and larger.

The parent colony inherited its zooxanthellae from its mother, and so on, back into the ages for thousands, perhaps millions of generations. Even some protozoans have zooxanthellae, and perhaps corals evolved from a protozoan stock that already had algal "symbionts." For that matter, we might also question where the zooxanthellae got their amazing little chloroplasts.

Chloroplasts of protozoans and plants were considered for a long time to be cellular structures produced to house chlorophyll molecules. Lynn Margulis of Boston University suggested, however, that chloroplasts may once have been free-living cyanobacteria that were "captured" by protozoans and that later evolved into multicellular plants. Indeed, like zooxanthellae, chloroplasts do have their own DNA; they do reproduce themselves; they are transmitted as whole organelles in the cytoplasm of the egg, and they do closely resemble primitive cyanobacteria. Cellular organelles called mitochondria, found in all cells of all plants and animals, also have their own DNA, can reproduce themselves, and are transmitted from parent to child in the cytoplasm of the egg. Perhaps they, too, were once free-living bacteria that joined with larger organic molecules to form cells.

The only difference between "cytoplasmic genes"—as mitochondria and chloroplasts are assumed to be—and zooxanthellae is that zooxanthellae can and do live outside coral cells and can even swim freely in the sea. Chloroplasts and mitochondria have become so specialized they can no longer live (as far as I know) as the free bacteria they once may have been.

At night, when coral polyps expand, the appearance of the colony changes dramatically. Whereas the daytime coral colony, or head, seems smooth, at night the coral head is a forest of hungry mouths each surrounded by long waving tentacles. Some corals have really big tentacles, so large that they cannot retract into the skeleton, and these wave day and night. The largest of these are the 10-millimeter-thick arms that cover the disc of *Heliofungia actiniformis*. Corals with the smallest tentacles seem to have none at all, such as the lovely *Argarcia fragilis*, which uses only ciliary action to move fine detrital material over the soft tissues to the star-shaped mouths.

Most stony corals, however, have tentacles that are only a few millimeters long and are unbranched. The soft-branching octocorals all have eight tentacles per polyp and these are fringed like feathers to increase their filter feeding surface areas. The polyps themselves range from less than a millimeter in diameter to almost 60 centimeters long. Most coral polyps, however, are between one and ten millimeters in diameter. Usually, the larger the individual coral polyp the smaller the whole colony, with the very biggest polyps—*Fungia*, for example—not forming colonies at all.

The tentacles of most corals are slow and clumsy. They are coordinated by a loose association of nerves that entwine around the body wall cells. There is no real brain, and the muscles with their associated body wall cells look like a tightly packed bunch of protozoans captured in an electrochemical net. The nerve impulses flow both ways in the neurites, which must further impede coordination. In addition, the nerve impulse creeps along at only 20 centimeters per second compared to 12,500 per second in some fish and cephalopod nerves. To make matters even more interesting, the coral nerves don't respond to the first sensory signal. They have to warm up in a process called "facilitation," which means that each stimulus makes the next nerve transmission a little easier. A coral tentacle, therefore, does not get wriggling until a number of rapidly repeated stimuli course through it.

It is clear that corals could never catch anything with such a system. But they have a weapon that is not dependent on nerve impulses. A zooplankter need only brush a tentacle and, *blam*, it is harpooned instantly by stinging barbs. The high frequency struggling of the harpooned prey eventually attracts the attention of the coral. More stinging capsules, called nematocysts, are shot to secure the victim. Then, slowly, the tentacle stuffs the food into the polyp's mouth. Ciliary whipping, mucus slipping, and muscular contortions of the throat work the food into the coral's gut.

At the base of the mesenteries that divide the polyp gut into pie-shaped sections are long mesenterial filaments. These help with the larger food particles. They protrude from the coral's mouth and wind around legs or fins, shooting nematocyst barrages into the prey. Then the filaments tug the food into the gut where they penetrate the morsel with a digestive hug. They secrete a powerful protein enzyme that breaks down the food into polypeptide gruel. As the digestive process reduces the prey to slush, the internal filaments tighten, further assisting in the digestion. The organic slurry is then enfolded by amoeba-like arms that reach out from the cells lining the gut. These cells form food vacuoles much as do amoebas and complete the transformation of prey into coral metabolites. These are absorbed by wandering amoeboid cells and distributed by ciliary currents through the polyp's cells and into the passages leading to other polyps. In this way those that did not catch anything also get fed.

Any undigested products are pushed out of the coral by contractions of the body wall. Ciliary currents and waving tentacles cast this refuse off the surface of the colony while numerous commensal creatures, including everything from protozoans to fishes, lend a hand—or rather a mouth—in the cleaning process.

Now it is time to take a close look at the amazing interstitial cells that get together to bud new coral polyps off the existing ones.

Among the most important tricks in the interstitial's repertoire—certainly the most melodramatic—is the cell's transformation into a stinging nematocyst, the cnidarian supergun mentioned earlier. It was, in fact, the amazing nematocyst that allowed corals to become the evolutionary success they are. The production and operation of this weapon is a highly sophisticated and ingenious process.

Consider one of the small, rounded interstitial cells nestled quietly at the base of the body wall cells. It receives an "impulse" from "somewhere" that a

microbasic mastigophore is needed in Tentacle 5, Battery 3. The inactive cell mobilizes, feeds, and grows to twice its former size. The nuclear membrane vanishes, chromosomes aline, instructions flick from molecule to molecule and the body wall pinches inward, squeezing the cell into two parts. One resumes its inactive role. The other, weapon maker *extraordinaire*, moves off into the microscopic corridors of flowing protoplasm, through the tissues, headed for Tentacle 5. How it knows where to go, when to stop, is its own secret.

But motion is not a distraction from the construction of the needed gun because the cell begins making it even as it moves off. Scientists call the weapon maker a cnidoblast. Inside its cytoplasm millions of molecules link together with electrical affinity. A space forms and this becomes a chamber as the vacuole wall molecules hold back the granular life that is the cell. The chamber is filled with a fluid. The cell nucleus moves next to the chamber, the better to supervise things. Simultaneously, the cell ingests a goodly amount of nutrients and grows larger.

From the code inscribed in its genes, the nucleus assembles and discharges chemical messengers which somehow move through the cell to the ribosomes. These are chemical factories that scan the messenger RNA molecules, determine what protein is needed, and assemble the required atoms into long-chain molecules that are then shipped into the now firmly established vacuole. An inner and then an outer wall of perfectly arranged molecules lines the chamber, grown in the way all crystals are grown, by selective attachment of the special molecules one to the next. The walls are smooth, transparent, and very strong.

After the gun case has been constructed, the gun itself crystallizes inside the case. It is not a simple thing. The crystal grows as a single entity, without seams, from the inner chamber wall. It is a long coiled tube armed with thousands of sharp spines. Chemical activity continues, and complex, specialized supermolecules are carefully stuffed into the chamber *through the nearly impermeable wall*. Finally, the tiny capsule is adjusted and moved into the leading half of the cell.

While accomplishing all this chemistry, the weapon making cell continuously alters the electrical potential of its own body wall; its protoplasm slides out to form pseudopods that move the entire factory through the coral tissues until it reaches Tentacle 5, Battery 3. Here, numerous other gun emplacements surround the weapon maker. In addition to other microbasic mastigophores, there are spirocysts to coil around corepod hairs and glue guns in the form of spiny holotrichous isorhizas. The entrenched gunners are moved aside by the new weapon cell.

A pseudopod snakes between the other cells to the layer of mesogloea in the tentacle wall. The mesogloea is a chitinous kind of jelly that holds the inner and outer tissues together. The cnidoblast's pseudopod anchors itself in this matrix and its cellular wall electrifies into a tough sheath to hold things in place. The nematocyst capsule is hefted round to lay against the cell wall on the outside of the tentacle where the gunner makes a small cone that sticks out into the open sea. Then, on top of the cone, the gunner extends a flexible, hair trigger, a bristle called a cnidocil. Tough supporting fibers grow inside the gunner's cells attaching the nematocyst to the anchoring stalk and supporting the installation.

The gun is now in position to fire.

Nematocysts are abundant on the tentacles, mesenterial filaments, and even in the stomach or body wall and the surface of the mouth. There must be thousands, perhaps hundreds of thousands of these weapons on each polyp. Fortunately, the polyp does not have to coordinate all these guns with its primitive nerve plexus: The guns operate for themselves. They are chemosensitive to the coral's hormones. Nematocysts are metabolically expensive to produce. The cnidoblast cell dies when the gun is fired, and so the cnidoblast holds fire until it is needed. Exactly how the cell knows when to fire has frustrated zoologists since the late 1800s. Scientists have poked the triggers with glass rods and nothing happened. They have doused them with chemicals, heated them, cooled them, flooded them wth juices from coral prey, shocked them and subjected them to a barrage of tests. The gun only fired when the nematocyst was ruptured or damaged.

The gunner patiently waits for the right conditions. While it waits, commensal protozoans bump clumsily into the ominous trigger and small fishes who live on the surface of the coral nestle happily in the nematocyst-armed tentacles. Isopods charge hither and yon unconcerned by the possibility of being blasted. Presumably, these little commensals have learned the secret chemical or tactile password that keeps the gunner from firing.

Even more amazing are some flatworms and shell-less mollusks who, while feeding on hydroids and corals, capture the dangerous weapons for their own use. They not only keep the gunners from firing when ingested, but they sort out the cnidoblasts from the other cells and their own amoeboid cells march the prisoners up to exposed dorsal tissues where the cnidoblasts are again put on guard duty. If a fish tries to eat the flatworm or the sea slug, the gunners blast away at the soft lining of the fish's mouth. This nematocyst recycling by flatworms was demonstrated in the 1920s when it was discovered that *Microstomum* went looking for hydras only when it needed more nematocysts. Normally, the flatworm would refuse to eat hydras when it had an adequate complement of stinging cells.

When the coral polyp is hungry, the gunnery sections are alerted. Then, should appropriate stimuli such as a live copepod, brush the tiny trigger, the gun fires. The guns are small, but the effects are potent. The average coral nematocyst is less than 50 microns in diameter. Some nematocysts are much larger, the record being held by a floating species called *Halistemma* that has 1.12-millimeter nematocysts with a tube several millimeters long coiled inside. The nematocysts of the infamous Australian Sea Wasp can pierce human skin and kill unwary bathers, and those fire coral (*Millepora*) cause painful burn-like stinging. Generally, however, coral nematocysts are too small to penetrate human skin.

Smaller creatures, however, are easy prey for these weapons. The instant the trigger fires, an electrochemical reaction changes the lattice of the nematocyst wall and water from the gunner's cytoplasm rushes into the chamber. The resulting hydraulic pressure pops open a molecular trap door just over the place where the coiled tube joins the inner capsule wall. The tube then turns inside out as it explosively shoots out of the opening. You can visualize the process by imagining a balloon with part of its wall extended into a long finger which is pushed inside. When the balloon is squeezed, the finger unfurls, inside out, with a pop. A sticky substance, combined with the high muzzle velocity and the sharp leading edge of the unfurling tube, gives the nematocyst real penetrating power. It needles right through the chitinous armor of its prey and continues to unravel deep into the victim's tissue. When the tube is unfurled, it becomes a long hypodermic needle. More water surges into the capsule and a virulent nerve toxin jets through the narrow-bore tube into the prey.

The gunner cell, anchored in its emplacement, holds onto the nematocyst while the prey struggles. Once the prey is subdued by the poison and safely on its way into the gut, the gunner gives up its capsule and is consumed by its neighboring cells. Meanwhile, impulses are somehow sent to another interstitial cell that a new microbasic mastigophore gun is required in Tentacle 5, Battery 3. Within 48 hours, it will be there, ready for action.

All of this means that the sophistication of corals is at a cellular level. The nematocysts and their gunners are the real food getters, and not the tentacles that merely serve as platforms for the battery emplacements and later as a big, uncoordinated arm to push food in the general direction of the mouth.

If all this feeding action sounds a bit uncoordinated and unlikely to succeed, it also looks that way when you observe it. The feeding success rate of corals is so poor that a sometimes heated debate has developed among biologists over the role of eating in coral nutrition. Some coral biologists insist that corals get all the food they need from the zooxanthellae; others maintain that corals are primarily plankton feeders. The latter group, to prove their point, fed plankton to corals and watched them devour it with obviously practiced ability. They point to the active mesenterial filaments and the perfectly workable tentacles as sure evidence that corals feed on plankton regularly. The opposing biologists agree that such conclusions seem reasonable, but after examining coral after coral in nature, even when collected at night, they can't find any plankton remains in coral guts.

The pro-plankton school argues that digestion is very rapid and perhaps corals only feed at certain periods during the night. Nobody has managed to catch them in their feeding act, they say, because nobody wants to collect them at midnight.

The anti-planktonists meanwhile wonder why zooxanthellae stay in the corals at all when they could just as well use the flagella they keep hidden in their chromosomes to whip off into the sea. What are zooxanthellae for, if not to feed the corals? A great deal of time and energy was spent showing that, indeed, zooxanthellae make sugars and metabolites that the corals utilize in their own bodies.

The obvious conclusion, it seems to me, is that both are right. Corals do feed on plankton, but not very often, and not very much, and not very well. Having spent many hours—day and night—watching corals, I have noticed two things: first, stony corals are not really designed as plankton feeders; they actually feed on something else entirely. Second, they can eat plankton, but I've never caught them doing it without outside help.

The only time I have ever seen corals capture plankton was when the corals had an abundance of plankton actually bombarding them, the abundance being entirely my doing. I shined my night light just off to the side of the coral head. The light attracted plankton like a porch light attracts flying insects.

Under such circumstances, I have watched for more than an hour as larval fish, polycheate worms, copepods, crab larvae, and rapidly moving things too small and too fast for me to identify ran headlong into the outstretched tentacles of more than twenty species of corals. Blinded by my light, the small animals crashed into the waving tentacles and then swam off unharmed. The corals themselves, just on the edge of my beam, did not seem to react to my man-made photons. In such unnatural situations I have seen corals catch and hold onto prey and even move them into their mouths. I have also, on occasion, seen their captured morsels stolen from them by other animals.

From such observations, I conclude that stony corals are not efficient plankton feeders and seldom capture the fast dodging critters whose sophisticated sensory gear is alert for just such things as tentacles. In fact, with the exception of such branching corals as *Acropora*, corals are not even approximately the right configuration for filter feeding, their surfaces usually lying horizontal, the polyps pointed upward toward the surface of the water. This feature increases with depth so that many species that form rounded colonies in shallow water, grow into big, flattened plates deeper on the reef. Their morphology seems designed to feed from above; notably from the sun and from the organic debris that descends upon the sea floor.

True filter feeding animals, such as soft corals, hydroids, feather stars, basket stars, and so on, erect a network of some kind, or else suck sea water into their feeding aparatus. Most stony corals don't follow that pattern and, while they are opportunistic enough to eat a plankter that bumps into a tentacle, their primary source of "food" is, no doubt, the zooxanthellae's busy solar energy factories.

Such production, however, requires many trace elements, especially phosphates and nitrates. And, as a good farmer, the coral is required to provide these to the plant cells within its tissues. An occasional planktonic animal provides a coral with some of the necessary phosphates and nitrates, but most of the needed minerals seems to come from fish.

One morning, during the Tektite II expedition to the coral reefs of the Virgin Islands, I made an interesting discovery. I had, for many nights, been venturing from the subsea habitat to observe corals. I surveyed one coral head after the other, trying to find a polyp in the act of eating plankton. It was a frustrating task and, other than the plankton concentrated by my night light or actually stuffed into the coral's tentacles by my fingers, I never found them with dinner in their tentacular clutches. But on this morning I actually witnessed a coral eating. In the daylight! And it was not eating a struggling animal; it was eating a fish fecal pellet! Specifically, it was the excrement from a *Caranx ruber*, one of a school overhead. I watched as another pellet landed on a colony of *Montastraea cavernosa*. Tentacles grabbed it and, after a few minutes, the pellet vanished into the polyp's mouth. Excited by my first observation of coral ingestion, I examined all the corals in the vicinity and quickly tallied 23 pellets being eaten by 11 species of corals.

During the day, many species of fish form dense schools that hover over the coral reef. At night, these move off into nearby sand and grass areas to feed. When they return to their daytime resting places, they digest their food and neatly package the remains in mucoid pellets which they drop onto all those hungry little coral mouths.

Even though the pellets have little caloric value, they are loaded with phosphates and nitrates much as are bird droppings. It makes perfect zooxanthellae fertilizer. Schooling fish form a giant, living net above the reef, catching planktonic animals and providing a constant rain of fecal pellets to fertilize the coral "gardens."

Nematocyst-laden tentacles and the mesenterial filaments are normally retracted into the coral tissue during the day. But when a fish pellet bumps down on the surface of a coral, the disc nematocysts zap it with harpoons and tentacles pop out to guide the catch into the mouth. I was especially impressed with the way brain corals trap such pellets. Their rippled valleys and walls form a natural sluice to trap the cylindrical pellets as they waft back and forth in the surge from the ocean waves. The instant a pellet lands in a valley (where the mouths are) of *Diploria labyrinthiformis*, the coral ingests a large amount of water, swelling the sides of the valley so they clamp shut over the fecal pellet within 20 to 40 seconds. Inside the puckered valley walls, mouths gape and mesenterial filaments writhe until the pellet is gone. In 20 minutes or so, the coral is again ready for another pellet.

I collected fecal pellets and dropped them onto every species of coral I could find. With the exception of the branching coral (*Acropora cervicornis*) and the soft corals, every species of stony coral on the reef gobbled them up. It was a far more efficient performance than the clumsy attempts to capture zooplankton that I had watched at night.

The coral reef can thus be seen as a giant protoplasmic web. The fish form a catchment system that extends like a great fan over the water column and sweeps out into the sand and grass beds. The corals are an organic depository that also grows the very substrate over which the fish hover. Thus, the coral provides a habitat for grazing stocks of fish, and uses the fertilizer pellets from the fish to grow and cultivate its own zooxanthellae "plants" to feed itself. A wonderfully efficient arrangement, and one that has made possible the growth of the massive coral reef structures we see today.

Reproduction begins with the interstitial cells. Responding to some unknown signal—the gravitational pull of the moon, the daily exposure to the sun, the relative abundance of food—the interstitial cells "decide" to become sex cells. They move through the coral tissues until they reach the area just behind the mesenterial filaments. This is a choice location where they can be first to get food. Later it will provide an exit out of the coral body.

Here, surrounded by zooxanthellae and coral cells, the interstitial cells undergo meiosis, resulting in the formation of sex cells, eggs or sperm, each with only half the genetic information needed to build a new coral.

Some coral colonies produce sperm, others make eggs. Some colonies make sperm one time and eggs the next and are called protandric. Others make eggs and sperm at the same time and are called hermaphroditic.

Sperm cells, when ripe, burst through the coral tissues into the gut and are ejected through the polyp's mouth into the sea. This is a concerted effort, a real ejaculation, triggered by environmental signals. Of the millions upon millions of sperm cells released into the ocean, only a few survive to find an egg.

Some species of corals may eject the passive eggs into the sea by the millions. Smoky yellow clouds of eggs merge with white mists of sperm over the reef. Most stony corals retain the eggs behind the mesenterial edges where they wait patiently for sperm cells to answer their chemical siren call. Responsive sperm cells wiggle into the mouths of the gravid coral polyps, push through the thin membranes covering the eggs, and dive into the cytoplasmic spheres. The DNA molecules of egg and sperm unite to become zygote, blastual, gastrula, and finally a ciliated planula larva which swims out into the sea.

Armed only with primitive abilities to sense light, temperature, metabolites and textures, the planula larva joins millions of others like itself rising from the parent corals into the sea where ocean currents whisk it away. It is a largely futile try at life. Hundreds of millions of young planulae start out from each large coral colony every year. Perhaps only one in a million ever finds shallow water again. Only one in a million will not be eaten on the long blind swim through a sea alive with animals that find planula succulent prey. And most of those that do make it will be snared or sieved out of the water by filter feeding beasts when they attempt to "land." Of those that do find a place to settle, most of them will perish from some passing predator, or they will be overgrown by algae or sponges or soft corals or other hard corals.

Luckily, a few make it to the size critical for survival, and thus begin another link in the coral chain of life.

Now that we have a little more understanding of the strange plant and animal brew that is living coral, we can examine the living assemblage called a coral reef. We accepted the individual coral polyp as a living entity, and we considered the whole colony formed by asexual budding a part of a single organism. But in reality, it isn't. It is made of numerous individual polyps, each of which is composed of a dozen or so different kinds of cells. Some of these cells can live and move on their own as plants or protozoans. On the surface of the living coral tissue are ciliate protozoans, fishes, flatworms and nematodes, not to mention bacteria and viruses that live only on certain species of corals. This multitude of "individuals" that lives inside and outside the coral tissue and even below it, growing in its skeleton, all works as a whole, and can be considered as a single superorganism. There is no definite line between the polyp and the other "cells" that form the coral body. They are all one great living unit. Even more important, there is no dividing line between the single coral head or colony and the other animals of the reef complex as life welds one "creature" to the next in food chains, respiratory chains, reproductive chains, growth chains. So when examining living corals, we must naturally consider all of the symbionts, predators, parasites, competitors.

Biologists have long viewed coral reefs as a "complex" living unit, and have measured their respiration and metabolism. By positioning ships upcurrent and downcurrent, they have been able to measure the phosphates, nitrates, and oxygen in the sea water that flushes through the system.

Paleontologists and geologists, while aware that the individual coral heads are discrete species, also see coral reefs as "species" and they study the growth of the entire assembly of animals over geologic ages by drilling into the skeletal remains of these titans.

From this larger perspective, we see the multitude of reef creatures, the fish, sponges, mollusks, nematodes, sharks, birds, men, as part of a single great organism; cells, like the cells of a coral polyp, move on their own, in response to rhythms of the whole reef entity, and play individual, if redundant, roles. As wind and tidal currents circulate the vast potential of sea water through the arteries and capillaries of the coral reef, the ocean becomes a living blood from which the host of cells may extract what nutrients and chemical elements they need to go on living and growing. The skeletons of corals, coralline algae, echinoderms, mollusks, and fishes all form the "bones" of the coral reef, carefully sculptured to obtain proper orientation to the sea currents, wonderfully grown into a porous structure of caves and tunnels as complex as any circulatory or lymph system in any living creature.

Let us continue our introduction to coral reef biology from this higher perspective, perceiving the fish as motile feeding extensions of the living coral reef, the algae as an organic cement, echinoderms as maintenance cells that cleanse the tissues. Further on, I will examine the vast movements and behavior of the whole complex as the reef extends ponderously through the millennia.

Just as a coral polyp has amoeboid cells that move freely through its body, distributing food, absorbing intruders, clearing away wastes, so the coral reef has mobile "cells" that perform similar functions. Thousands of species of fish, echinoderms, annelid worms, mollusks, crustaceans, pycnogonids, protozoans, flatworms, nematodes and so on—a dazzling display of creepy crawlers and flashy swimmers—are eternally trimming here, adding there, keeping the giant organization in prime condition.

Tracing the relations among all these moving creatures and the corals is an impossible task, but some of the pieces fit easily together.

One morning I dropped anchor next to a large patch reef off the southern coast of Eleuthera in the Bahama Islands. The water was clear and I could see the yellow and orange of the shallower corals even before I leaped in with mask and flippers. It was a magnificently healthy reef with the coral growth as prolific and diverse as any I had seen. It was surprising, actually, because I had just come from a patch reef not 100 meters away that was very unhealthy looking. While the healthy reef swarmed with a great variety of fish and invertebrates, the unhealthy one had a bleak look. It was covered with many large dead corals, and the few remaining smaller ones were being smothered by a thick coating of a broad-leafed algae.

A comparison of both reefs showed one major difference: sea urchins. The healthy reef was loaded with sea urchins. Long, black spined *Diadema*, green *Echinometra*, small *Lytechinus*, all tucked away in the coral waiting for night. The other reef had no urchins at all, not even small ones.

Sea urchins make up the maintenance crew that keeps algae from becoming too abundant on the reef. Fish, for some reason, seem to leave the large green fronds alone. Without the sea urchins, the algae simply take over, growing everywhere and smothering the small coral colonies.

Sea urchins also play a vital role in helping corals to heal wounds. Torn coral tissue can become infected with a blue-green alga. The tiny algal threads grow in huge numbers forming a blue-green mat of fibers that spreads over an infected coral head like a cancer. Such growths, perhaps over a period of months, attack the living coral tissues until the whole colony is destroyed. At night, the *Diadema* bristle forth like an army of urban street cleaners. The urchins have hydraulically controlled tube feet—several hundreds of them—tipped with suction cups. These carry the spherical animals up vertical coral heads, along the roofs of caves, anywhere, in their endless search for algae. Many times I've come upon a big black *Diadema* carefully eating away the infectious blue green algae from small wounds on the coral reef. When urchins clean off the area they do so completely, even removing the infected part of the coral skeleton.

There was, however, no obvious reason why one

reef had urchins and the other did not. We found many Bahamian reefs without urchins and, on one of them, we planted a colony of *Diadema* to see if we could catch the urchin-eater at work. The black urchins fell to work at once gobbling up the algae, but the next morning half of the population of *Diadema* was gone. A few scattered spines and bits of broken urchin plates were all that remained. Although we dived day and night, we never managed to find out what was eating the urchins. Whatever it was—probably a large fish—it did an efficient job; a week later there were no more urchins on the experimental reef.

The problem, at least off Cape Eleuthera, did not seem to be man-related, and it must have been going on for some time as the corals themselves had altered their shape under the influence of the algal fronds. Instead of forming rounded, domed colonies, many of the corals formed tall pillars, being unable to grow out to the side because of the fringe of algae that crowded in on them.

In Florida, I found a similar lack of *Diadema* on a similar algal-choked patch reef. Just south of the famous Pennekamp State Park, Hen and Chickens Reef is a massive ruin compared to what it was when I went to graduate school. As late as 1965 it was a healthy reef with lush coral, fish, and invertebrate growth. Ten years later it was a mess. Algae grew everywhere and the blue-green algal infection, so deadly to corals, was evident on the few remaining live coral heads. There had been a great deal of controversy over what killed Hen and Chickens. To me, the answer seems obvious. The lack of *Diadema*, usually very common on Florida patch reefs, had caused the reef to die in a green tide of algae. But what caused the elimination of the sea urchins? And what has kept them off the reef for ten years? We will come back to sea urchins and patch reefs later, but now let us continue with reef "cells" of another sort.

One night, in sixty feet of water on the outer edge of a reef in the Virgin Islands, I watched a coral attempt to swallow a small fish I had given it to eat. I happened to notice the serpentine arm of a brittle starfish projecting from a crevice and resting on the coral tissues. It was pointed right at the little fish and, just as I wondered if the brittle star could feel the vibrations of

the fish through the coral flesh, another arm appeared. Then still another snaked into view followed by a green, disk-shaped body with red polka dots and two more arms carried the starfish rapidly over the coral. The starfish whipped one of its arms over the fish, yanked it out of the coral's tentacles, and lurched back to its cave with the fish packed under one arm like a lunch box.

Since then, I have seen many serpentine brittle star legs lying quietly on the surface of corals at night. Perhaps they are using the corals as a living food web—spider fashion—just as corals use fish as a living food catchment system.

I mention this to show how the food flows from one part of the reef animal to another, just as the food flows from one polyp to another in a coral colony. For whatever is captured from the open sea forms organic molecules that enrich the greater body of the reef: a body with millions upon millions of mouths collecting its food from the sea just as your billions of body cells capture their food from your own blood.

There are few spaces within coral tissues not occupied by a working cell. Similarly, there are few habitable areas on the coral reef that are not occupied by some creature. There is a kind of harmony in both cells and reef animals, with each component doing its own thing in concert with all the others. This means that control systems must exist to prevent one "cell" from being cancerous and outdoing the others. And these control systems make the crowded life on the sea floor seem, at times, a giant battle for space, sunlight, and a solid foundation.

Unlike the cells in their own bodies that are quite orderly in their growth, coral colonies are not always content to accept their alloted space. Thus, two coral heads may settle near one another and then grow together. When they meet, they compete. It is a "king of the hill" kind of battle in which one will dominate the territory. I once saw two brain corals waging furious battle on the wreck of a steel ship in the Dry Tortugas. Where the two colonies met they had grown into a broad, flattened battle zone. They were lashing out at each other with their heavy-duty mesenterial filaments. These extruded from each colony and were thrust into their opponent's tissues. They were digesting each other. The leading rows of polyps of both colonies had ejected their zooxanthellae (as corals under stress are apt to do) and were a colorless, bloated mass of dying tissue.

A year later I returned to the wreck and the battle. They were still fighting. I guess such fights can go on for a long time because digesting your opponent is a way to gain strength to go on fighting and, since both colonies were about the same size, they had equal powers of endurance. Even so, one colony had clearly won and was overgrowing the other, killing it by cutting off sun and sea with an expanding ledge of coral skeleton.

Many species of corals maintain their growing room by beating off encroaching organisms with nematocyst-laden tentacles, or—as their neighbors grow within reach—by simply digesting them with mesenterial filaments. These filaments seem capable of a respectable boarding-house reach and the growing zone around coral colonies is at least a centimeter or so in smaller polyped corals, up to 8 or 9 centimeters in big-polyped species.

Having nematocysts and rope-like filaments with which to eat your neighbors does not work in all cases. The rapidly branching corals, for example, grow into tall thickets that advance steadily along the reef flats growing high above the massive corals. From their elevated position, they cut off the sunlight and water supply to the corals in their growth path, in effect starving them out and then simply growing over the dead skeletons.

I recall one lonely star coral boulder awash in a thicket of staghorn coral. By peering down into the orange thicket of staghorn coral around the yellow—green star coral, I could see the shapes of smaller corals that had long since smothered. The sides of the star coral were already dead. Only the top surface still lived in the sunlight while the staghorn branches lapped at the living tissues like frozen crystal flames.

Soft corals, because they do not need to secrete such large skeletons, grow faster than hard corals. Generally, however, soft corals form bushy structures that lift the polyps high into the sea. They do not directly compete with the massive reef building corals, even though they may grow alongside of them. Some soft corals, however, find it easier to grow over the top of coral skeletons than to make their own. These have developed a special layer of tissue that seems immune to nematocyst blasts or digestive corrosion. This tissue forms a crust that allows the soft coral to overgrow corals with ease. Thus, on some reefs, the encrusting tissues of *Erythropodium caribaeorum* can be seen as a brownish-purple blanket over what used to be massive star corals, brain corals, and so on. It is a kind of skeletal piracy that may help regulate coral growth on the reef while giving the enterprising soft corals a place in the sun. Sponges, like the chicken liver, *Chondrilla nucula*, can also overgrow coral colonies, blocking the light and life from the coral.

As long as the whole reef animal is "healthy" these little ebbs and flows of life seem orderly and beneficial to the organism. A balance is maintained by echinoderms that consume the algae, sponges, and the soft corals that are more easily eaten than stony corals. Thus, the populations of each seem somehow stable.

The skeleton of the coral is also subject to decay. Coral skeletons are chock-a-block full of animals. Many species of clionid sponges, for example, secrete acids that help their amoeboid cells chip away the delicate coral crystals, dissolving them to sea water again. In the vacated space the sponges form a network of tunnels, gradually making the coral reef more and more porous. While tunneling into coral, the sponges circulate water through their bodies and into the coral crevices, in effect behaving like both heart and blood vessels for the reef. A multitude of other organisms tunnel into the coral colony, constructing a capillary system for the reef.

Lithophaga (rock-eater) is a clam that drills almost perfectly circular tunnels through coral skeletons. Special glands on the edge of the clam's mantle secrete an acid mucus that softens the coral while the rasp-like edges of the shells twist and turn, wearing away the aragonite. In some wave-beaten areas where the coral is dense and cemented with smooth algal mortar, sea urchins grind away at the coral with crystal teeth, carving a niche for themselves in the surf zone and providing homes for a multitude of other creatures.

The slow dissolving, drilling, chewing and tunneling is a normal and essential part of the reef. It creates space for hundreds of species of small animals that form an important base for the "in house" animal food chain. Worms, foraminiferans, ciliates, isopods graze on bacteria, diatoms, protozoans and algae, and themselves provide nutrition for crabs, shrimp, lobsters, larger worms, and fish. A layer of diverse creatures (bryozoans, ascidians, hydroids, stylasterid corals, sponges) lines the sea-washed caves and tunnels with firmly anchored filter-feeding bodies. Each hidden animal of the reef quietly finds nutrients in the passing ocean water and turns these into organic tissue. When the reef animals spawn, the long process of capturing nutrients from the sea is inverted and their bodies yield up their accumulations of organic fuel in the form of swimming larvae. Trochophore larvae, tadpole larvae, planula larvae, eggs and sperm by the billions are wafted into the sea from the reef tunnels. Most larvae are immediately consumed by the surface filter feeders—the soft corals and crinoids, small fishes, worms— so they in turn can provide the food for larger fishes, invertebrates, reptiles, birds, mammals.

Smaller coral skeletons are completely devoured by the destructive actions of the rock-eaters but, generally, the tunneling animals seem to maintain a balance, and the reef continues to live and grow.

Living corals, being thin watery blankets of flesh embedded in aragonite boulders, are hard to eat. In addition, since more than half their biomass is made of plant tissue, the carnivorous coral feeder will have to consume about 50 percent plant tissue, tissue that it might not be able to digest. Herbivorous animals are faced with the difficult task of grinding through aragonite to get only a small percentage of plant tissue. As a result, coral has prospered in an environment relatively free from major predation.

Some fish—the butterfly fish, for example—with tiny mouths and vast determination, nibble all day long at exposed coral tentacles and seem to thrive on such fare. Another creature is a worm with bristles that can sting human flesh. This worm, called the bristle worm or *Hermodice carunculata*, finds a branch of coral the right size and shape and swallows it. The worm is normally only a centimeter or less in diameter and about 20 centimeters long, but its whole front ends opens up into a truly impressive mouth that can engorge its way over a 4-centimeter-thick branch of razor sharp coral cups for some 10 or 15 centimeters. His body wall becomes a mere iridescent sheen through which you can see the raised coral cups. When the worm is finished, the branch is a lifeless white. A few other animals—the parrot fish and some species of crabs and shrimps—manage to eat coral, but not as a regular diet. They pose no threat to reef survival.

To my knowledge, there is only one really successful coral predator. With sixteen arms, long ultrasharp poisonous spines, and a beautiful pattern of red and green, *Acanthaster planci*, the crown-of-thorns starfish, is the prolific coral feeder.

The starfish feeds by extruding its stomach out of its mouth and spreading it like a blanket over the polyps. It digests the coral tissues—plant, animal, and commensals—right in their little coral cups. When the coral is only a delicious organic soup, the starfish absorbs the nutrients into its fleshy, orange-colored stomach. After a few hours of feeding, the *Acanthaster* sucks in its tummy and glides off leaving behind a glowing white patch of coral skeleton which, within 48 hours, is coated with a grey-green algae. Under normal conditions, however, the crown-of-thorns starfish is not a problem—just one more biological control mechanism.

Scientists describe four "kinds" of reefs: atolls, barrier reefs, fringing reefs, and patch reefs. As with "kinds" or types of animals, reefs sometimes have quite different genetic origins. Some have one group of corals dominating the structure; others will have different species in the same niches. Atlantic atolls, for example, are formed by entirely different species, and they often begin quite differently from Pacific reefs. But the fundamental idea of the reef and its relation with the sea are the same everywhere. The basic reef designs are found over their whole global distribution between the tropics of Cancer and Capricorn.

The shapes of reefs, of course, reflect their earthly foundation. They are determined by the original topography of the rock on which the corals began, the ocean currents, and what lies beyond the edge of the sea (continental reefs differing greatly from mid-ocean reefs in overall milieu). The circular body of atolls may form on top of submerged sand banks, as Alacran Reef in the Gulf of Mexico, or on the peaks of long dead volcanoes, as most Pacific atolls. Their final structure depends on the gross environmental parameters that surround them as they grow.

Geologists have debated the formation of atolls for years, ever since Charles Darwin examined their "growth stages" in various parts of the Pacific. According to Darwin, the magnificent circular coral atolls began on the flanks of marine volcanoes. These cone-shaped mountains were built up from the ocean floor perhaps a hundred million years ago. After their molten youth, the mountains were assaulted by rain, wind, and gravity, and they began to compact and slowly to subside beneath the sea. At some point, about 50 million years ago, some of them became encircled by a growth of stony corals. Even then corals were not newly evolved organisms; dating back another 100 million years to the Jurassic period when they evolved from the feeble reef corals of the Triassic.

But the mountains, like the one that later was named Enewetak, "came alive" as a coral reef creature only fifty million years ago when the volcano finally sank beneath the long Pacific swells. Then the fringing coral reef became a great circular ring in the sea. While it began as a fringing skirt around the sinking mountain, it gradually developed into an upward growing ring as the volcano sank lower and lower.

Enewetak's volcano sank at the rate of 51.9 meters per million years throughout the Eocene. It slowly steadied to 39.6 meters per million years in the Miocene and, some ten million years ago, it slowed to 15.2 meters per million years. The subsidence of the volcano, of course, lowered the coral's substrate year by year and the whole structure would have vanished completely were it not for the steady upward growth of the great coral city. Millimeter by millimeter, as the earth sank, the coral organism built its greater body from sea water to keep within reach of the sun.

Actually, the coral probably could have grown faster, but limited by the mirrored interface of sea and sky, it was held just beneath the low tide mark, easily keeping pace with the slowly sinking volcano. The subsidence of the mountain, in fact, was an earthly "regula-tor" for the atoll's growth. In times when the mountain halted its decline, the coral stopped its megagrowth, balanced by cycles of construction and destruction until the mountain subsided further into the deep.

Today, such remarkable coral atolls as Bikini, Enewetak, Kwajalein, Wotje, and Ailuk are the oldest living beings on earth. So old, yet continually young and growing. Today, Enewetak's great skeleton reaches down 1.25 kilometers into the sea to rest on a volcano whose crest is 3.2 kilometers above the sea floor. Kwajalein, majestic in its antiquity, sits atop a 1.98-kilometer-high skeleton.

To say that coral atolls have been alive all that time is not to imply they have had an easy, uninterrupted growth. Geological drillings have demonstrated that atoll life became very difficult several times through the ages. The sea is not a stable environment; it is strongly influenced by what happens in space—passing dust clouds, for example—as the planet and its star scream around the galactic core at some 300 kilometers per second. When the earth cools, the sea has periodically yielded itself up to the land as crystal snow caps. When the Earth-solar thermostat flips to chill, the increased volume of water bound in ice and snow at the poles lowers the sea level. And, while coral can manage upward growth in response to earth's dynamic movement, it can not grow backwards. When the sea is trapped on the land as ice and snow, the great body of the atoll becomes stranded in deadly air.

Fortunately, however, although the sea level has dropped as much as 180 meters from time to time, the living atoll managed to survive by living deeper and deeper along its older skeleton. The living coral thus became a fringing reef again skirting the emergent coral mountain. Rain and land creatures flowed onto the raised mountains and, in time, the very structure of the coral skeletons changed from biological aragonite to geological calcite. Then, as the thermostat clicked again to warm, the ice melted and the sea rose to immerse the whole structure again and the living coral climbed back to its former topmost position.

Using ^{14}C, ^{230}Th, and ^{234}U dating techniques, geologists have shown that the upper 10 meters of corals on Enewetak are all less than 6000 years old. Below that, from 10 to 48 meters into the skeleton, the corals were greatly altered, having been subjected to atmospheric and terrestrial biological changes. This weathered layer covered corals that were between 100,000 and 130,000 years old. Samples taken from the skeletons 80 to 191 meters below the surface proved to be between 160,000 to more than 700,000 years old. The weathered layer of coral skeletons is known as the Thurber Discontinuity and has shown up in cores of coral reefs from the Atlantic, Indian, and Pacific Oceans, proving that the modern reefs were exposed to air due to glaciation drops in sea levels from 8,000 to 100,000 years ago.

At Kwajalein, other discontinuities have been found at even deeper levels—335 and 847 meters from the surface—which may correspond to even older glacial periods.

One way we can recognize atolls as superorganisms is by their constancy. They reproduce themselves, growing into similar body forms with specialized body parts performing definite functions to keep them alive as whole, growing entities. The overall shape of an atoll is no more "accidental" than the overall shape of a domed brain coral. Like all animals, the atoll is a blend of its genetic past and the environment that molds these genetic sub-units into a larger pattern. These giant creatures of the sea, like the corals that help construct their skeletons, look a little different from one place to the next, but their basic components are functionally the same.

The atoll is a circular reef surrounding a deep lagoon. Rimmed by reef yellow and island green, the turquoise lagoon is a zone of protected water in the open sea. The lagoon is a highly specialized and important part of the atoll ecosystem. The overall shape of the lagoon is formed by the reef corals of the outer wall and by the submerged rock on which they grew. The many passes that allow water to flow in and out of the lagoon are organically structured and maintained, as are the many specialized features within the lagoon.

Typically, there is an inner reef flat that slopes down to a 20-meter-deep shelf circling the edge of the lagoon. The remaining lagoon floor is fairly flat and about 60 meters deep. Patch reefs and thickets of coral abound on the shallow shelf, and coral knolls rise here and there from the lagoon floor in towering pillars of life.

Lagoon water owes its lovely color to plankton, organic substances, and a drizzle of calcium carbonate that precipitates from chemical and bacterial action in the warm shallows. Lagoon corals, forever protected from the violence of the open sea, grow more branches that are slender and thinner leaf-like blades than their outer reef siblings. Many species of fish and invertebrates and plants live only in the atoll lagoons, seldom, if ever, venturing to the seaward slopes.

The lagoon floor is blanketed with white sand, peppered everywhere with countless holes and burrows. The sand is a community crowded with bacteria, protozoans, worms, mollusks, echinoderms, crustaceans, fish, eels, and a multitude of other creatures of various sizes, shapes and descriptions.

The sand is, in fact, part of a living structure, produced by the creatures that live in it or near it. It forms the skeleton and provides the protective habitat and food for thousands of species of plants and animals that are inseparable from the sand. And the creature-cells of the sand move their skeleton, the small mineral crystals churning and flowing in constant living turmoil. A dome placed on the bottom shows the sea floor metabolizes in a fluctuating day-night rhythm.

Like the cells within an animal body, the creatures of the lagoonal sands are in a constant state of change. Their bodily functions continuously generate new sand and break down the old sand. At Bikini, the 20-meter-deep shelf lining the lagoon is made from protozoans known as Foraminifera that live in great numbers on the inner reef flat. When the Foraminifera die, their shells are washed into the lagoon to form a ring often several miles in width, piling up here and there to become part of the surface of the shelf. In deeper lagoon areas, a calcareous alga, *Halimeda*, grows so abundantly that its flat limy leaves form the major part of the lagoon floor. In still deeper areas, sand from the coral knolls mixes with a still different foraminiferal fauna to produce the living bottom.

Many other plants and animals contribute their skeletal remains to the lagoon sediments and the major contributors vary from one atoll to another. However, we can always see the lagoon floor as a product of atoms transformed by sunlight into a complex assembly of organic matter vibrating in the tropical sea. These moving crystals have an intricate food web: Fish eat sea cucumbers that feed on Foraminifera that feed on bacteria and diatoms from sunlight or decaying organisms. And let us not forget the filter-feeding animals that lift tentacles, mucous nets, and ciliary sieves into the sea water moving over the sand.

The lagoon fauna and flora is a vital part of the whole coral atoll energy flow. These collect and produce nutrients for fish and invertebrates whose domains extend for miles across the sand. The lagoon is, in fact, a giant plankton trap and solar energy collector.

The lagoon and the reef passes may be thought of as a communal plankton net energized by the gravitational pull of the sun and the moon. Twice each day the sea rises and falls and Enewetak's lagoon, as one example, fills and empties with some 500 million cubic meters of sea water, each drop of which contains a variety of microscopic organic creatures. The giant atoll feeds with gusto at the reef's high energy passes where the water is funneled through a maze of grasping tentacles and mouths.

Many tons of plankton manage to escape this gauntlet to enter the lagoon's turquoise tranquillity. Here, in the calm, warm water, diatoms bloom and zooplankton feed and grow. Larvae, washed in with the tide, hasten to change into their new form as echinoderms, fish, crustaceans, and corals. They are ready to settle down after their sea voyage that usually lasts a few days. Many of these new settlers become morsels for the lagoon creatures who were there first.

Oceanic zooplankton, that is scooped up by lagoonal tides, circulates slowly in the warm swirl of lagoon water. The tide that carries the plankton into Bikini's 37-kilometer-wide lagoon does not sweep it back out as the moon-pull moves on over the earth. Within the lagoon there is a complex circulatory system. In addition to the in-and-out tidal movements of the passes, the wind creates a pair of counter-rotating currents superimposed on a vertical overturning of the lagoon water. These currents efficiently move tidal water away from the passes so the water that is discharged with the fall-ing tide is only partly made up of the water that entered with the rising tide.

Thus, the zooplankton that enters in the night (when it comes closer to the surface of the sea to feed) mixes with the rich algal blooms of the lagoon and by dawn the plankton is well fattened. As the sun rises, the plankton heads down into the cool depths to discover that there is no deep water, only a sandy bottom with coral knolls alive and hungry for chubby zooplankton. The lagoon, therefore, not only captures huge populations of zooplankton, it also cultivates them with organic waste products from the host of reef creatures— and then gobbles them up at dawn.

The creatures of the reef passes benefit greatly from the huge lagoon. The tidal water needed to fill the plankton trap assures a vigorous rushing current which would not occur without the relatively enclosed lagoon. Twisted branches and shelves of corals along the pass walls provide an increased surface area for the filter-feeding creatures. Sea fans and soft corals are jammed together, vibrating in the swift flow of the tides. Sponges, hydroids, feather stars, and ascidians abound. Fishes and sharks school in the passes, swimming continually to remain in place. And, in the turmoil of life and growth at the passes, feeding becomes a full-time task. Normal territorial boundaries seem to be overlooked as the crowded reef organisms bulge into the rushing sea and dance in the swirling tidal rips.

The construction of the lagoon passes is therefore a critical part of atoll life. There is often a deep pass on the leeward side of the atoll. At Bikini and Enewetak, the large pass is as deep as the lagoon. Many smaller passes and caves connect the lagoon with the open sea and these somehow keep from growing closed. One creature that may help keep the passes open is the crown-of-thorns starfish. These voracious coral feeders are seldom found on outer reef faces. They live just inside the lagoon passes in clusters of fifteen to twenty large individuals.

The starfish are not alone, however. Other coral predators enjoy the fast pace of the passes. The corals themselves help shape the passes by growing faster into the current rather than along its flanks.

There are few passes on the windward side of the

atoll where ocean waves stumble over solid reef. Should we dive into the deep blue world of the open sea, we would find the windward reef wall abounding with hovering fishes, clouds of zooplankton and swift, streamlined sharks. Above, at the air-water interface, we could see rolling, mirrored surf washing up into the corals and vanishing onto the reef top where corals are scarce, low and flat under the constant foam of ocean waves. The outer face of the reef is a maze of corals formed into protruding buttresses and channels, ledges and caves. The vertically arrayed, undulating ridge-and-valley construction provides the atoll with an increased surface area for feeding and growth, as well as a hydraulic relief system to absorb the energy of the ocean waves.

The valleys or "surge channels" continue up to the smooth, hard algal ridge that crests the leading edge of the atoll like enamel on a tooth, preventing erosion and organic decay. The ridge is made of a dense calcium carbonate secreted by calcareous algae (*Porolithon*) that thrive in the high energy environment. Some of the surge channels become a network of tunnels under the smooth, cement-hard reef flat. At Bikini, the power of the breaking waves (estimated at 500,000 horsepower per roller) separates a half-a-meter head of water which slides over the flat to the lagoon no matter what the state of the tide. It is this moving sheet of sea water that brings life to the reef flat communities of coral, algae, and Foraminifera. The algal ridge is absent elsewhere on the atoll and, in fact, is missing from atolls not in the trade wind belts. In Atlantic atolls and the monsoonal atolls of the Indian Ocean, the top of the reef is lower, with respect to tide level, than the atolls with algal ridges. Coral growth is usually more prolific in areas without the strong algal ridge, apparently to counter the increased wear and tear of the exposed portion of the reef.

The south and southwest sides of Bikini and Enewetak are normally protected from ocean waves. Here the coral grows a finer, more delicate structure and often actually overhangs the deeper portions of the atoll wall. When typhoons come, some of these corals break away and sections of the coral wall, sometimes weighing tons, may tumble to the lower slopes and terraces.

The northern side of Bikini and Enewetak is almost always protected from strong waves and these reefs are richly developed. The coral does not form wave-breaking surge channels but twists into caverns and ledges in which fish and invertebrates can meander for kilometers without once venturing into the open sea.

From a human view, the islands of atolls are of special interest because that is where humans live: the reef's men-cells, Polynesians or Micronesians or Tourists. The islands are long, narrow, small, flat, low, sandy. The largest are on the windward reef flats where debris and sand is constantly thrown up from the sea. Most of them at their highest point are only 3 or 4 meters above the reef flat. Bikini has 26 named islets and Enewetak has 33. Interestingly, the islets are not very stable although a layer of hard beach rock generally helps anchor them. The smaller islands on the windward side slowly erode on the seaward side. The sand migrates around to the island's lagoon side, so the small islands actually wander in from the sea to the lagoon. It is a transient, cyclic parade of sea, mineral, plant, and animal: a slipping, sliding dance of life.

We have only touched on one level of atoll zonation in the description of the major body parts, and even these differ from one atoll to the next. Scientists have studied atoll form and function in great detail, producing over 1100 pages with more than 600 plates and figures, in one series of publications on Enewetak and Bikini alone. There are hundreds of other books and periodicals concerning atoll biology. Almost every conceivable part of the atoll has a name of some kind; merely to list the body parts would require a library. In addition, the zones of life on an atoll knows no limits; for corals of reef types and, within themselves, zones of tissues, zones of behavior, zones of cells, and so on. So, rather than sink into the depths of smaller synergetic patterns, let us move the other way and examine the largest patterns. Let us examine how our megabeast functions relative to its whole environment.

First, we must conclude that the atoll organism functions very well. It is not only large (Bikini's skeleton massing some 1000 cubic kilometers) and old (50 to 60 millions of years) but apparently indestructible. What other animal could have survived, as did Bikini,

21 megaexplosions, direct hits with powerful thermonuclear weapons? Enewetak had even more powerful nuclear bombs detonated on it, and one of its islands was totally atomized, and the vegetation was seared from several other islands.

As amazing was Bikini's stoic survival of the damage wrought by the 42,000 men involved in the atomic tests, who lived on the tiny atoll islets, or on the 200 ships anchored in the lagoon. To add chemical insult to the atomic injury, the whole area was dusted with DDT, inundated with untreated sewage and chemical wastes from the ship and shore facilities, flooded with fish poisons for the hundreds of major scientific collections, and on Enewetak even blackened by massive oil pollution during military action.

Geologist Harry S. Ladd, a senior scientist who was a part of the atoll survey program, commented in 1973 that "Atolls and their buildings are well-nigh indestructible." Surveys showed the miraculous ability of the living reef organism to heal its atomic and chemical wounds. Only ten years after hostilities between man and atoll simmered down, a very healthy reef environment had returned to the devastated areas, even into some of the craters left from the nuclear explosions.

There is an aura about the coral polyp, as well as around the whole atoll that is quite real and measurable, albeit invisible and intangible.

Around each individual coral animal is a space of some centimeters that is not within its body, but it is within its reach. That space is part of the coral although you will not find the coral in it. In the same way, each reef creature has its space, its territory. While these often overlap between the motile and the sessile creatures, when animals compete with each other, these spaces can be as physical a limit to individuality as skin or shell. Thus, the small damsel fish (*Pomacentrus*) chases away any animal—even humans—from its nest area while laying its eggs under a living coral. A grouper will tolerate or eat smaller fish that swim in its territory, but he will do battle with another large fish—unless, of course, the other fish is much larger and eats little groupers.

I have often seen this aura of invisible tension around reef fishes. It is not generated only by the individual organism. It is a synergetic interaction of both the animal generating the aura and those perceiving it. It also reflects the state of mind of the animals. I have seen a barracuda hover in the midst of a giant school of anchovies. The anchovies formed an almost solid mass, but as they swam past the cuda the mass parted and a perfectly cylindrical tunnel appeared in the silver shoal of fish with the cuda dead center. The wave of fish allowed exactly for the predatory potential of the larger fish. The tunnel tapered off about a meter behind the cuda's tail, but no fish swam in front of the barracuda's mouth. This display showed exactly where the behavioral aura began and ended, something the anchovies obviously could perceive and avoid.

So the reef does not end with the sea floor. It continues upward into invisible domains of fish territories that reach to and beyond the sea's surface. It extends even into the air where birds establish fishing and nesting territories that include a considerable area within which the atoll "lives." So, too, the living feelers and the invisible territories of the reef bulge out into the sea where they are constantly challenged by the greater oceanic predators.

This behavioral aura changes drastically between day and night. As dark approaches, sea birds return to their roosts from their fishing excursions. Beneath the waves, the fish that school over the reef during the day break formation to venture into the lagoon or along the reef flats for food. Herbivorous fish, all of which seem to feed during the day, look for some safe hole where they retire for the night. Parrot fish construct a delicate bubble of mucus around their sleeping bodies as a warning against moray eels or other nocturnal predators. When the night guard—the nocturnal feeders—go on duty, their coral caves and crevices will be inhabited by colorful angel and butterfly fish. Down from his plankton feeding station comes the iridescent blue chromis and up from the dark cave comes the big-eyed, bright red cardinal fish to take his place.

The invertebrates arise: spiny sea urchins ascend to feed on the reef top. The crown-of-thorns trundles out from hidden recesses and casts its stomach over the coral polyps. Basket starfish with hundreds of thousands of arms creep from unseen caves; thickets of twisting arms are shaped into baskets to net passing plankton. In the lagoon, gastropods erupt from the sand, gliding this way and that. Sea cucumbers toss off their blankets of sand and lumber over the sea floor on hundreds of hydraulic legs, mopping up diatoms and Foraminifera as they go.

If the reef is a single entity, it must have a nervous system. And, indeed, it does. Special nerves by which the "cells" communicate. There are at least three such systems within the atoll body, and they are organized into a loose network similar to the two-way nerves that coordinate the cells in a polyp's body.

The first of these systems is a generalized, hormonal communication system that, to some degree, reaches all of the atoll cells. It operates with complex organic molecules discharged into the atoll's blood (the sea) by the members of the coral reef body. Mostly, it communicates information about sex, territorial and behavioral limits, location and condition of prey, proper settlement sites for larvae, and who knows what else. Female corals, for example, emit molecular signals that are picked up by male corals of the same species and probably are picked up also by filter-feeders who feed on liberated sperm cells. Fish, mollusks, sponges, all the reef cells, exude their special chemical scents to the sea and sniff and taste for replies. Metabolic communication thus functions to coordinate the whole atoll complex so that the cells all know what to do and when to do it. Probably, the same sort of mechanism is used to tell the quiescent interstitial cells within coral tissues when to activate and what to make of themselves when they do.

The second "nervous system" is sound. Every moment of the day and night sound signals report myriad intricate events and coordinate billions of muscle movements among atoll "cells." These vibrations, like ocean waves, are carried through the sea water without actually changing the water itself. No molecules and no atoms carry these impulses, but all atoms and molecules are moved by them. Sound can carry a wide variety of information at the amazing rate of 1500 meters per second. Just as our much slower electrochemical nerve impulses cause an arm to bend or a hand to grab, sound vibrations from one part of a coral reef "cell" elicit

muscle movement and specific behavior in other parts. Usually, the "messages" are important and the resulting movements are vital for survival. Many of the reef sounds are inaudible to human ears, but we can, of course, clearly hear human voices, bird songs, groupers' grunts, the rattles of groups of snapping shrimp, and the quacks of lobsters.

Third, visual displays transmit highly complex messages among all animals with eyes. This includes most animals above the cnidarial level of development. At any given moment on the reef, vast amounts of information are exchanged by visual displays. Fishes signal one another about a multitude of different important biological functions—even altering the color of their skin, forming spots or lines as their function or activity changes. A fish might signal hunger by developing a black band across its eyes (to conceal where it is looking). A smaller fish reacts by racing into a protected zone and altering its color to match the background. Octopus turn red when they are hurt, white when they are angry, iridescent blue when hunting, and whatever the bottom color and texture is when they want to hide.

Such combinations of signals coordinate the feeding, reproduction, movement, and distribution of the many reef species and their individual members.

Fringing and barrier reefs are much younger than their atoll cousins. Continental land masses and the large islands along the borders of the tropical seas are more active than the older mid-ocean volcano domain where atolls live. Continental land masses play a game of tilt-and-uplift that confuses things, while the sea level rises and falls with ice-age supertides.

Fringing reefs are simply young reefs that have grown on the fringes of islands or continents. They are usually made of organisms that are more resistant to turbidity and sand. Most of their corals are small. The life expectancy of these colonies is short because rain water and silt from the land mass can damage them. In favorable environs, however, fringing reefs can develop into magnificent displays of coral architecture. On small, high islands, zonation of the corals is similar to the outer coral walls of an atoll: the windward side ribbed with long buttresses and surge channels to dissipate the power of surging waves. Generally, the leeward side of islands has the most beautiful coral growth, harbored in bays or coves along the shore. Usually these displays are built on submerged terraces that probably resulted from wave erosion of the shoreline long before the corals were firmly established. An interesting feature of almost all island fringing reefs that I have examined is that they are often isolated, separated by long miles of rather barren rock and algae that, for no known reason, have not developed reef formations.

Barrier reefs form on the outer edges of a submerged platform, thus creating a lagoon between the reef and shore. Although younger than atolls, barrier reefs are often much larger. The Great Barrier Reef of Australia is 2300 kilometers long, and in places extends over 200 kilometers offshore. Although the main reef area encompasses more than 140,000 square kilometers, the actual living reef growing on this part of Australia's submerged continental shelf is only about 17,000 square kilometers. It is not a continuous, solid reef development, but is broken up into some 2425 subreefs that average less than 3.5 square kilometers in area.

The history of the Great Barrier Reef has been extensively investigated. Like many other barrier reefs, its present day form is only 12,000 to 13,000 years old and the active reef-building complex is only some 100 meters thick and is laid down on top of sand or foraminiferal ridges that were once—some 20,000 years ago when the sea level was about 100 meters lower than it is today—above water. At that time, the area where the Great Barrier Reef now lives was a low-living terrestrial plain swept with large river systems, hills and valleys. The sea lapped at the foot of a 200-foot-high cliff. All the usual movements and cracklings of the earth's crust and the powerful forces of erosion and sedimentation shaped the platform that, when the seas returned, became the base for the coral reefs. Some of these terrestrial formations, such as old river beds, still slice the Great Barrier Reef into sections. Other parts of the land's features are blunted by coral growth. Reef corals have grown upward as much as 100 meters in some areas, easily keeping pace with the sea as it gradually climbed the cliffs and washed up over the lowlands to reach its present level some 5000 years ago.

The time of the rising sea was a time of growth.

It did not take long—only about 13,000 years—for the reefs to complete their scaffolding and fill in the spaces with the skeletons of reef life. On the seaward edge of the reef, long groove-and-spur formations absorb the energy from wind-driven waves, using them to drive the circulatory system of the reef organism. On the landward side, the reefs are broken into thousands of smaller segments and patch reefs that lie along the lagoonal channel between reef and shore. Barrier reef tops and passes seem much like atoll reef tops and passes except there is a greater mass of living things on the barrier reefs.

Barrier reefs of continental or high island masses are "fed" by the land as well as by the sun and the sea. Along the coastline, on the inside of the lagoonal channel, the estuaries and rivers are lined, mile after mile, with deep green mangrove swamps. In the roots of these unique salt water trees, a great variety of fish and invertebrates spawn and nurse. When they reach an effective swimming size, the fish migrate out. For a time they inhabit the rich inshore fringing reefs, then in lagoon patch reefs, and finally they settle into some community of the outer reef.

Many reef fish and invertebrates go through their whole life cycle on the reef, as they do on atolls, but the "extra" faunas from the mangroves and inshore reefs give the barrier reefs their aura of biological wealth.

If the life on barrier reefs is richer than on atolls, it is also more hazardous. The greater fish population is only part of the biomass increase. There is also a tendency toward increased plant fertility, especially in areas of extensive farming on adjacent coastlines. Nutrients added to the sea from land runoff tends to promote blooms of phytoplankton that, along with terrestrial silt, make the water murkier and slow coral growth. This is compensated by the increased availability of nutrients to the shallower corals that grow in terrific profusion. The zooplankton population soars upward as the plant population increases, thus helping to support additional masses of fish. On the vast expanse of the soft sea floor behind the reef, great beds of sea grass and algae extend for kilometers, generating more fish and invertebrates to add to the biological fuel of the reefs.

All this makes fringing and barrier reefs more sensitive to shifts in their environment. Man-made disturbances can have far more drastic results here than on atolls.

The whole reef structure, be it fringing, barrier, atoll or patch, is constructed by the combined effort of all the reef animals and plants. Stony corals form an interlocking, highly porous framework which is then filled by the skeletons of the other reef plants and animals. Mollusks, ranging from giant clams whose valves weigh hundreds of kilograms, to tiny gastropods with shells only as big as a letter on this page, participate in the reef-building process by adding their skeletal remains to the coral framework. Echinoderms, soft corals, sponges, foraminiferans, and calcareous algae metabolically construct the blocks and manufacture the sand that fill the coral frame.

Growth of the whole reef complex is difficult to measure. Most rates have been extrapolated from growth rates of individual corals, a difficult and perhaps misleading exercise. Using cores of coral skeletons, growth rates as low as 0.02 centimeters per year have been obtained over 70 million-year periods. However, this overlooks the fact that coral growth is dependent on the sea level. Once the corals grow to the low-tide line, they can only wait—in equilibrium—until the sea level rises again.

Establishing growth rates of modern reefs is made even more difficult by the fact that the sea level has been more or less stationary for the past 5000 years and the corals have been at a standstill for some time. They are still actively growing in places where coral growth probably has not reached maximum for various hydrographic reasons. There is a possibility, too, that once a standstill environment develops, other ecological conditions develop that help maintain a steady state of growth and decay. Such balancing controls are obviously at work today.

Patch reefs deserve a moment's consideration. These small, ovoid reefs are usually within the protection of a lagoon. As a result they are a place of special quiet. The water is usually not very clear where patch reefs grow, but the coral growth is delicate and varied, and these reefs swarm with fish and invertebrates.

Patch reefs are very much alive and seem to exude a glow of "youth." They are very "wealthy" as reefs go, because of their small size in relation to the grass or algal flats that may extend for miles around them. The grass flats, themselves, are nurseries for a multitude of fish and invertebrates. Once these grow to a certain size, however, they look for shelter where they can hide when they are not feeding. Patch reefs are ideal for the purpose, and they are constructed and protected by a concerted fish and invertebrate symphony of animal togetherness.

Protection is needed, for the mounds of coral are ever in danger of being overgrown by the luxuriant vegetation of shallow lagoon waters. Fortunately, the numerous herbivorous fish and sea urchins that live in the patch reefs enjoy their maintenance labors. In fact, they are so efficient that patch reefs can be seen from the air as dark mounds of corals surrounded by a moat of white sand in a dark green sea of vegetation. The characteristic white band of sand or rock around the reefs is primarily caused by the grazing activities of parrot fish and surgeon fish that stay near the protective coral caves when not foraging for food.

In some places, however, sea urchins—especially the black spined *Diadema*—create and maintain the band of white. During the day they hide in crevices in the coral. At night they emerge on their multitude of spiny legs and their hydraulic suction-cupped tube feet to eat the algae growing on the reef and in the zone adjacent to the reef. In some areas, at night, the sand buffer zone is almost completely covered with grazing sea urchins. One patch reef off Key West, Florida, suffered the loss of its entire *Diadema* population in a single day as I and a few helpers carefully moved them to a chicken-wire holding area in the sea grass near the reef. In two weeks, there was not a green thing alive in the pen, and virtually everything that could not get away was eaten. When the urchins were released a month later, they left a 6-meter-wide trail of ravaged vegetation leading directly back to the reef. Where the trail crossed the sand halo, its clear whiteness showed markedly against the green-white of the old zone that was already densely coated with young algae. In a few weeks, these algae were eaten off by the urchins and the patch was once again set apart from the vegetation by a clean white apron.

Like all organisms, reefs can die from natural causes. Perhaps the most common form of coral death comes from a combination of tide and storm that leaves whole reefs high and dry and then soaked with pouring rain. Such storms have left large sections of shallow water reefs dead or dying, the tissues alternately exploded by invading fresh water and stripped from their skeletons by thundering waves. Rivers of silty water from rain-soaked lands need only wash over such injured reefs to further damage them with a thick layer of silt and consequent lack of sunlight.

Most reefs, however, have evolved to handle such situations, especially where hurricanes, typhoons, or cyclones are common events. Thus, although two or three big storms blow over the Great Barrier Reef each year, only three cases of extensive coral damage have been reported in the literature, and these were only in localized patches. Rain-damaged reef tops are surrounded by living corals, usually only a short distance below the dead surface corals. The damaged reefs thus are quickly recolonized by reef creatures, and storm damage is normally repaired within a few years. In the case of a major coral kill, repairs were made within fifty years.

Atolls and mid-ocean island reefs generally suffer even less from such storms. The only notable damage is tissue loss from some of the shallower colonies and some broken corals, or tipping of cantilevered coral shelves. Even broken corals still provide plenty of live material for regrowth. Repairs start even as the storm charges over the horizon to new areas.

Sea level changes have left reefs both too high or too low for continued coral growth. But coral reef life can move—however slowly—downward as well as upward, by larvae settling on the new bottom as the sea rises or falls. So, although the reef in any one location may be killed by changing sea levels, it hardly matters from a biological view: The coral reef organism simply relocates itself, dancing and dodging with the agility of sex and the speed of generations.

During the ice ages, sedimentation increased and temperatures decreased, shifting the limits of coral survival back and forth over the years. When water temperatures dropped and sediments shuttered the light, only a few sturdy corals survived on the reef, and there was a shifting of growth rates and predator-prey relationships. When the interglacial period came again and the seas warmed and cleared, the old species that had survived in pockets of tropical warm water repopulated the old sites. Their siblings, meanwhile, had changed into new, reproductively isolated species, and had altered their optimal growing conditions. In some cases, as with the two Atlantic species of *Siderastrea*, the new species tended to live closer to shore where it could survive the higher sedimentation rates and the cooler winters better than the older one, which stayed in clearer, more stable water. A few reefs are known to have been killed by volcanic ash and even lava flows, but this—like storm damage—is only a localized problem. The lava itself will one day be colonized from surviving, nearby reefs.

While such major catastrophes have been a normal part of coral history and have, no doubt, helped evolve the great multitude of coral species and other reef organisms, it is the present-day coral deaths that concerns man in his role as caretaker of the planet.

In this connection, natural diseases are of interest—if indeed they are natural diseases. Several times in the recent past a mysterious plague has killed vast stands of corals, leaving the reef a smoldering wreck. The best documented case happened in the Dry Tortugas, off the Florida Keys, in 1878. The Tortugas' shoals and banks had been covered with thickets of staghorn coral, *Acropora cervicornis*. Then the water of the lagoon turned black with the decay of dying corals. The so-called "dark water" was probably the result of the dying *Acropora* rather than its cause. Repeated coral surveys from 1905 to 1975 showed that the dark water completely destroyed the *Acropora* thickets except for two small areas near Loggerhead Key. *Acropora* rubble littered the submerged banks almost everywhere, showing it had been very abundant before the kill. The two small centers of living *Acropora* slowly repopulated the area and today it is again the most abundant coral, its dense thickets growing everywhere. In many parts of the Dry Tortugas the *Acropora* thickets have overgrown whole patch reefs, smothering the slower growing coral heads with rapid 10 to 20 centimeters-per-year growth.

A similar case of dark water was reported at about the same time in Cocos-Keeling in the Eastern Indian Ocean, but no samples were taken to determine the agent of death. The commercial sponge fauna of the Florida and Bahama reefs suffered a similar disaster in 1919, 1936, and again in 1939. Because of the commercial interest in sponges at the time, the disease organism was isolated and found to be a marine fungus named *Spongiophaga,* a sponge eater. Normally, the diversity of the tropics is such that undersea invertebrates are seldom found in large numbers, closely crowded together. Sponge farmers, however, had sharply increased the density of sponges and the once-rare disease organism, *Spongiophaga,* suddenly flourished. The superabundance of *Acropora* on the banks of Tortugas might have created a condition where a similar fungus disease suddenly went wild, spreading from one part of a thicket to susceptible neighboring colonies.

The Tortugas, after a hundred years, did manage to regain their former abundance of *Acropora.* Since coral reefs are notably diverse when things seem to be going well, the plague may be a helpful and natural biological control mechanism for removing a dense concentration of one species. My own surveys of the Dry Tortugas' reefs showed that there was a greater diversity of fish and invertebrates on reefs with many species of corals than there were around the unispecific *Acropora* thickets.

For years diving scientists have been warning us that the reefs of the world are in trouble, and from Guam to Puerto Rico there have been many instances of whole reefs dying from one form of pollution or another. But recent trends provide some basis for cautious optimism. Less is heard these days from those who want to drill for oil on the Great Barrier Reef, or who would turn the reefs of Palau into ports for supertankers. For the time being, at least, atom bombs are not being dropped on atolls. Popular opinion seems to have turned strongly in favor of our living planet.

History teaches that once a problem has been defined and understood, man can act constructively. The environmental movement has fought many successful campaigns and it continues to gain momentum. Slowly, with faltering steps, civilization does seem to be moving toward increased compatibility with, and the sensible management of, our environment.

this is the garden: colours come and go,
frail azures fluttering from night's outer wing
strong silent greens serenely lingering,
absolute lights ...

This is the garden. Time shall surely reap
and on Death's blade lie many a flower curled,
in other lands where other songs be sung;
yet stand They here enraptured, as among
the slow deep trees perpetual of sleep
some silver-fingered fountain steals the world.

MILLEPORIDAE

STYLASTERIDAE

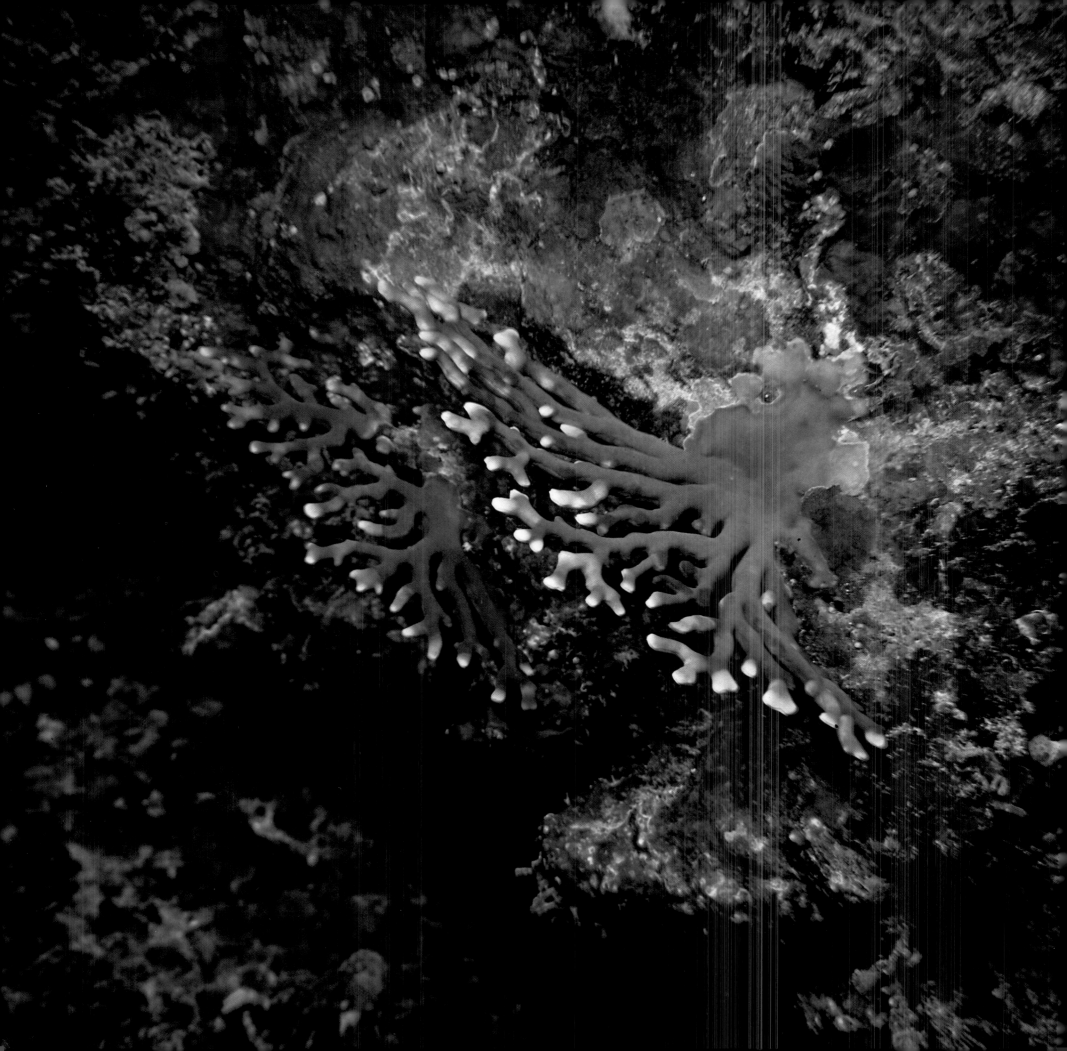

ANTIPATHIDAE

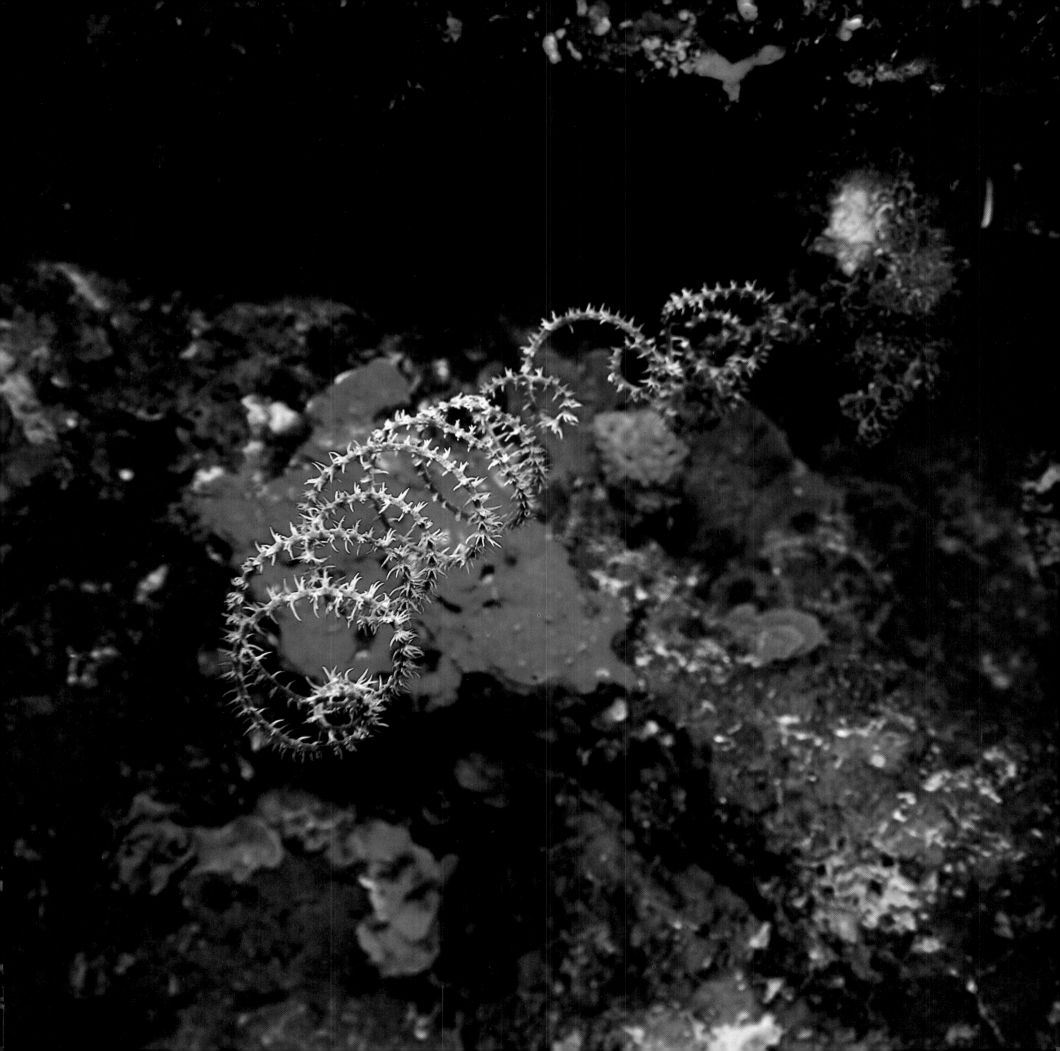

CLAVULARIIDAE

TUBIPORIDAE

ALCYONIIDAE

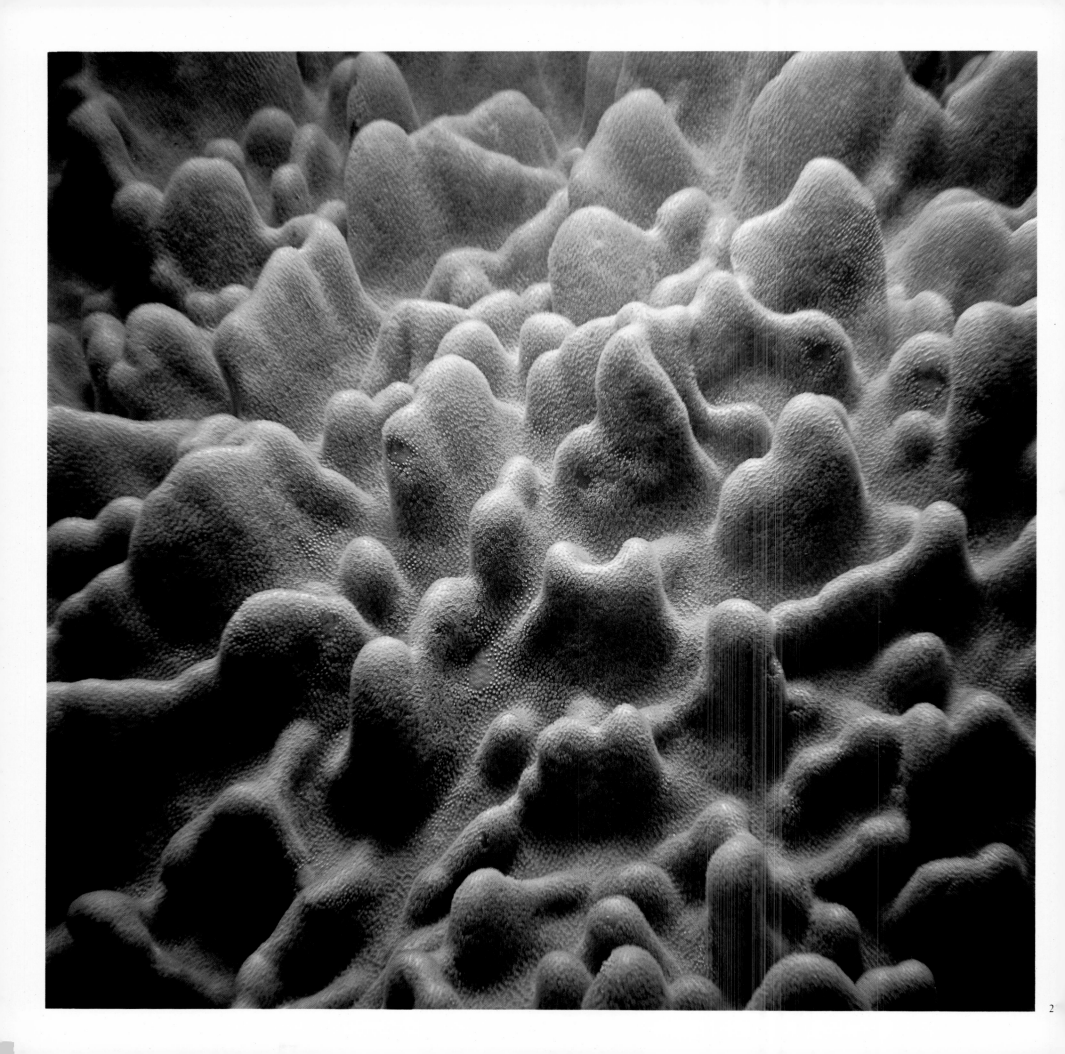

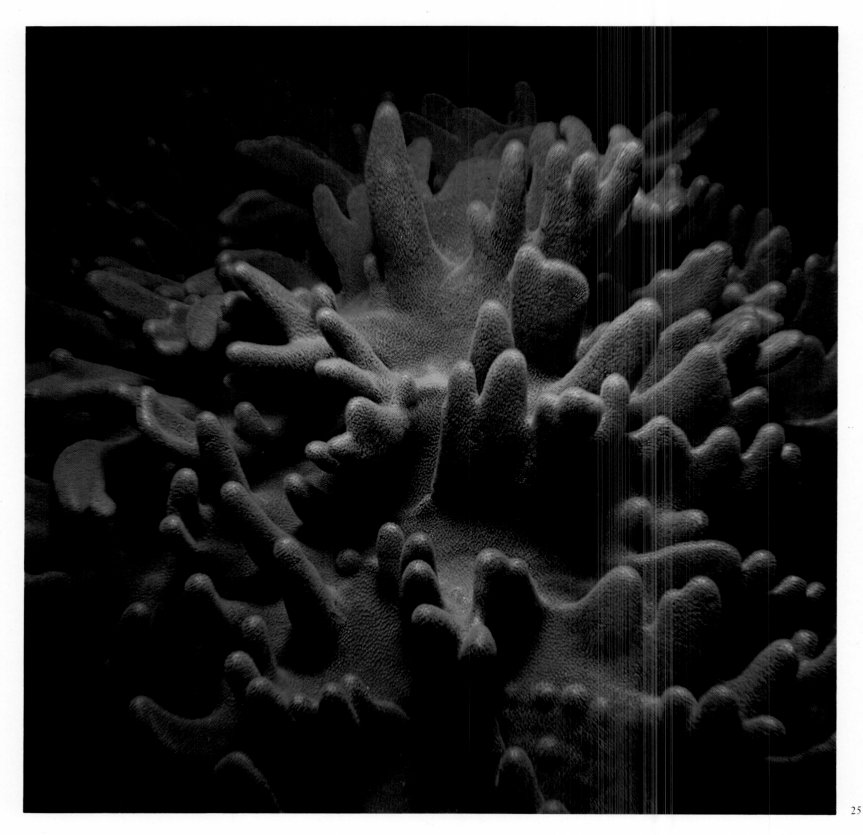

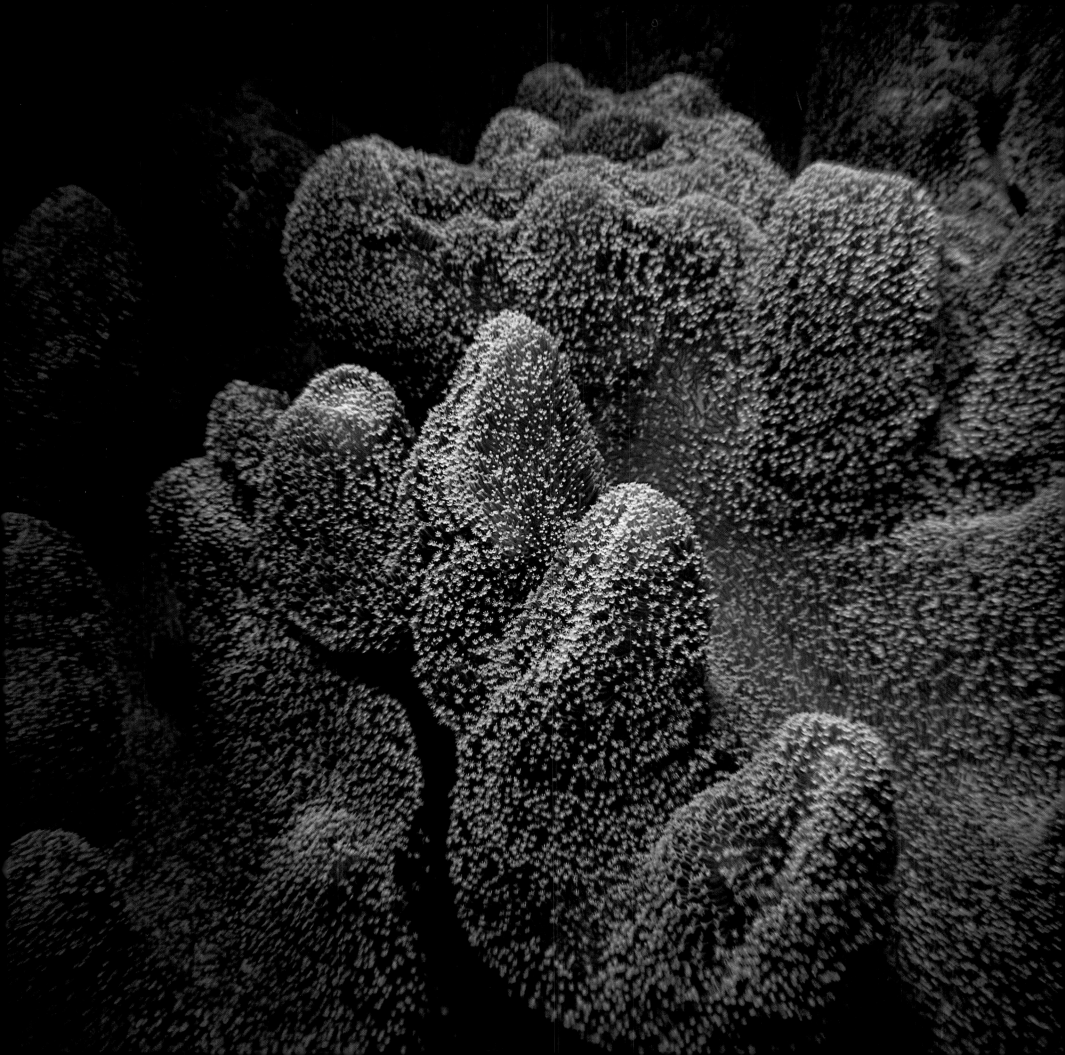

NEPHTHEIDAE

NIDALIIDAE

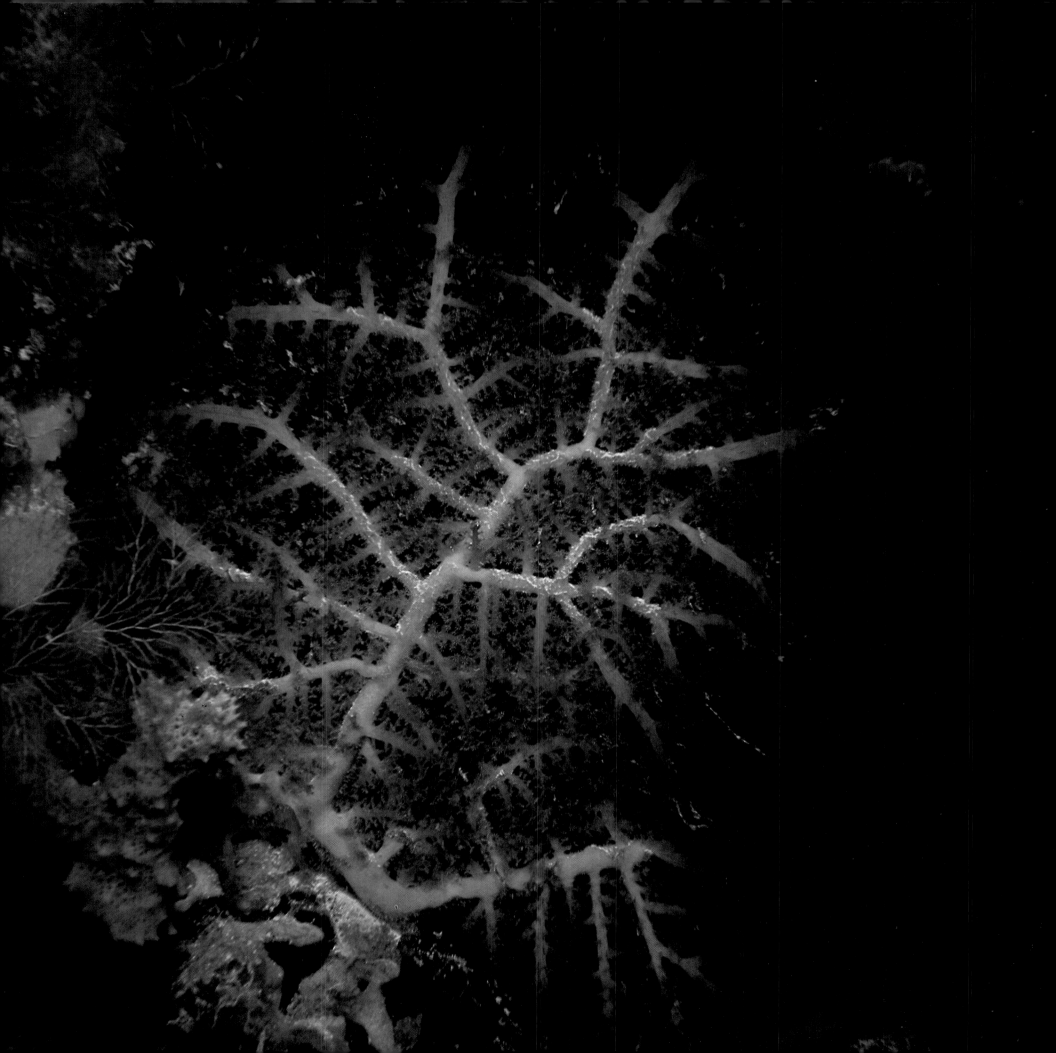

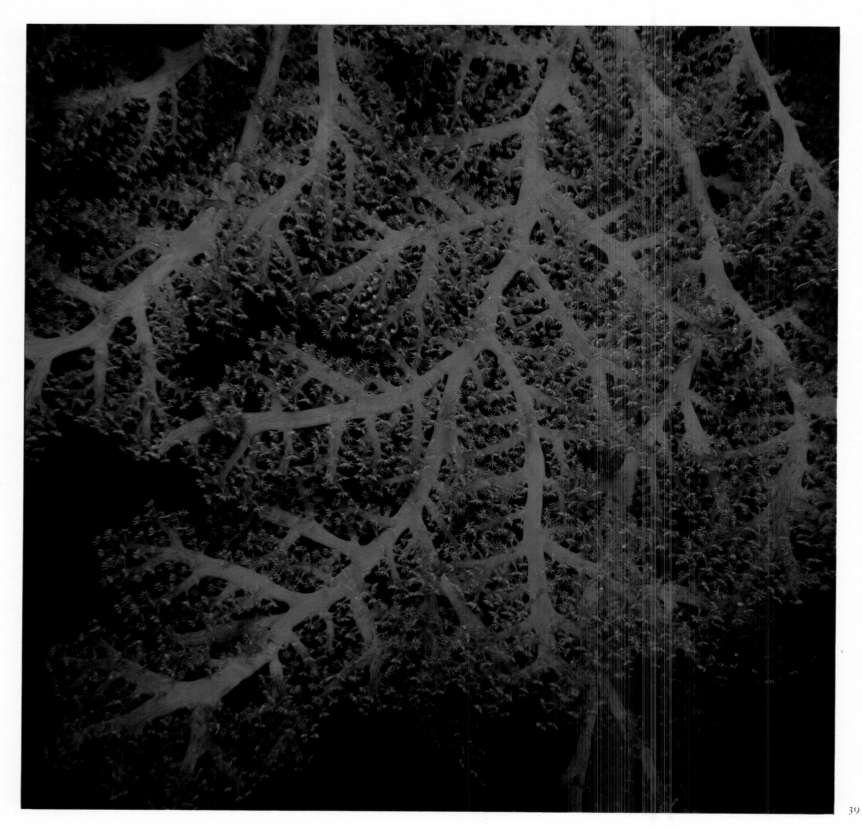

BRIAREIDAE

SUBERGORGIIDAE

MELITHAEIDAE

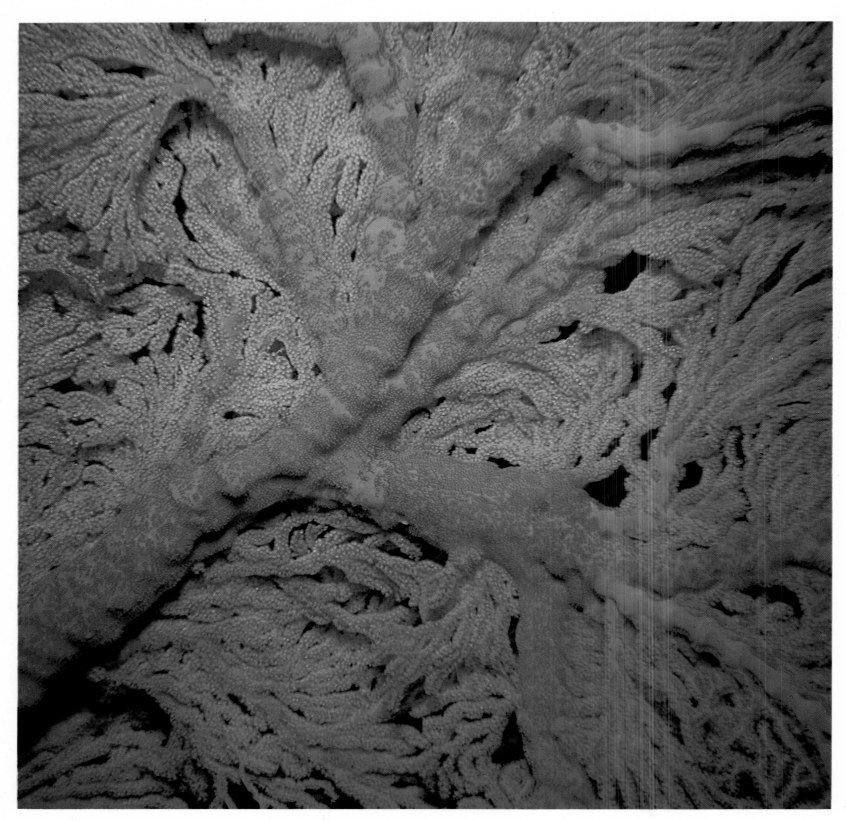

48

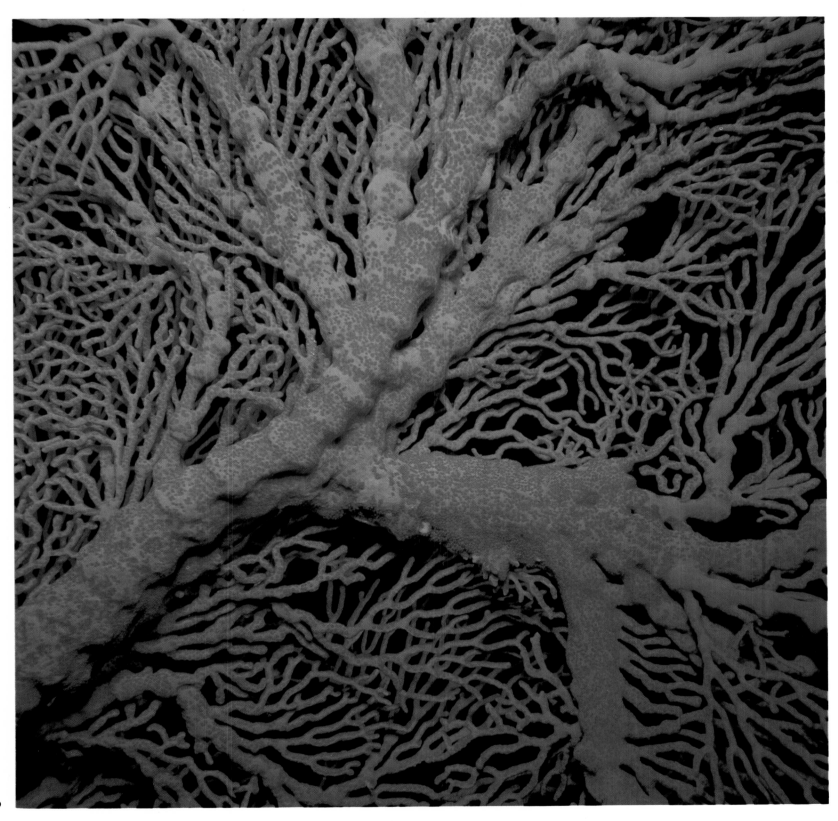

49

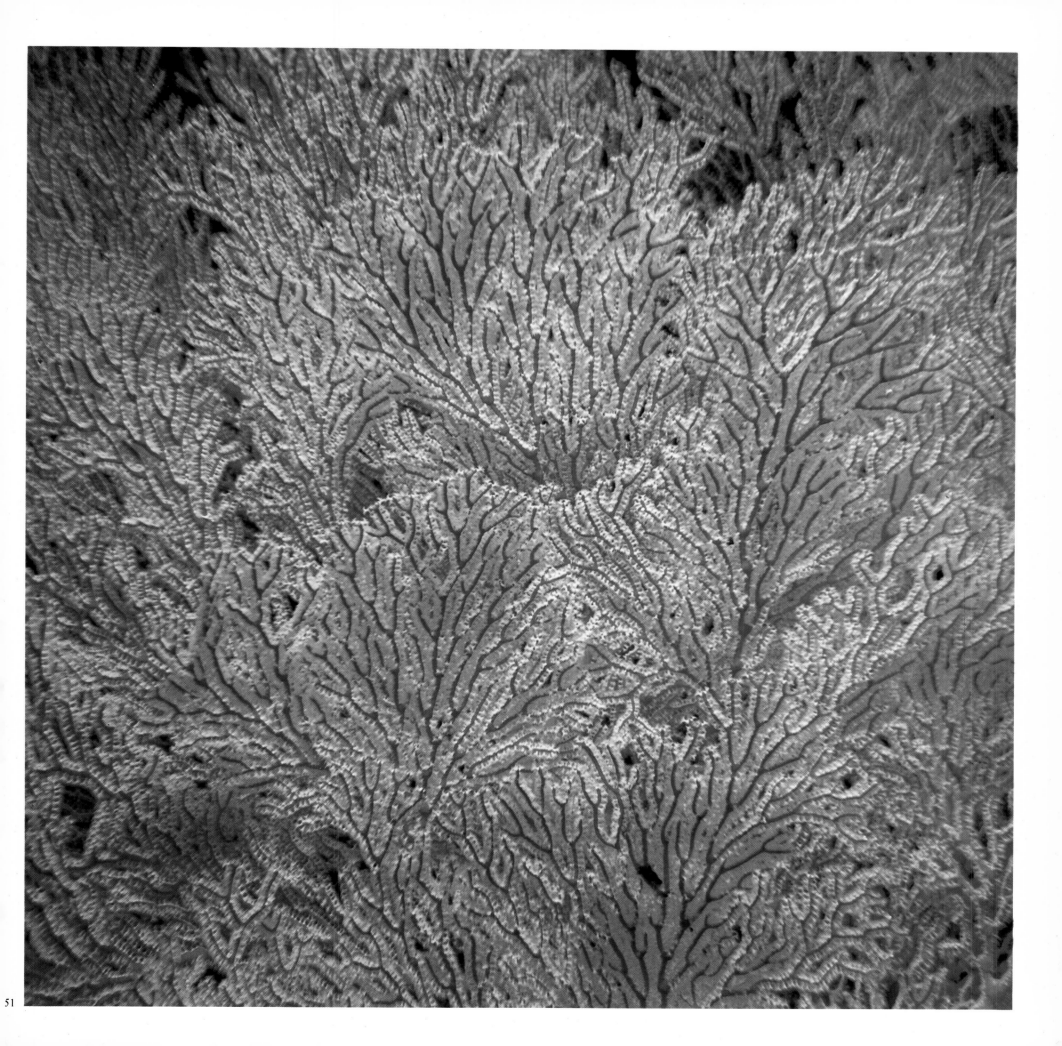

51

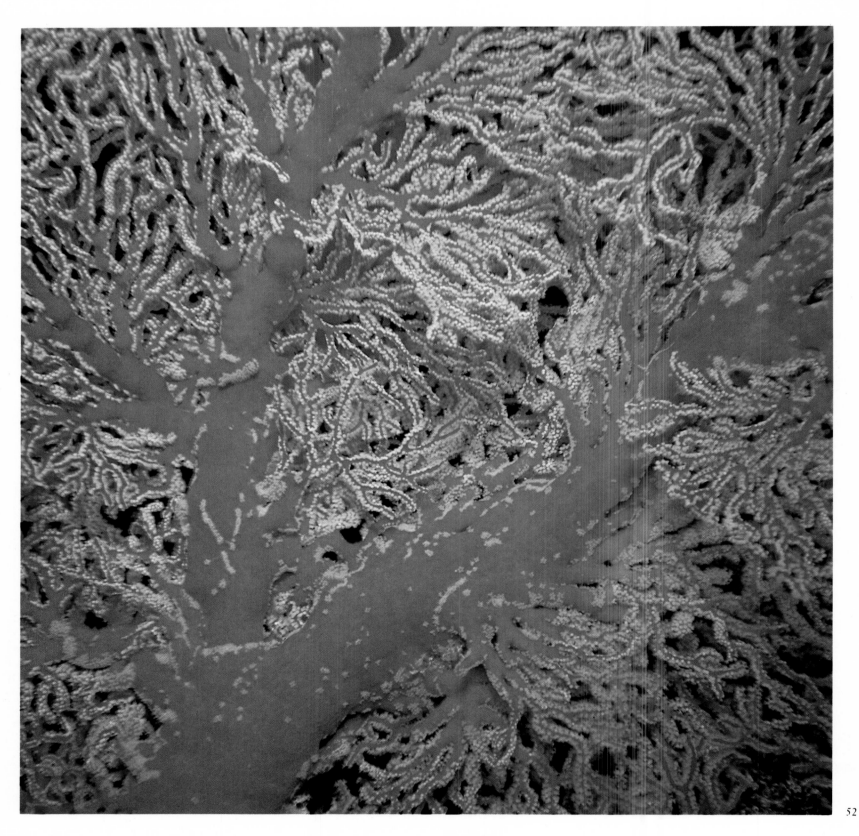

PARAMURICEIDAE

ELLISELLIDAE

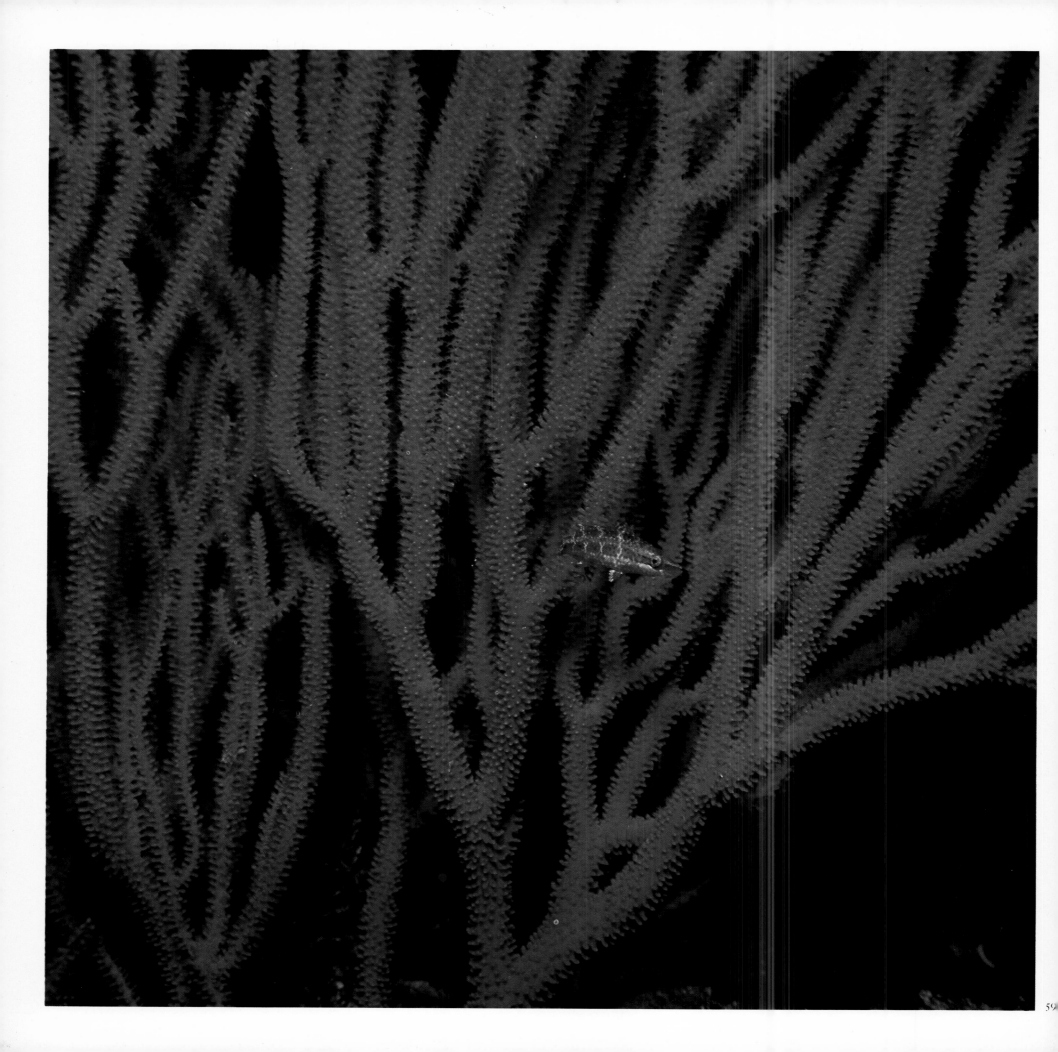

CHRYSOGORGIIDAE

PENNATULIDAE

HELIOPORIDAE

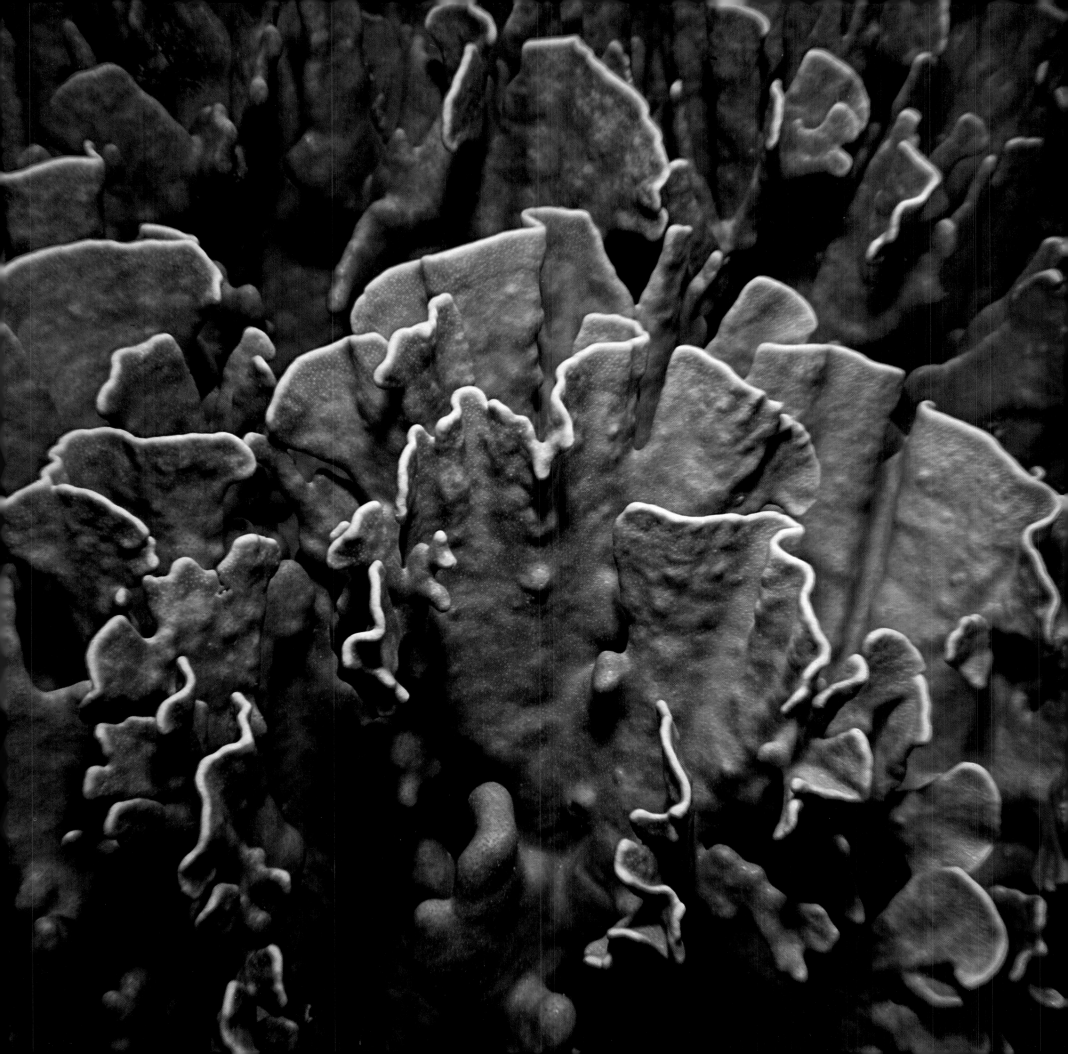

THAMNASTERIIDAE

POCILLOPORIDAE

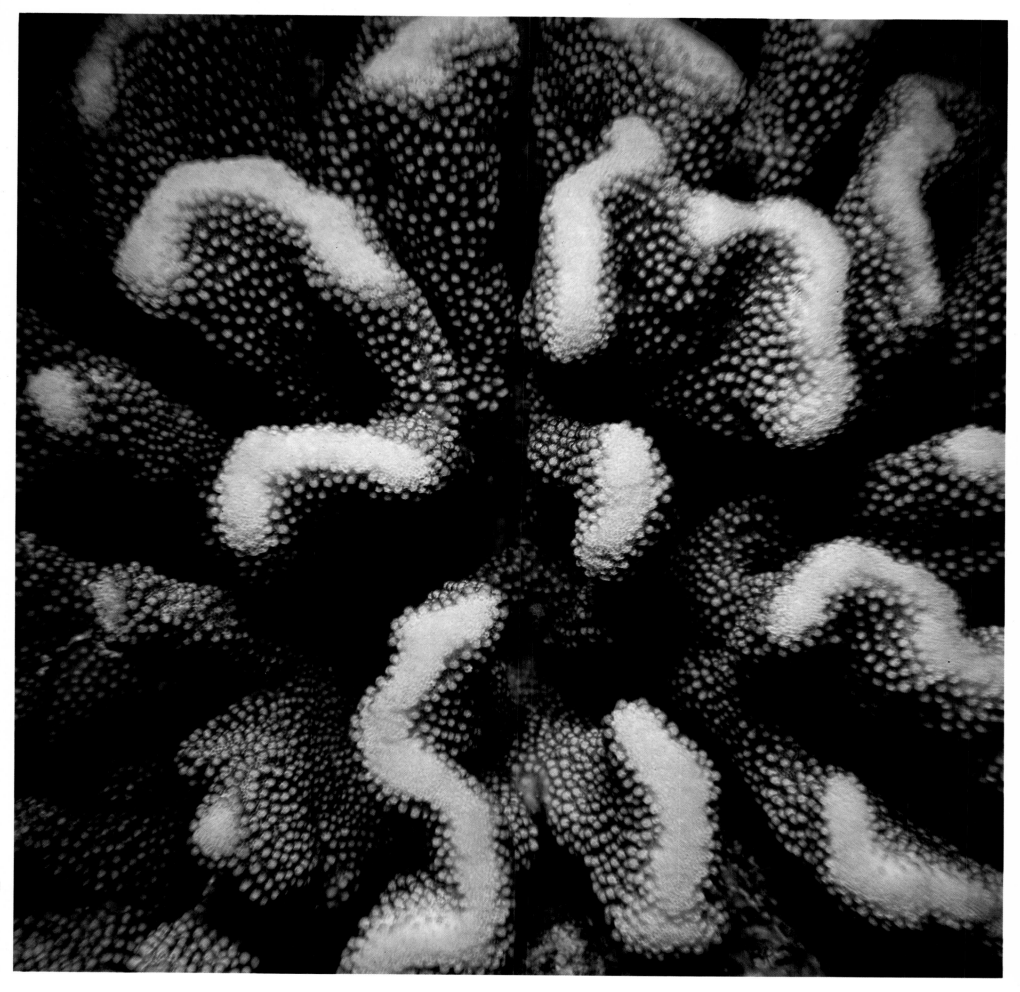

ACROPORIDAE

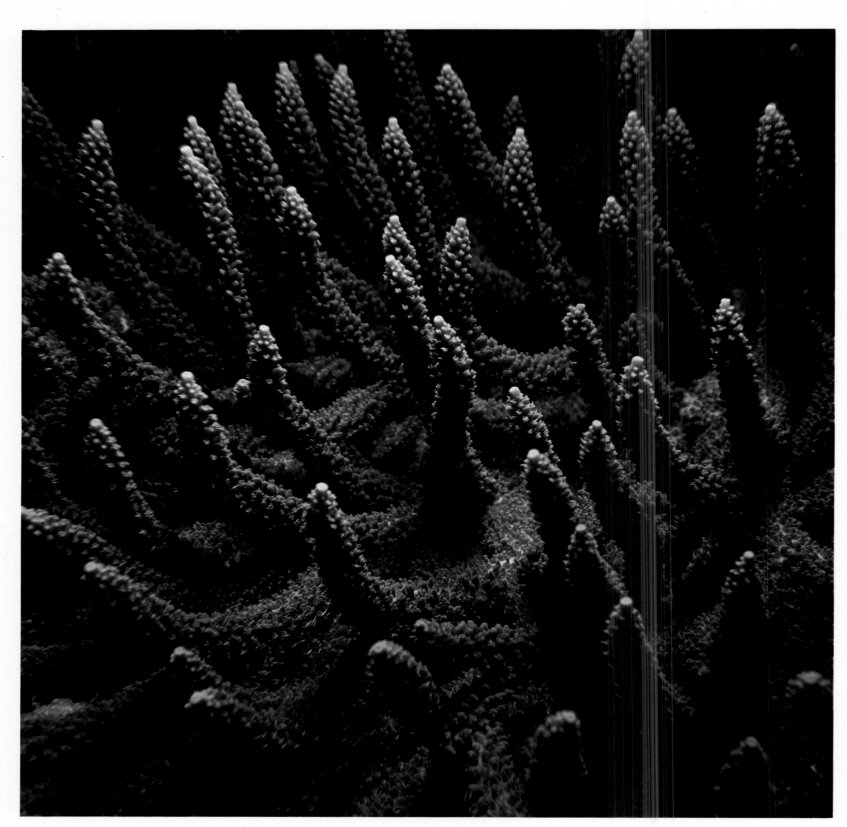

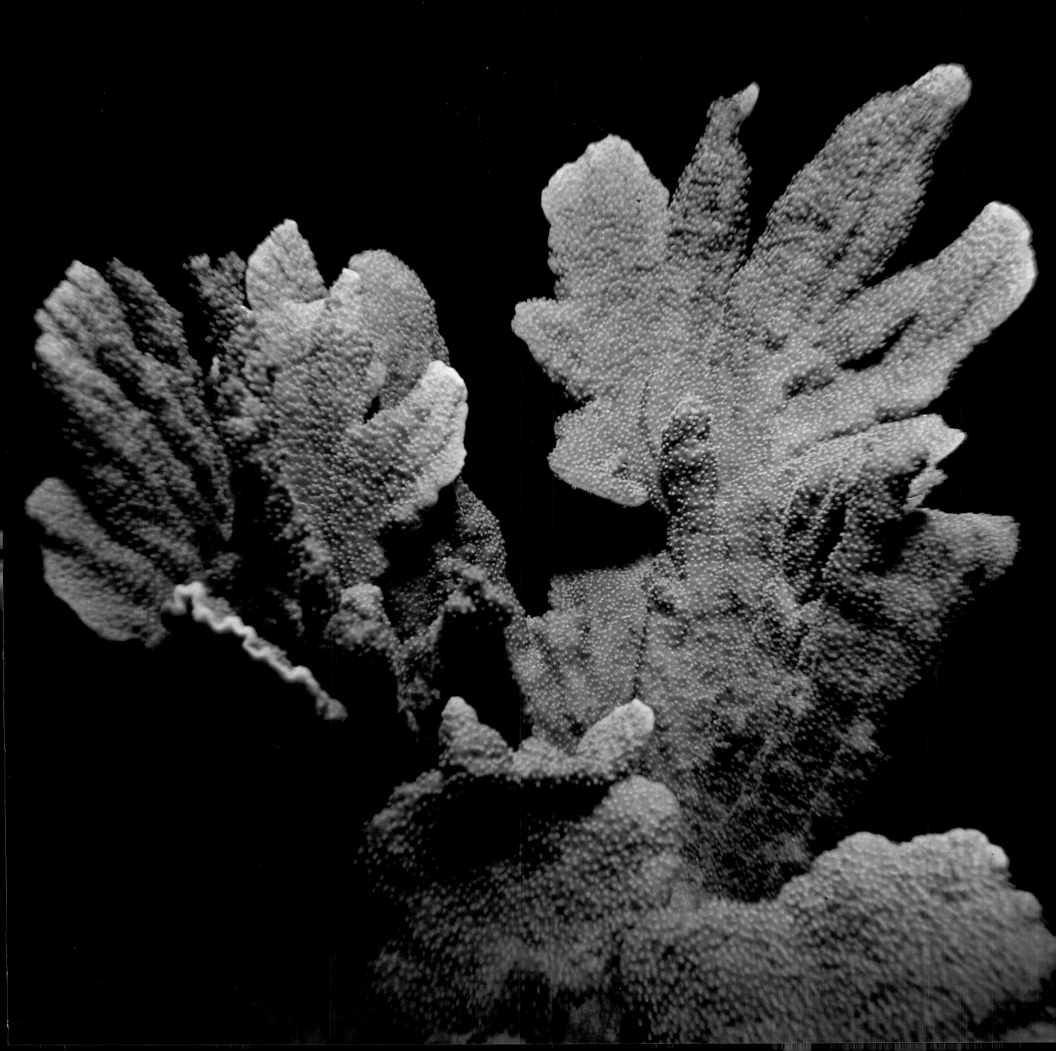

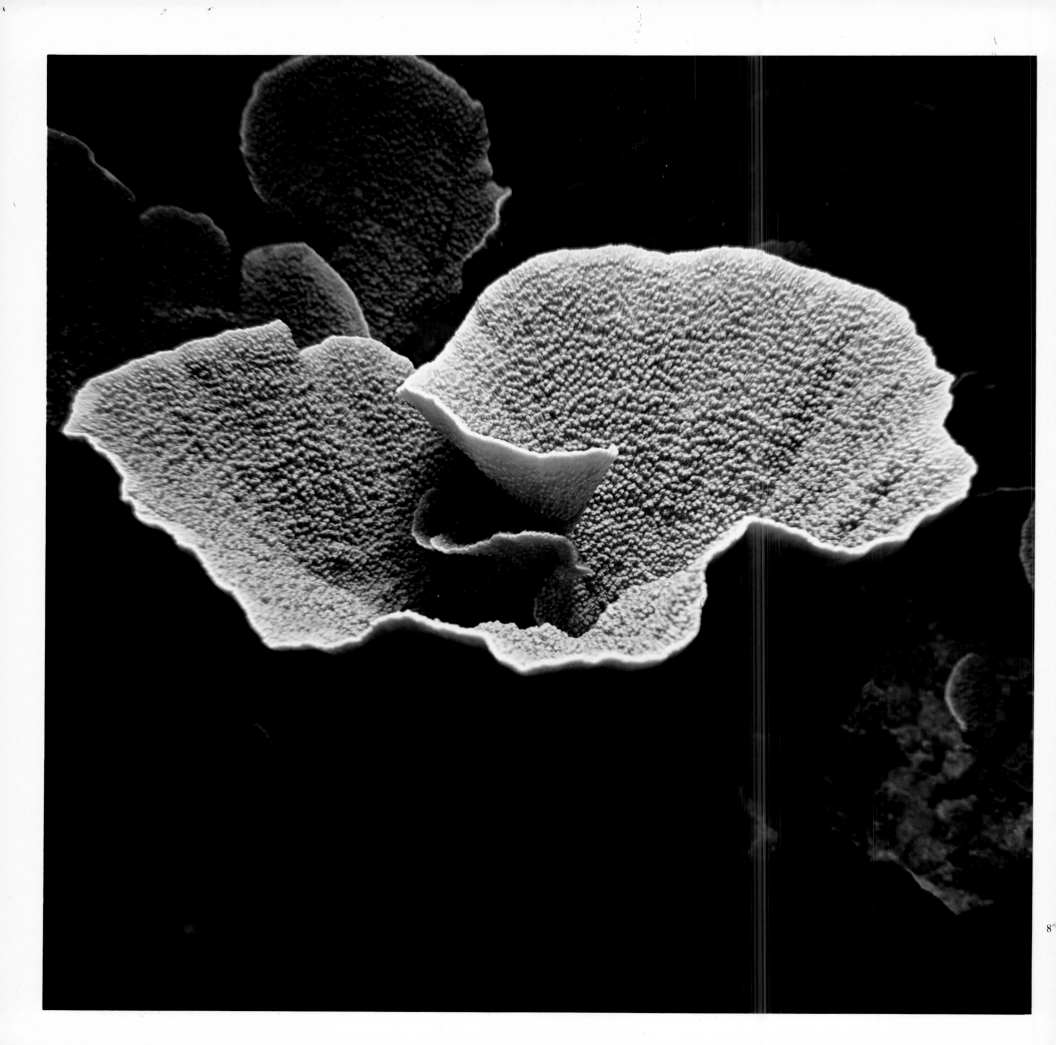

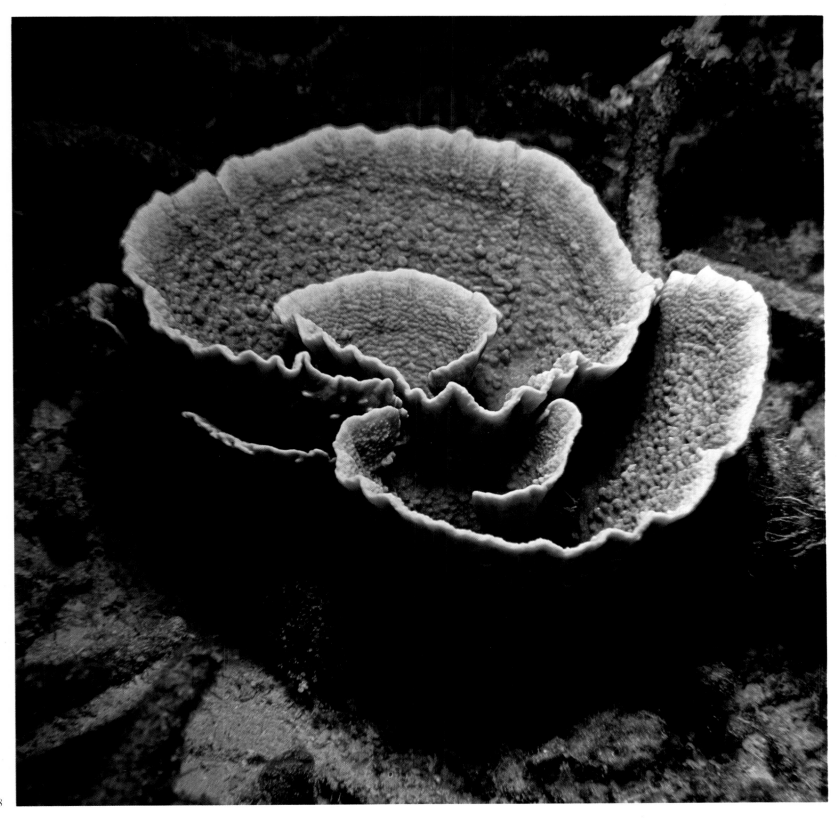

AGARICIIDAE

94

95

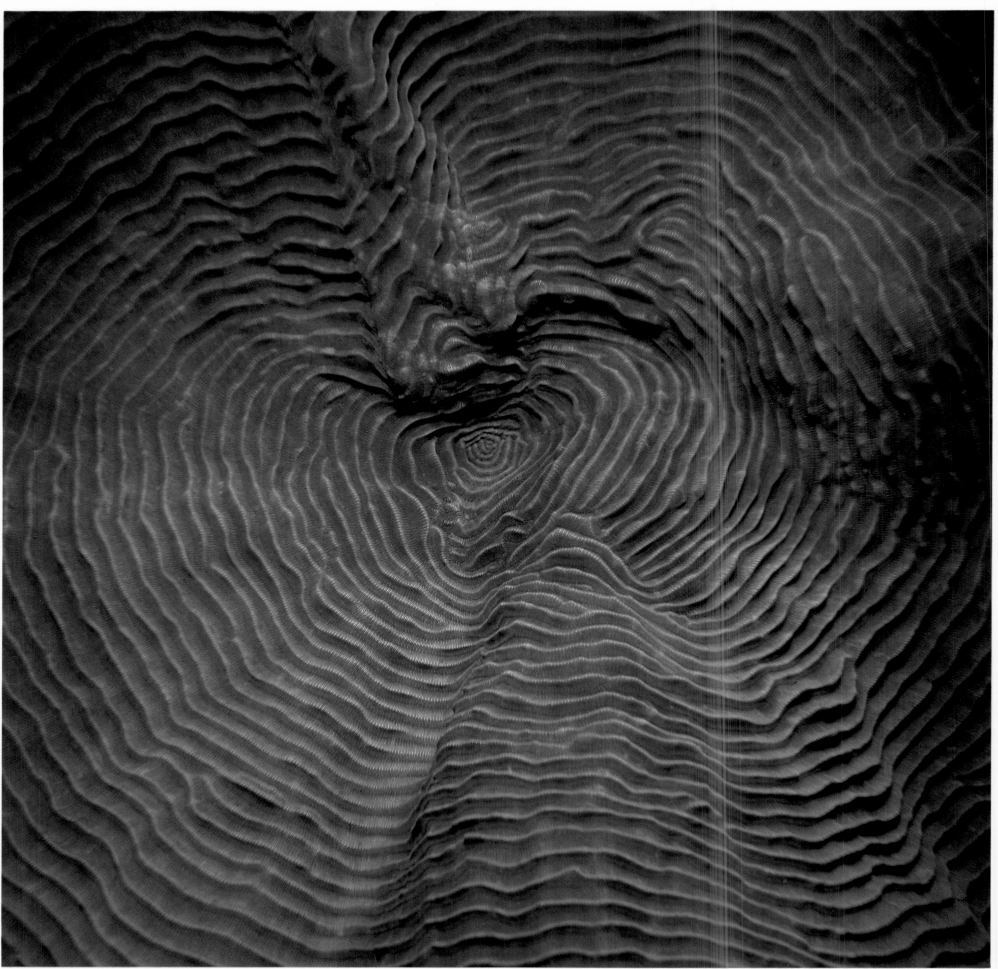

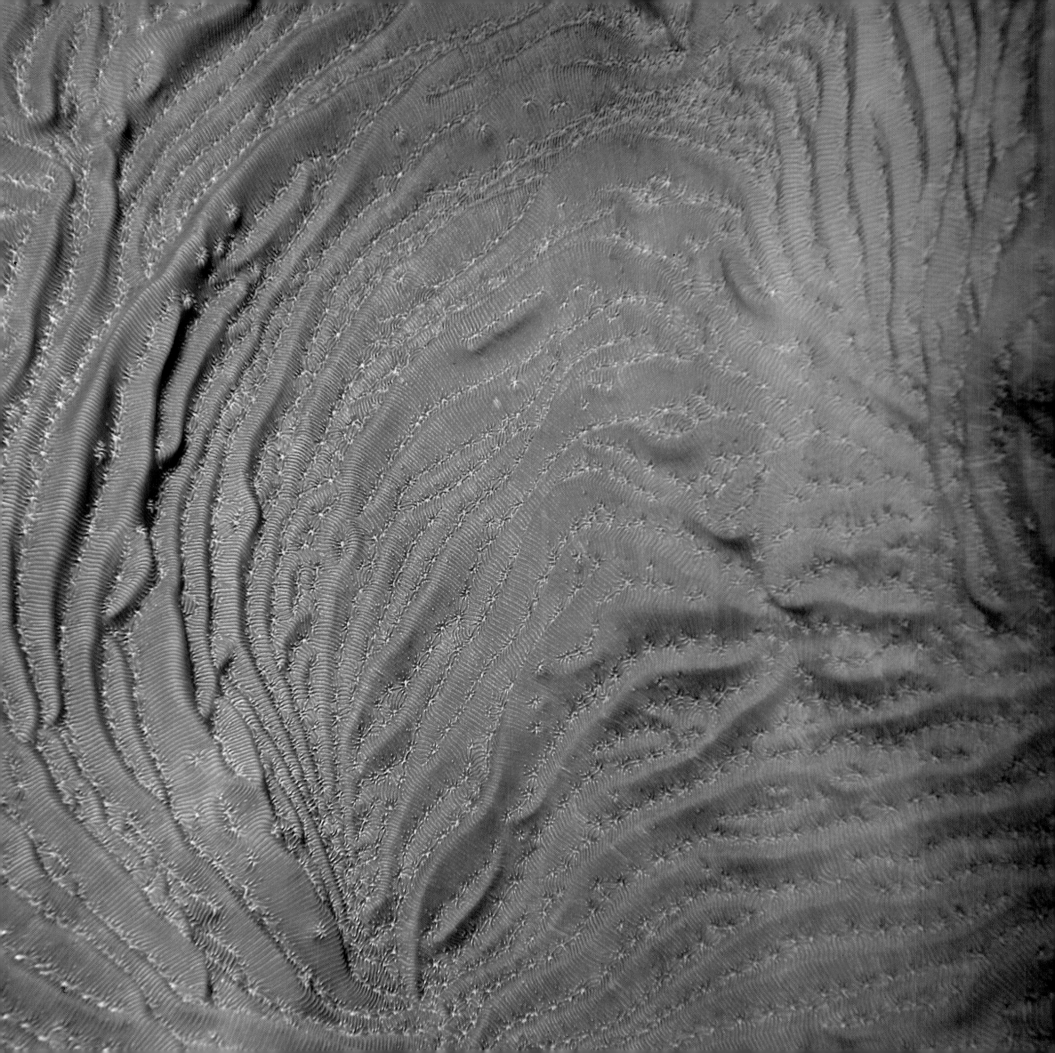

FUNGIIDAE

PORITIDAE

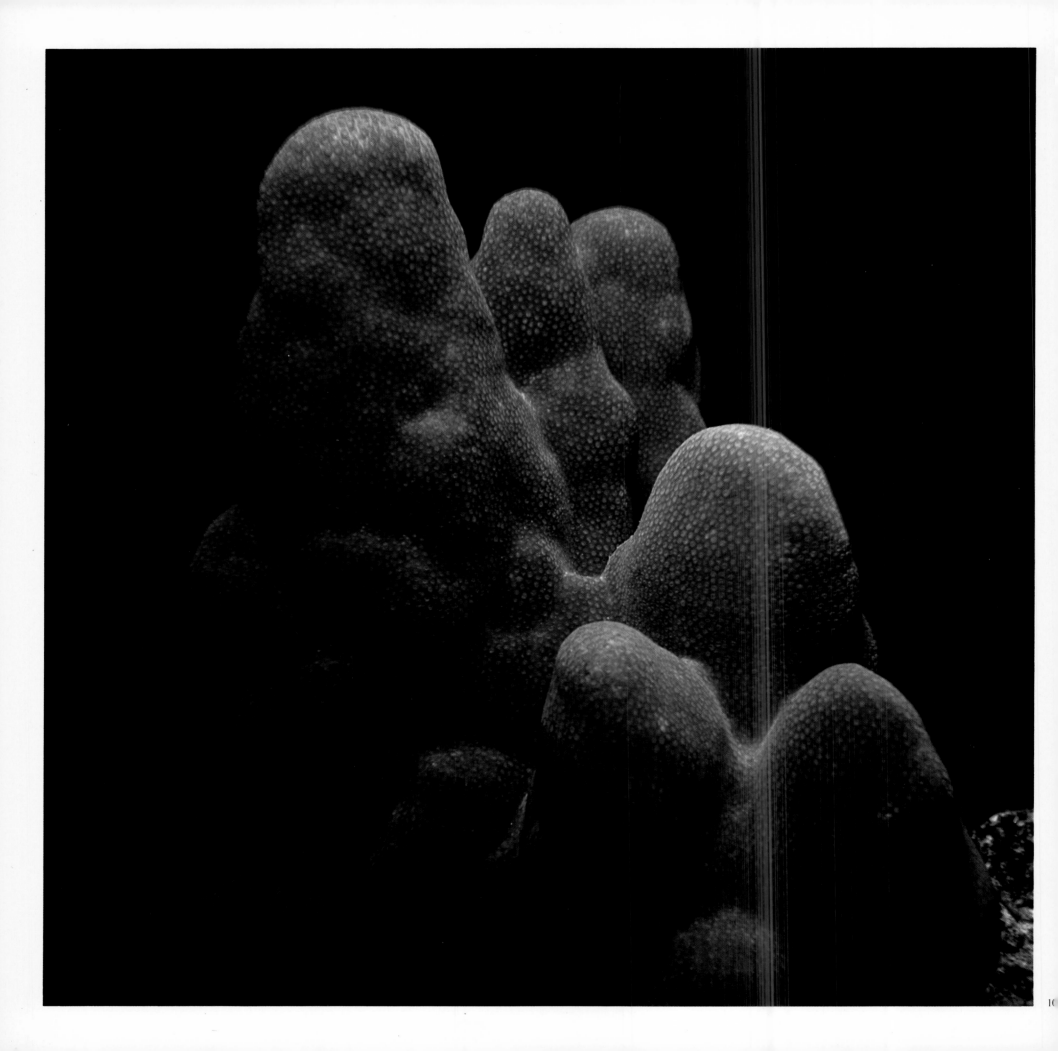

108

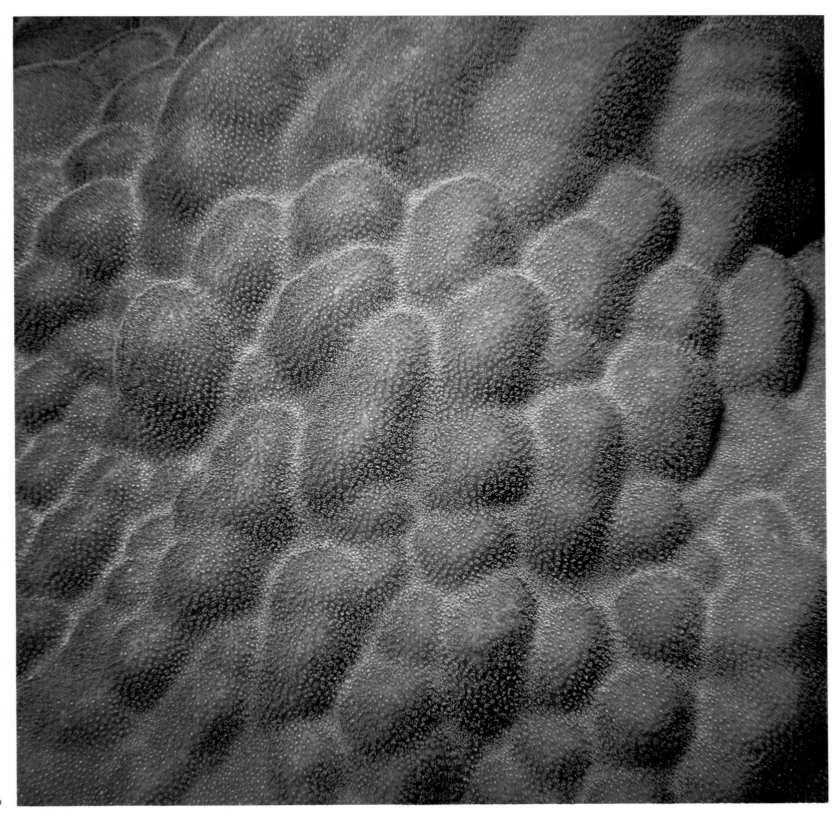

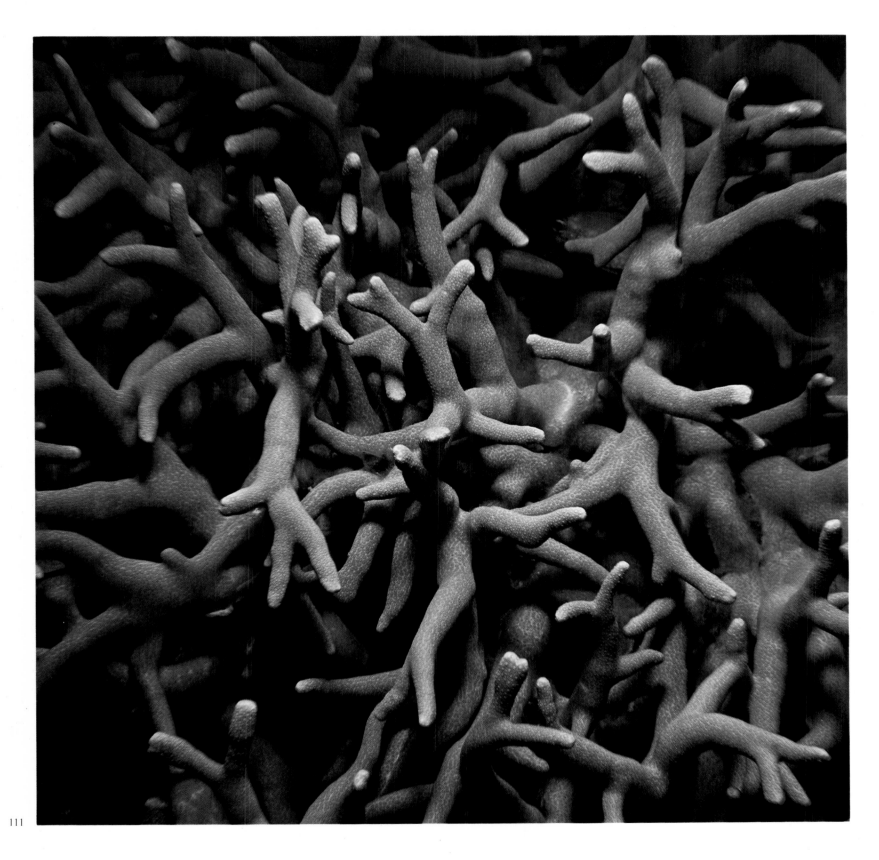

114

115

FAVIIDAE

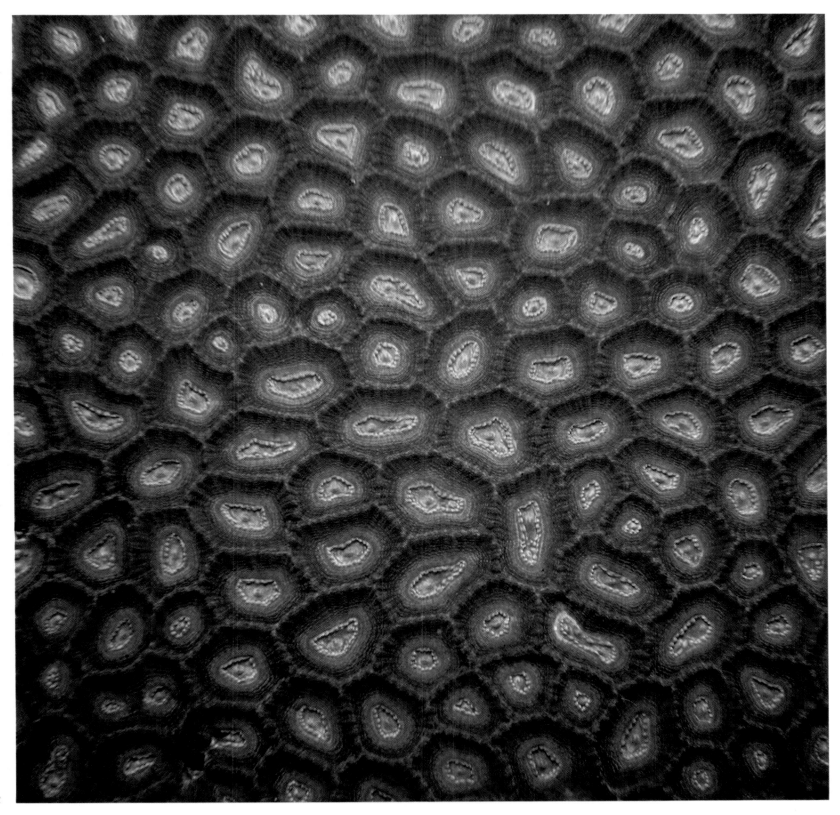

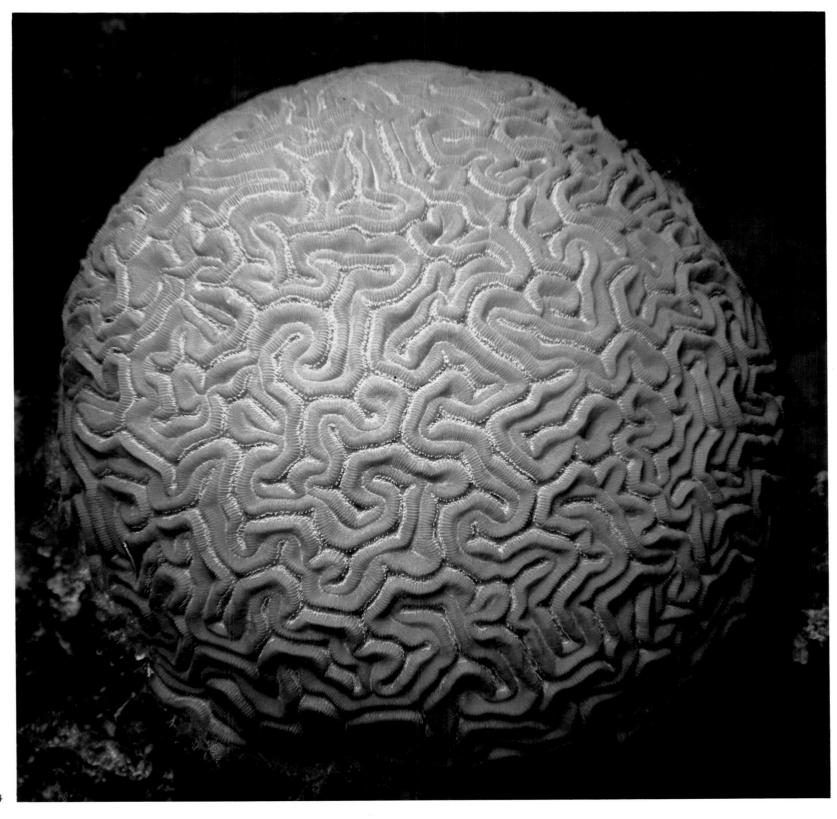

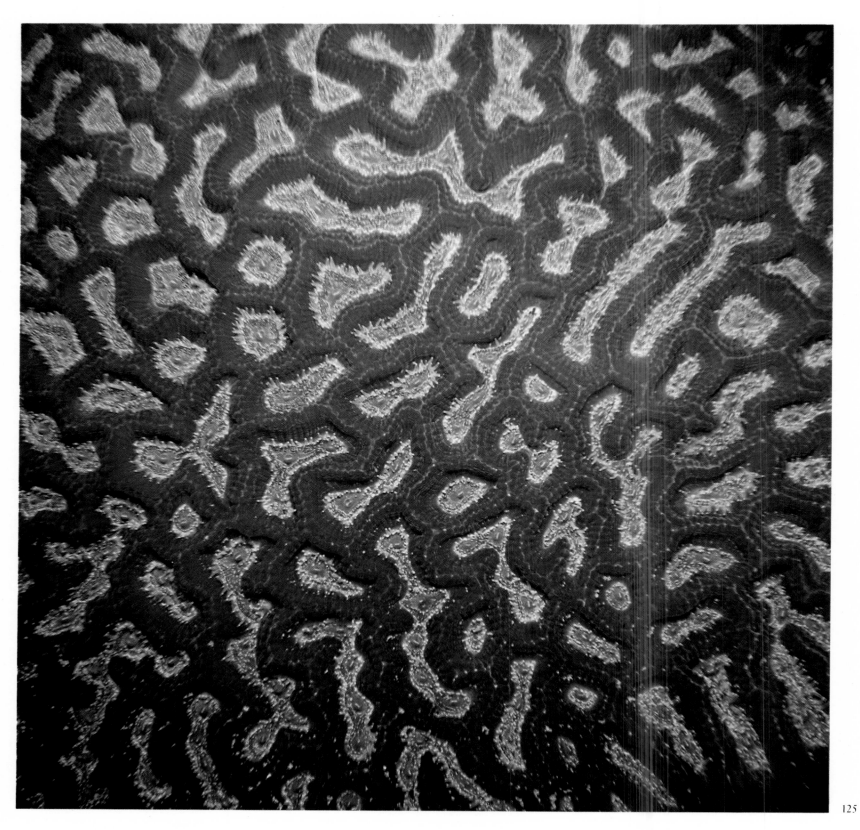

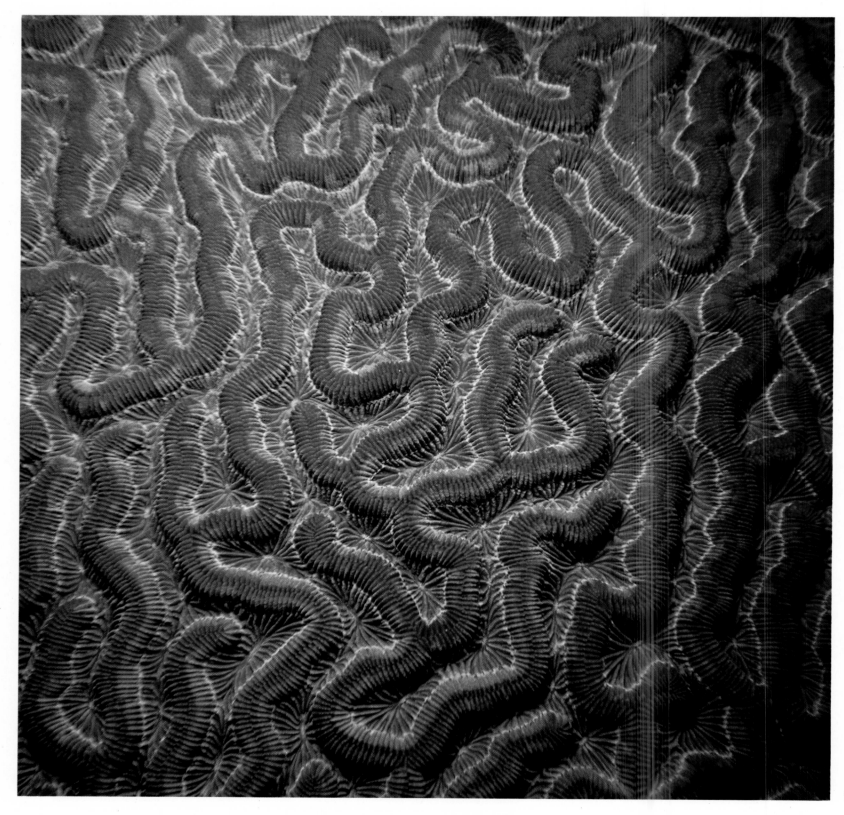

131

OCULINIDAE

138

MEANDRINIDAE

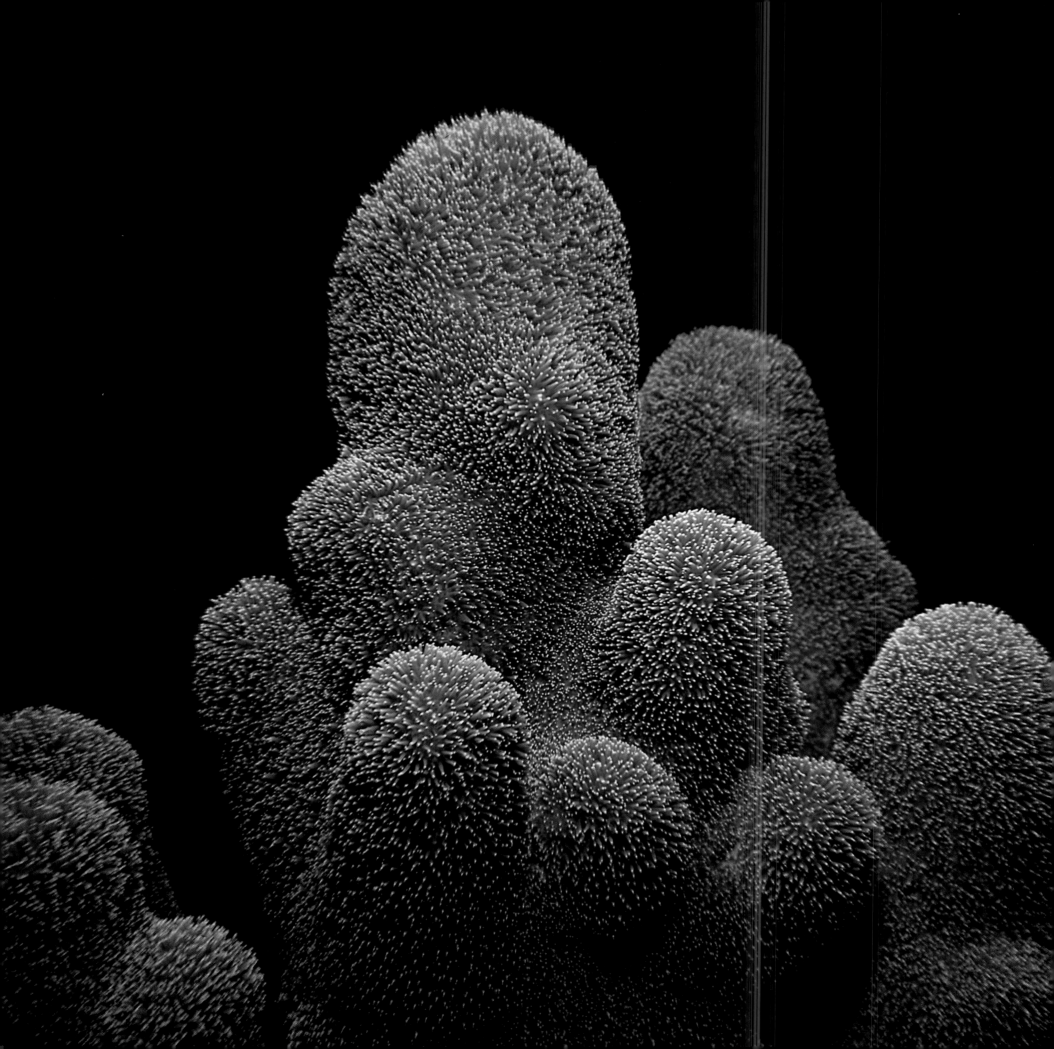

MERULINIDAE

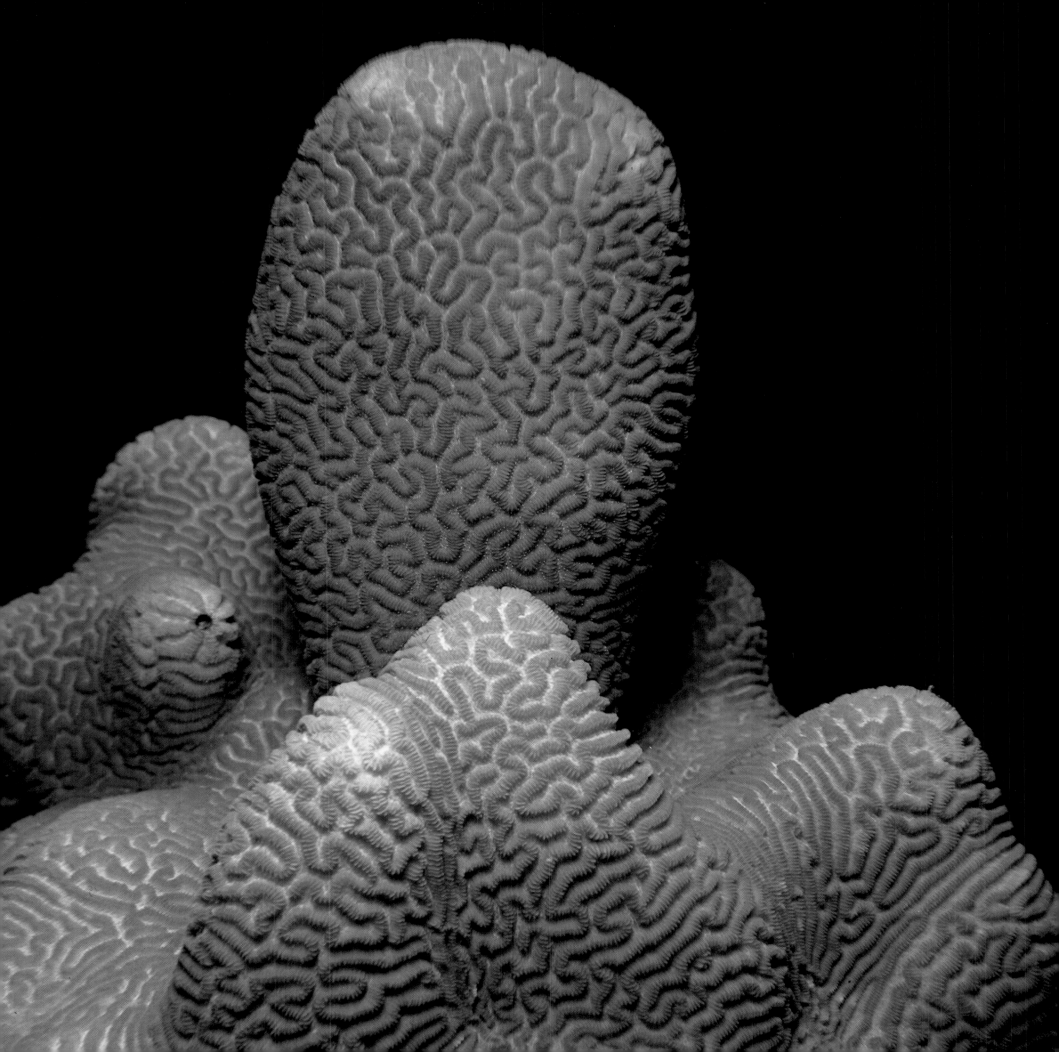

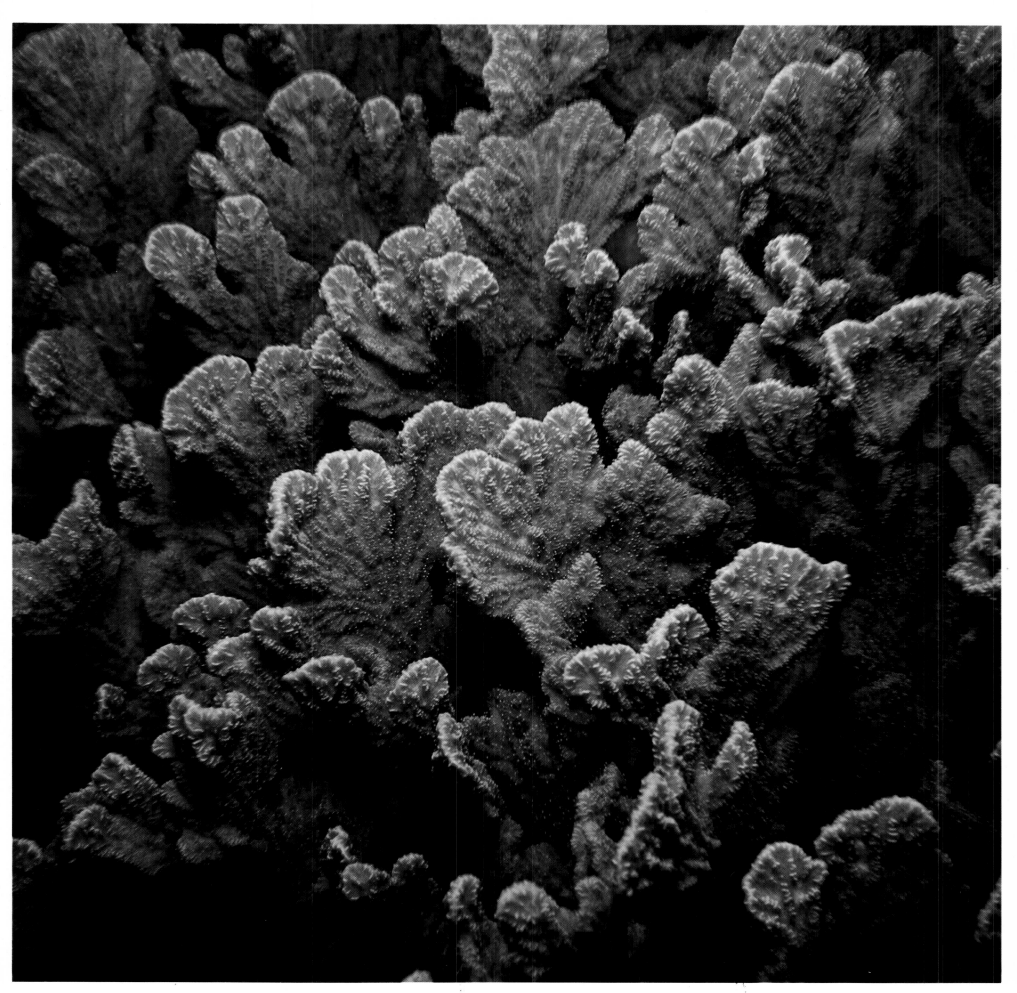

MUSSIDAE

151

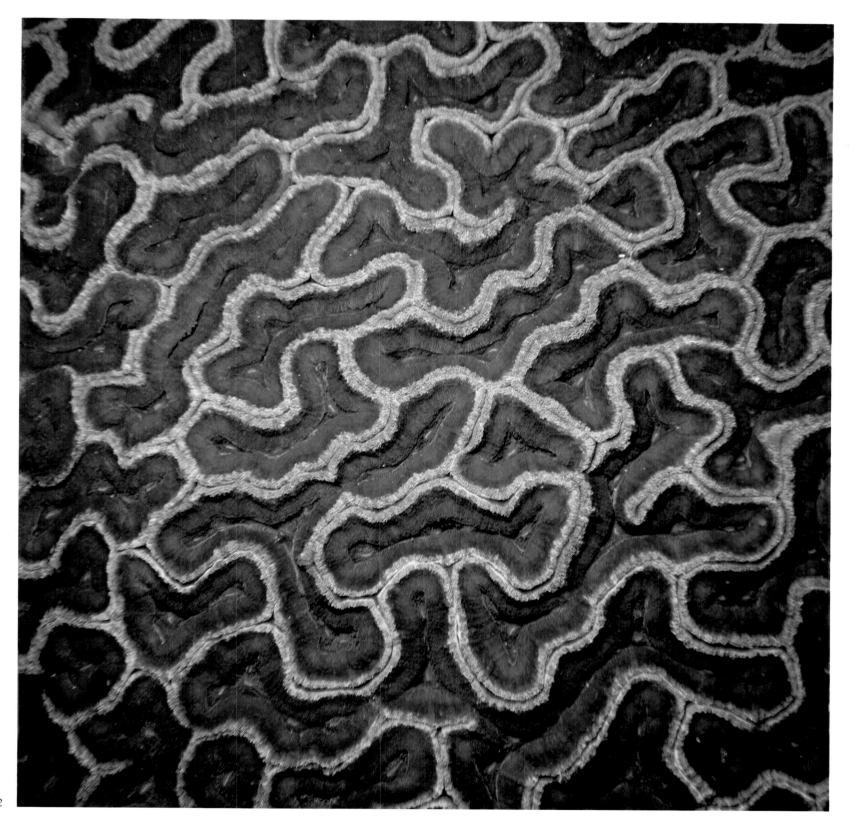

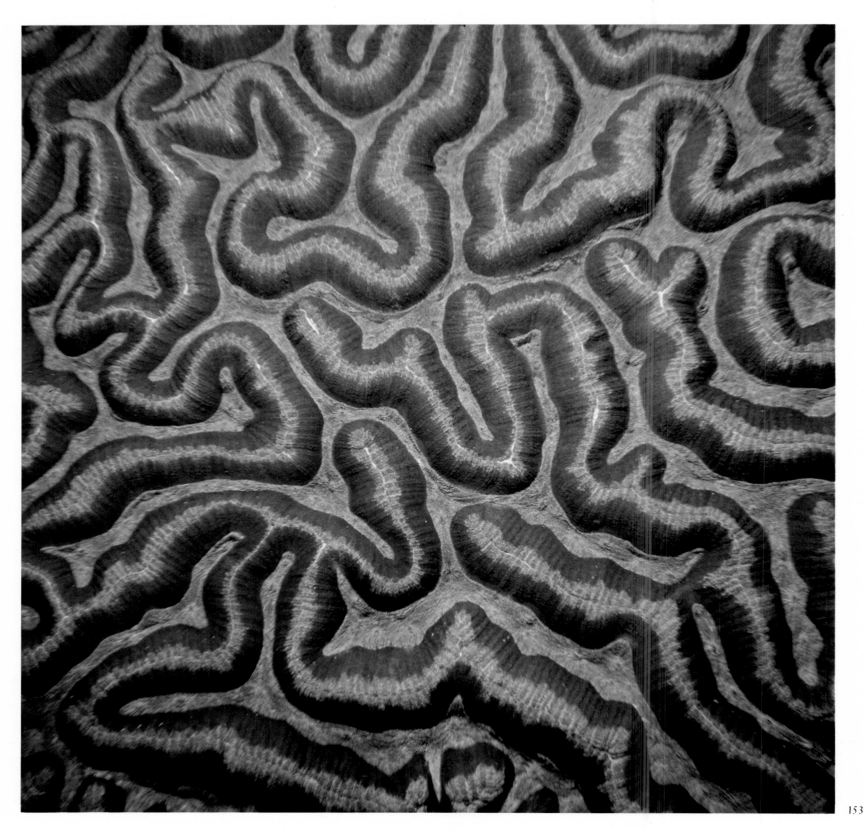

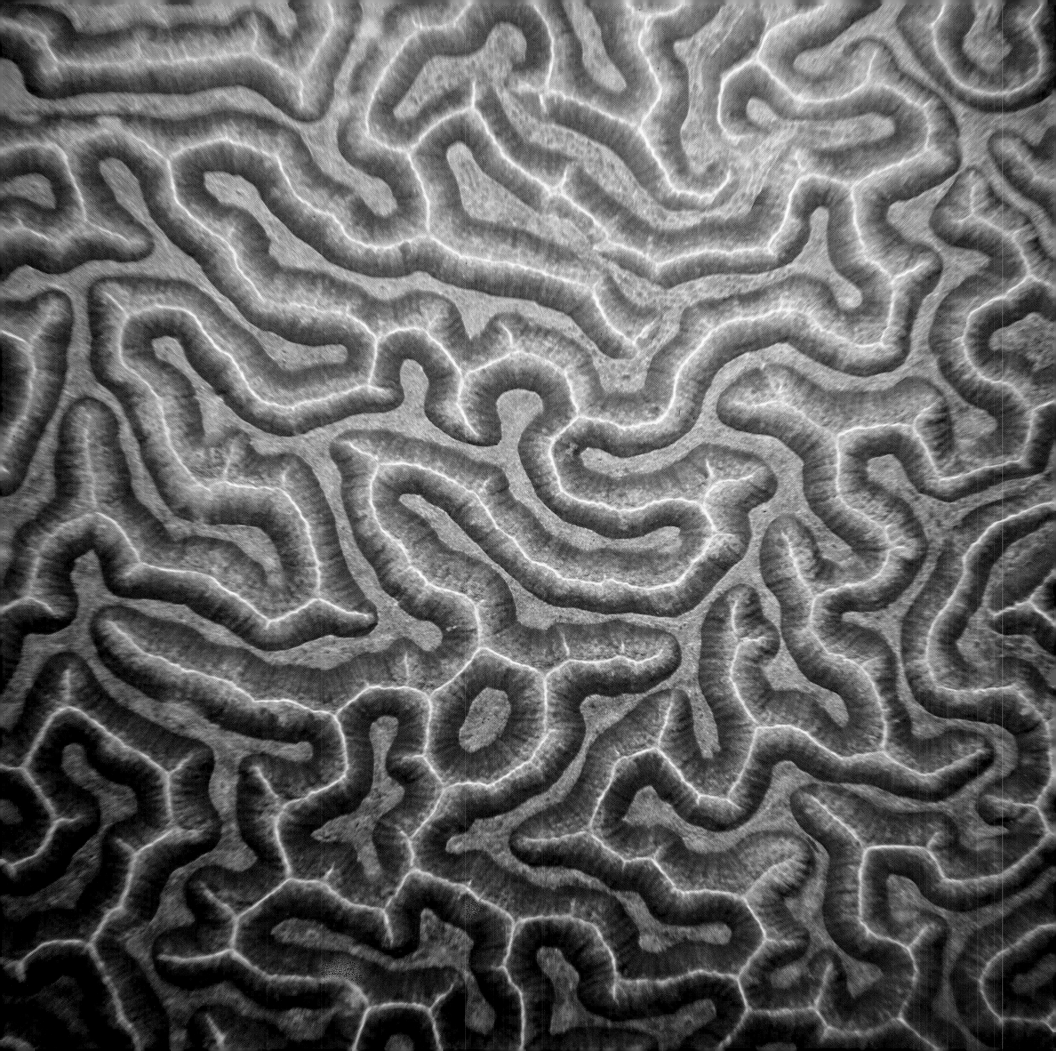

PECTINIIDAE

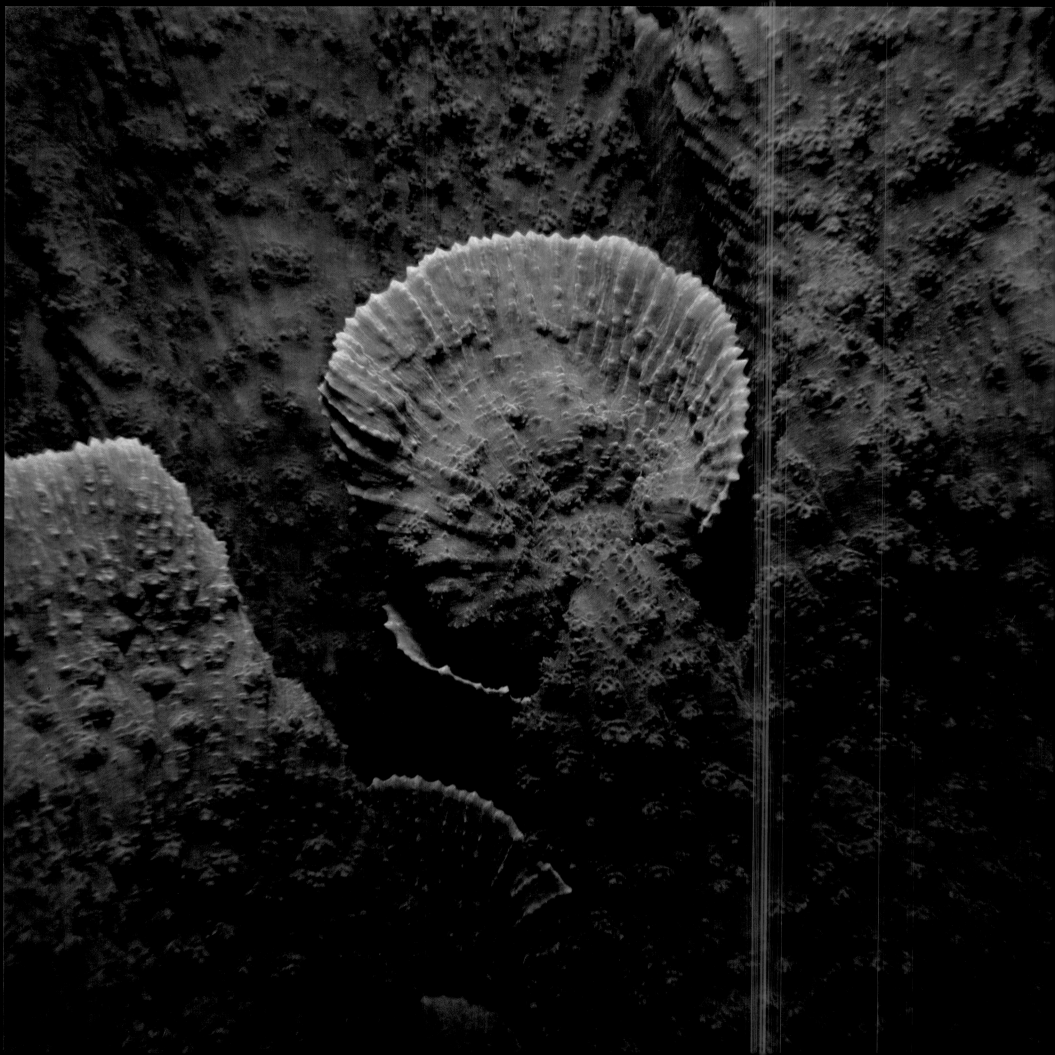

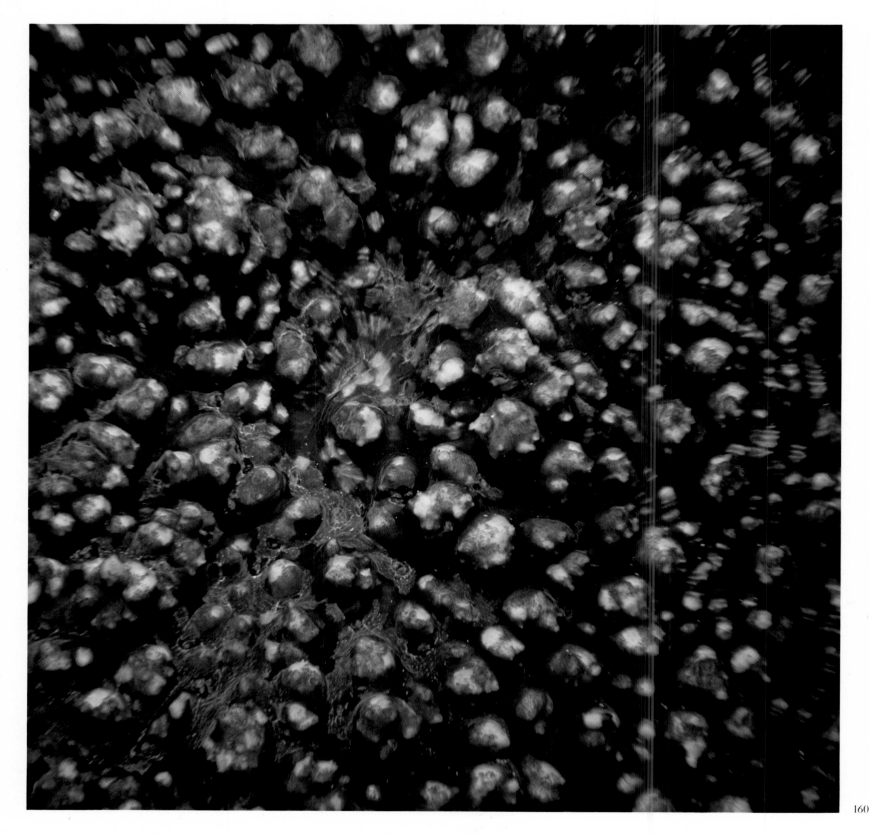

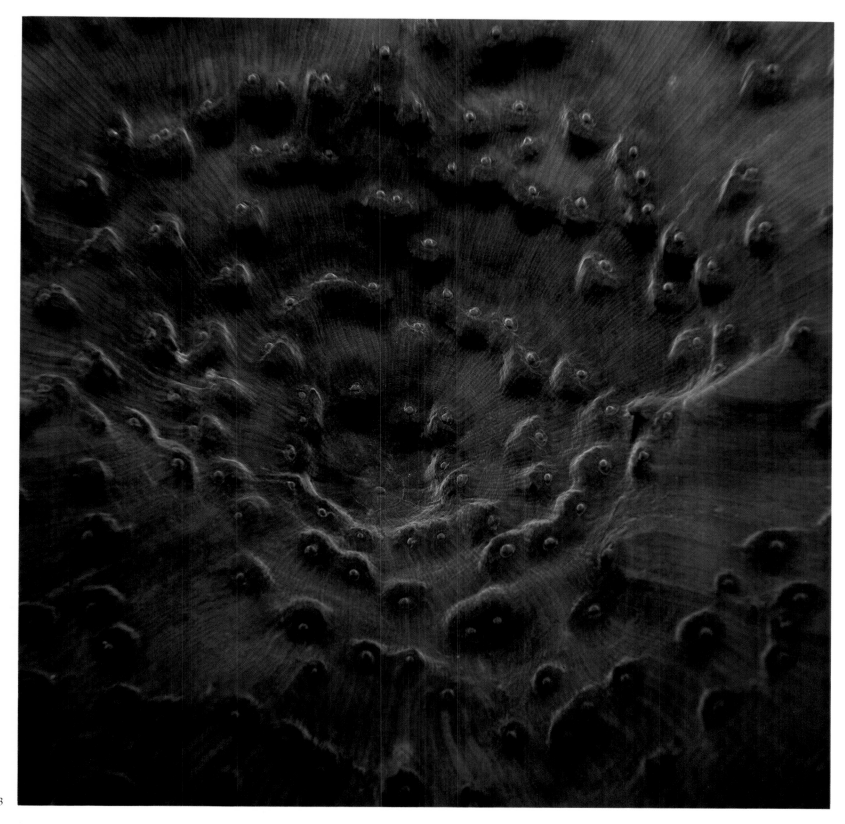

165

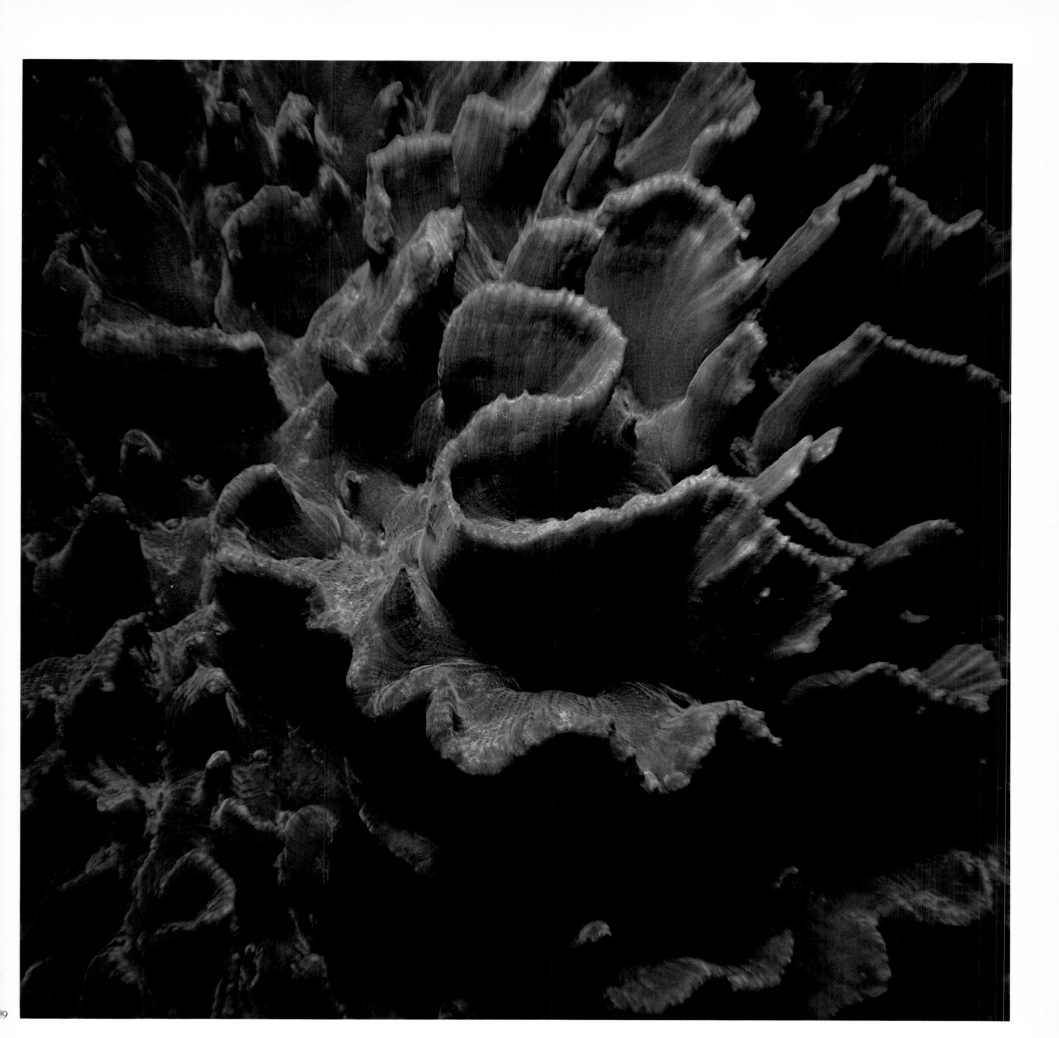

EUSMILIIDAE

DENDROPHYLLIIDAE

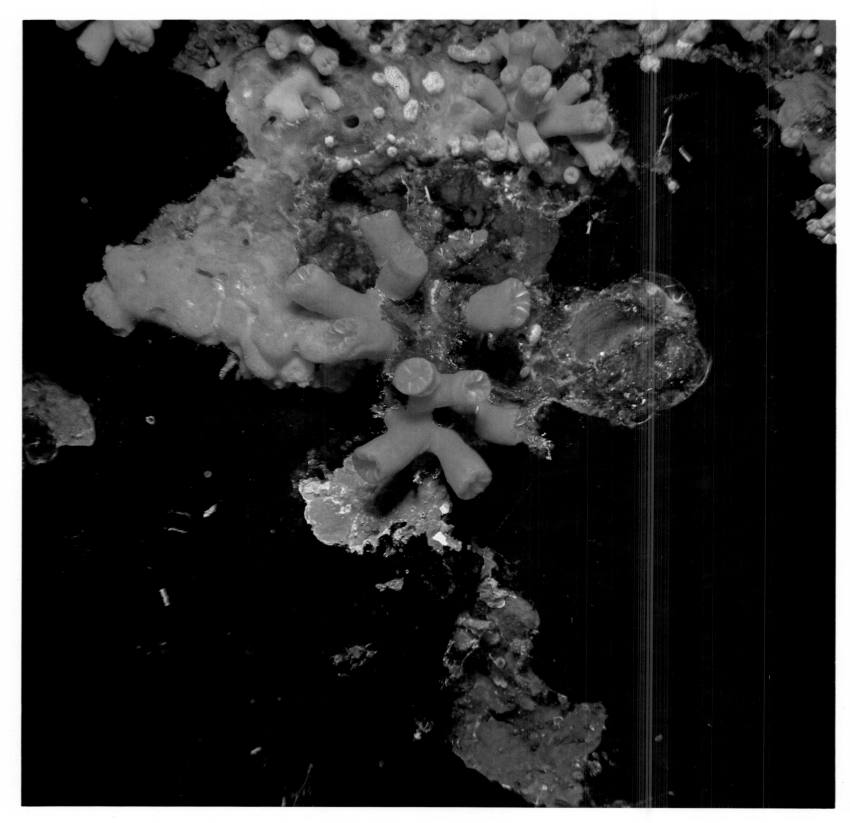

181

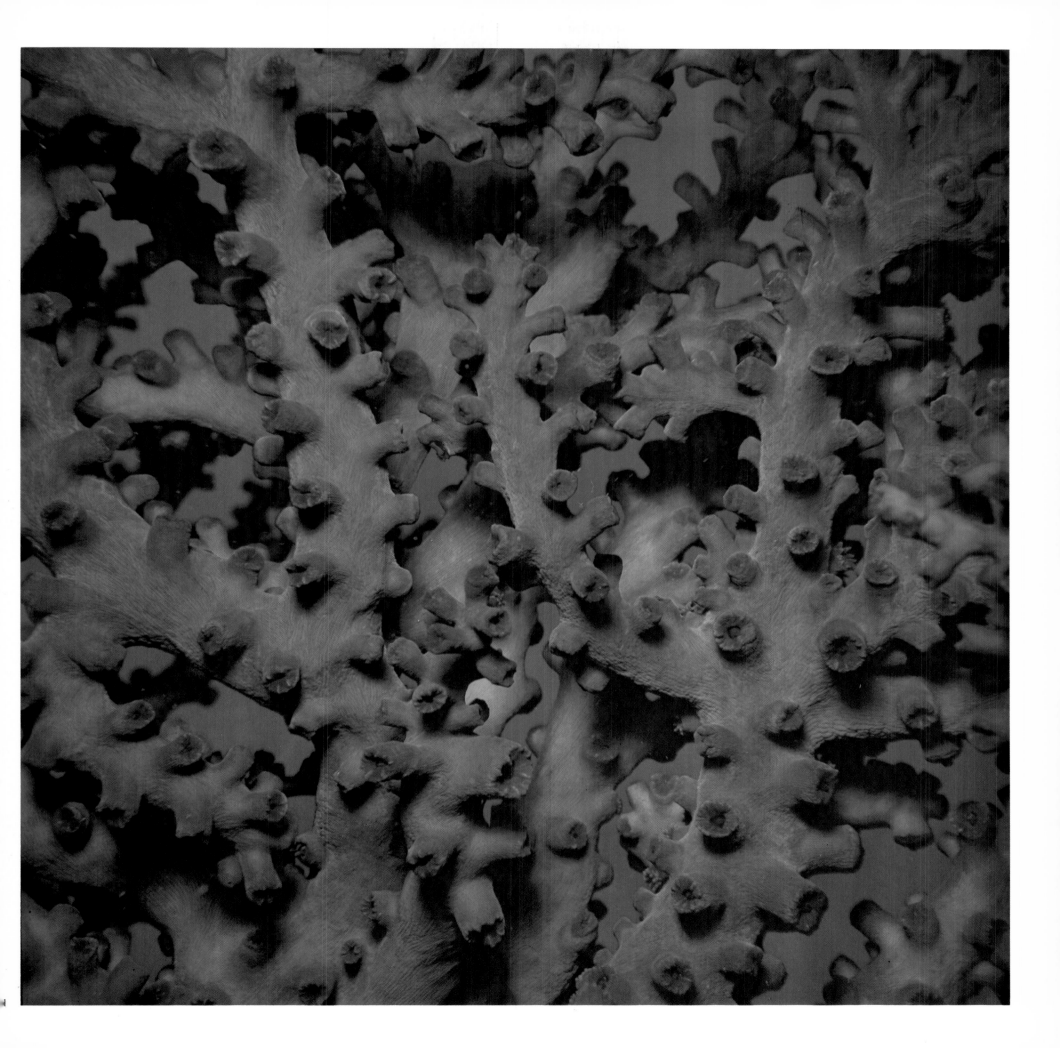

"Good morning," said the little prince.

"Good morning," said the flower.

"Where are the men?" the little prince asked, politely.

The flower had once seen a caravan passing.

"Men?" she echoed. *"I think there are six or seven
of them in existence. I saw them, several years ago.
But one never knows where to find them.
The wind blows them away. They have no roots,
and that makes their life very difficult."*

"Goodbye," said the little prince.

"Goodbye," said the flower.

To the visually oriented, words are a distraction. We see before we speak, and hear before we understand. An overlay of words helps us to see and understand anew, but it is that first vision which most excites us. Words will never replace what my eyes have seen. The recorded depth at which a coral lives is of little importance beside the beauty of the living coral.

Not long ago I projected my marine life photographs at a party. Before the slide show I told the small group there would be no running commentary. Despite this announcement, one woman persisted with her questions. Finally losing my patience, I said, "Do you see this creature? Imagine yourself underwater and suddenly you come upon it. Who is there to question?"

Books take from us as much as we learn from them. Do we always need guide books to see? The guide book carried to its ultimate absurdity is apparent at Buck Island reef in the American Virgin Islands. Here, an "underwater trail" is dotted with cement blocks displaying pictures of fishes and corals, appropriately captioned. These guides to reef navigation destroy the beauty of the very landscape they try to explain. I never studied photography to "see" through my camera. Seeing has been an extension of my delight in what there is to see, from infancy and childhood until now. I once explained to a friend, "You begin loving colors as they hang over your crib, a rainbowed mobile of fish bellies. Your eyes easily reach further than your little hands."

Virtually all the scientific names and taxonomic information for this book came after a lapse of many years. As it should, the photographic experience came first. I have maintained this priority in the book. A caption adjacent to each photograph would make convenient reading but why mar the vivid patterns which delight us? As Juliet reminded Romeo: "What's Montague? It is nor hand, nor foot, nor arm, nor face, nor any part belonging to a man."

My photographs are more important than my commentary. Yet I value the scientific approach enough to deal with each coral in depth, rather than in a rigid five-line caption format. My experience with a coral cannot be expressed in a caption. The commentaries are fitted to the corals, not to the limited space beside a photograph.

Corals do not live on a reef taxonomically arranged, but many family members do inhabit the same or similar environments. In *Living Corals* every coral is arranged taxonomically, which allows the reader to see, for the first time, similarities and differences among related corals, and among more distant relatives. One can gain a sense of life's flow, why species are alike and yet have diverged phylogenetically.

Beginning with my first roll of film, I kept simple records on caption cards. These field notes have provided most of the data accompanying each coral commentary. All data are recorded much as a scientist writes collection information on a tag that accompanies a specimen. Every data card and specimen is keyed to the numbered roll of film, sharing the same number. A typical roll number for Belau reads, 646-5, which is the 646th roll of film exposed on my 5th trip to Belau, 17 October 1971. My roll numbers are not necessary in this book, because the caption card information on the Poppy Coral for roll 646-5 is part of the data for plate 157. I mention this system because an underwater photographer engaged in serious documentary work must keep comparable records. All depths were recorded with a diver's depth gauge calibrated in feet, but feet and meters are given here.

My formal education in marine sciences occurred twenty-two years ago at the University of Miami. I completed one undergraduate course in marine biology and another introductory course in oceanography. At the time, it seemed to me that a formal marine sciences education only prepared students for a career in commercial fisheries. My interests centered elsewhere. The scientific approach rubbed off, however, giving my photographic work and the uses of it a measure of scientific discipline. Moreover, I gained an awareness and vision sufficient to roam at will in a very wide domain. As my projects grew in complexity, lingering deficiencies from an incomplete schooling in marine sciences taxed the patience of my advisors and even mine. While working on *Living Corals*, my defects seemed to me greatly magnified. Reportedly, an atomic physicist saw the space between atoms so magnified that fear possessed him when he walked across the floor, the firmness of which he seriously questioned. It is these spaces through which I swim, not content to remain in the shallow end of the pool. If awarded a full scholarship to the university of my choice, I would choose the sea. I would not trade an hour of many years underwater for a semester of classrooms. My informal studies, bolstered with considerable help from my scientist friends, provided sufficient background information to supplement my undersea experiences.

Among the many scientists who helped, two have been exceedingly patient and generous. Dr. Frederick M. Bayer and Dr. John W. Wells have worked extensively and with dedication to give scientific validity to my projects. Before I designed *Living Corals* in 1974, Dr. Bayer provided a general arrangement for the corals based upon the taxonomic arrangement in the *Treatise on Invertebrate Paleontology* R. C. Moore, Editor (Part F) Coelenterata Geological Society of America, University of Kansas Press. Anyone seriously interested in the study of corals should own the *Treatise* for it encompasses many families not represented here and although it is illustrated only with ink drawings, readers may become familiar with the larger taxonomic context.

During the course of my photographic work, I collected and air-mailed to Dr. Bayer several hundred coral specimens. Many were photographed and are among those illustrated, but most were collected nearby from a colony of the same species. When at all possible, I did not collect the photographed coral to avoid defacing something beautiful. Over the years, the corals grew and I documented their growth. I feel great pleasure knowing most of my corals are still alive. My mind perceives them in their various locations on the reefs of Belau. Their aliveness keeps the reef alive in me.

Having received the specimens from Belau, Dr. Bayer devoted countless hours to their identification to determine scientific names to provide the proper taxonomic arrangement for the illustrations. In Dr. Bayer's estimation, a dozen or more of the collected corals are new to science. During years of study, aided by the scanning electron microscopes at the School of Marine and Atmospheric Sciences, University of Miami, and now at the Smithsonian Institution, Washington, D.C., Dr. Bayer has made photographs of corals, utilizing black and white Polaroid prints. He assembled overlapping composites and will eventually publish them to illustrate a variety of coral spicules and structures. The many soft corals Dr. Bayer studied are partly identified by the form of their spicules. He could not give scientific names to the dozen or so new species because a revision of the genus, and possibly the family, must take place before generic and specific names can be applied with certainty. The new species are mostly soft corals, although several stony corals are new to science.

Thirty-one coral families are represented in this book. Information in the brief introductions to the seventeen families from Milleporidae to Helioporidae, as well as technical, morphological and physiological descriptions for each coral, was supplied by Dr. Bayer. Material for the fourteen remaining stony coral families, from Thamnasteridae to Dendrophylliidae, and the more technical information about each coral was supplied by Dr. Wells. Other than the photographs, my contribution to the commentary derives from years of swimming underwater among the corals, observing their distribution and population densities, their growth and behavior, and a host of details and impressions.

In December of 1973, Dr. John Wells assisted me at the eleventh hour with information about coral reef geology for the general text to *This Living Reef*. He crash-tutored me on a wintry weekend at Cornell University, after which I drove home and wrote my text in nineteen days. John Wells and Pie, his wife, were infinitely generous. They allowed me to telephone almost any time, day or night, seven days a week, until the 15,000 words were written.

In undertaking a major book about corals, it is fortunate that Dr. Bayer, a soft-coral expert, and stony-coral expert Dr. Wells, have continued with their help. Both men have devoted a lifetime to corals and were major contributors to the *Treatise*. I consider myself immensely lucky to have these two noted scientists contribute so much of their time and expertise to *Living Corals*. Behind the scenes, one begins to appreciate why scientists have slow schedules. In my books I have attempted to close that time lag between the acquisition of certain marine science knowledge and its dissemination to the public. Libraries of knowledge still await funds for research and eventual publication in appropriate journals. My commentaries are a modest link between the knowledge of working scientists and the public, but the book, I trust, will serve marine scientists as well.

The commentaries are divided in the following manner: there is a taxonomic classification for each family by class, sub-class, order, sub-order, and family although some groups have no sub-class/sub-order divisions. Following the classification, each family is introduced with a brief description which touches upon its morphological characteristics, the numbers of known genera and species, the known geographic populations and the depth range. The commentary on each coral is prefaced with relevant data: the common name, scientific name and author who first described the species, and the year his description was published. If the species was later transferred to a different genus, parentheses enclose the original author and date. If the coral is a new species or cannot be given a name, its generic name is followed by the word "species" in normal type. If a coral's classification is not entirely certain for want of a specimen, its scientific name is followed by a question mark. Others, even less definitely identified, can only be compared with a known species pending a technical decision, and the generic names of these are separated from the specific names by "cf.," the technical abbreviation for "compare."

All common and scientific names are followed by the coral's size as illustrated in the book. The majority of corals are shown approximately life size or $\frac{1}{4}$ to $\frac{1}{3}$ larger. This was intentional on my part to give the reader a feeling for corals as they actually appear under water. The locality is followed by the approximate depth at which the coral lives in feet and meters. Coral behavior is greatly influenced by the time of day; "Day" or "Night" indicates when it was photographed. Also included is the day, month and year the coral was photographed. The United States National Museum catalogue numbers for collected specimens of the corals illustrated in the book conclude each set of data. Not every coral was collected, but those that were are deposited in the permanent collection of the National Museum of Natural History of the Smithsonian Institution in Washington, D.C. If the actual specimen was photographed, the catalogue number in the data reads: Photographed: USNM No. 58497. If the collected specimen was not the one photographed, the catalogue number reads: Similar: USNM No. 58498. Generally, only one specimen of a coral was collected, but sometimes it was necessary to collect several. Therefore, a coral may have one or several catalogue numbers. If no specimen was collected this is indicated.

In addition to "Photographed" and "Similar" specimens, there are "Holotype" and "Paratype" specimens. A holotype specimen is so designated as "the type" by the original author in his published description. There is only one holotype of a species but when the author bases his description on additional specimens, he may designate them as paratypes. Several specimens of a new species collected for Bayer and Wells have been designated by them as holotypes and paratypes.

In certain instances a coral's common name was taken from local usage although the majority resulted from personal associations. At a time when I lacked scientific names for most corals, the "common names" made it possible to record a Chalice Coral from one depth and a Staghorn Coral from another on the same roll of film. Recently, I was amused and delighted when a scientist at the Smithsonian Institution told me about a person who called the museum to inquire about Douglas Fauklner's common name for a particular coral. In that moment I experienced the pleasure a coral taxonomist must feel when publishing the description and name of a new species. Yet oddly, publication of the common names in this book unburdens me of the need to hold them in my head. Common names are easy to remember, and therefore more useful. Unfortunately, they are only "common" to people sharing the same culture. Everyone cannot associate a certain *Siphonogorgia* with cotton candy but a scientific name is specific to one coral, irrespective of what Philippine Islanders, Solomon Islanders or we choose to call it.

The reader may be somewhat bewildered by a blizzard of unfamiliar words. For this reason, many facts about corals might reach beyond one's present interests. Nonetheless I have tried to include as much information as time permitted, hoping the commentary will whet the reader's appetite to explore further those subjects not sufficiently explained or included here.

There is no unified body of published knowledge on corals. What literature there is consists of a wide scattering of scientific papers or old hand-illustrated books costing ten and twenty times as much as *Living Corals*. Unfortunately, little specific information is known about the natural history and behavior of most corals. Studies have centered more on their classification than on their biology.

My commentary is only a patchwork of facts, many pro-

vided by scientists and supplemented by my own observations and impressions. In a hop-and-skip way, I have touched upon the seasons, lunar phases, tidal changes, minus tides and currents, light intensities both day and night, and how corals are affected by them. Other factors affecting a coral's life are the amount of cloud cover, rainy and overcast days and ocean storms, where they live and why, and how depth and habitat shape their lives. Coloration in corals is explored, as is reproduction and growth, aggression, and the separation of the sexes among the colonies of many species.

However fascinating, the above aspects of the lives of corals are known only in a scattered way. The life history of only a few corals has been investigated. Scientists such as Richard Randall, Carden C. Wallace, Judith Land, and the late Thomas Goreau have made extensive underwater studies on coral distribution, their growth and behavior. A scientist could devote a lifetime to one family or genus numbering a dozen species and not exhaust his subject, but corals are many and researchers few.

In reading through the commentary, one soon discovers that almost all the corals were photographed in Belau from 5 October 1967 to 17 April 1976, a time span accounting for 158 of the 194 photographs. This lopsided emphasis on Belau was intentional, for nowhere have I encountered quite so rich a coral world in so wondrous a setting. Many of my earliest photographs made in Belau are valuable to this collection. Amazingly, the 11th exposure on my first roll of film made in 1967 is plate 100. This brief five-week trip to Belau inspired two books: *This Living Reef*, completed and published in 1974, and *Living Corals*, in need of a text, was nearly complete. The five year delay in publishing *Living Corals* allowed Bayer and Wells more time to review the specimens and make taxonomic changes toward a more complete list of scientific names. It is most likely that the United States National Museum numbers would not be included here had the book been published several years earlier. Both Bayer and Wells raced against a deadline to make possible much of what is included.

If one has a fascination for dates, a glance through *This Living Reef* and *Living Corals* reveals that both books lived their days together in Belau, even though many photographs in *Living Corals* were made later, during the summers of 1973 and 1974. A map of Belau is not reproduced here to aid the reader. In *This Living Reef*, however, most of the coral locations are designated on a map of Belau. The 36 remaining photographs of corals were made in Australia, Papua New Guinea, Solomon Islands, New Caledonia, Loyalty Islands, Galápagos Islands, Honduras, Belize, Florida, Bahamas, Vancouver Island, and the Red Sea.

The photographs included are selected from more than 50,000 images beginning in 1962 with a trip to the Society Islands and concluding in 1977 on a trip to the Solomon Islands. My earliest coral photograph, the Merlet Leather Coral, was taken in New Caledonia on 4 February 1963, an experiment with natural light. This living sculpture is a source of great pleasure to me, for the image embodies the purest expression of my love for the abstract and for corals. The image in my mind swims easily and I follow like the Emperor in the Chinese fairy tale who splashes down the stream in pursuit of the golden fish. The Emperor imagined he was chasing a fish made of gold, but our true wealth is in Nature. She abounds with colors and patterns—butterfly wings, cuttlefish eyes, orchids and wildflowers, spiraled shells and sun-shaped clouds. Corals are not the only, or even the finest, expression of Nature's unceasing love of color and pattern. Nevertheless I have devoted more photographic time to corals than to any other being in the sea for they are one of this planet's great legacies.

Douglas Faulkner
13 June 1979

1. Scarlet Sea Fan *Melithaea* cf. *albitincta* (Ridley, 1884) • 3 feet high • Southwest Wall, Cheleu Island, Ngemelis Islands, Belau • 60 feet/18.3 meters • Day • 24 August 1974 • Similar: USNM No. 58576, 58577

The rays of the sun provide the silhouetted Scarlet Sea Fan with needed heat and light. The sea fan consumes plankton, relying on oceanic currents to bring food. Seasons, winds, currents and tides are inter-related, for they and the planet are governed by the Earth's varying relationship with the sun, moon and the long, slow tug of the stars.

2. Antler Fire Coral *Millepora murrayi* Quelch, 1884? • 1½ life size • Northeast Reef, Macharchar Islands, Belau • 20 feet/6.1 meters • Day • 18 October 1967 • Similar: USNM No. 58503

This Antler Fire Coral expresses the beauty of form in living things. In a seeming "still life," one sees the flow of the past into the present. The very simple use of light from above accentuates the poetry and drama of the fire coral's existence.

3. China Coral *Siphonogorgia* species 1½ life size • Southwest Wall, Cheleu Island, Ngemelis Islands, Belau • 70 feet/21.3 meters • Day • 8 August 1973 • Photographed; USNM No. 58578

A China Coral is attached to the ceiling of an outer reef ledge 70 feet beneath the surface. Its growth is directed downward into a current which flows through the tunneled spaces of the reef.

Although I collected a portion of this coral, its identification was not possible. There are some 40 different but very similar *Siphonogorgia* species from Caribbean and Indo-Pacific waters. Most of them, however, inhabit the Indo-Pacific.

By the use of the scanning electron microscope at the Smithsonian Institution, Dr. Bayer determined that each of the millions of spicules which comprise the coral has the shape of a spindle. Each tiny spicule is composed of calcite. The China Coral's flexible skeleton is made possible by the separation of each spicule from those around it. Were the spicules cemented together, the coral would be considerably more rigid and less suitable for a life broadside to the current, incapable of flexing with the water's variable flow.

4. Monument Valley Maze Coral *Pectinia* species • ¾ life size • Northwest Reef, Malaupaina Island, Solomon Islands • 120 feet/36.6 meters • Day • 19 May 1977 • No specimen

The spires of this Maze Coral from the Solomon Islands are reminiscent of the buttes of Monument Valley in Utah. The ridges increase water contact with the coral's surface, providing the colony with a greater flow of plankton. Moreover, the algae permeating the coral's flesh have increased exposure to sunlight.

Corals assume their shape partly in response to water conditions. In the quiet lagoons and coves they grow more elaborate forms, compared to the more austere shapes subjected to strong wave conditions on open ocean reefs.

5. Juliet's Lace Coral *Stylaster duchassaingi* de Pourtalès, 1867? • 1¼ life size • Baai Village Reef, New Britain, Papua New Guinea • 125 feet/38.1 meters • Day • 21 November 1976 • No specimen

Among the corals of warm, shallow-water reefs, lace corals have the most delicate structure. Generally, they live under ledges away from direct sunlight, which they do not require, for no algae live in their tissues. A large population of Juliet's Lace Coral lives below 100 feet off New Britain Island, growing on sponges, algae-covered ledges and on the open reef at 125 feet and deeper.

Lace Corals have porous skeletons because they grow quickly in contrast to the very slow-growing jewelry corals that form non-porous structures of considerable strength. The jewelry corals generally live between 600 and 1500 feet beneath the surface, though several species inhabit depths to 7900 feet.

6. Sally Ann's Daisy Coral *Goniopora* "Solomon Is. 3" Bernard, 1903 • 1½ life size • The Wreck, Bait Grounds Entrance, Ngeruktabel Island, Belau • 90 feet/27.4 meters • Day • 18 June 1971 • Similar: USNM No. 47093

A young colony of Daisy Coral grows on the war-damaged hull of a Japanese freighter. The ship was bombed by American military personnel during an air-raid over Belau near the closing days of World War II. Metal now rusts on the lagoon floor, but the ship's surface is a flowering garden of marine life. The exact date of the ship's sinking is known, so scientists could study the rate of previous settling and future animal growth there. Young Daisy Corals often seem to be found living only on wrecks while the larger colonies are easier to locate on lagoon reefs. Encrusted wrecks provide fascinating assortments of easily located organisms for photography and continued study.

7. Ngel Reef, Ngel Pass, Ngeruptachel Island, Belau • Day • 17 April 1976

At 3:36 P.M. on April 17th 1976, the water surface of the lagoon dropped below the uppermost branches of the corals living on the reef-top. The tide fell to –0.2 below mean low water, according to the official tide tables for Belau. Next month the tide fell as much as –0.6, on May 14th, several days after full moon. The increasing pull of the sun and moon during equinox causes the sea level to fluctuate below the tide level at which many reef-top corals grow. During minus tides the currents swirl in and out of the passes from the lagoons to the ocean beyond. One can stand atop a reef and watch the water recede from above and around the corals.

The tidal fluctuation builds and diminishes over a period of one week. The minus tide falls each day until it reaches a maximum low for one or two days. Then as the combined gravitational forces of the sun and moon diminish, the tides return to normal levels.

Minus tides destroy many thousands of reef-flat corals, and limit the upward growth of those that survive. In Belau the minus tides begin in April and reach their maximum low of –0.6 in May and June. By July, they diminish and then cease until the winter equinox returns.

A dedicated reef-watcher may observe the daily and monthly progress of the damage. When exposure to air, rain, and sunlight is severe enough, the coral and the flesh covering the skeleton washes away as the rising tide re-submerges the colony. A lower minus tide returning the following afternoon reveals whitened branches of de-fleshed staghorns and other corals. All unexposed coral branches are still covered with flesh. As the water continues to recede each day more of each colony is exposed. On April 13, 1976, no minus tide occurred. On the 14th at 1:37 P.M., the tide was predicted to be –0.1. April 15th at 2.09 p.m., the tide dipped to –0.4, and was repeated on April 16th at 2:51 p.m. The last minus tide for April occurred at 3:36 p.m. with a –0.2 tide, as seen here.

Weeks later, I let my boat drift over the top of the reef. Many coral branches were clothed with brown algae. The reef no longer looked like a snowfield when the first minus tide of May occurred. Algae-covered branches protruded from the water as successive minus tides revealed more of the devastation.

When May's minus tides dropped below April's devastation, a lower zone of coral died, creating a new band of white separating the algae zone above from the still-living animal below. Once the destruction ends, each coral's newly-exposed skeletal zone becomes overgrown with algae.

These semi-annual minus tides shape a reef and the corals on it causing certain colonies, including *Porites lutea*, to grow into "micro-atolls." Minus tides kill off the polyps except those living around the sides of the colony. The living polyps continue to extend the colony outward in the shape of an atoll. Even reefs build outward because living space for corals stops at the ocean surface.

8. Monet and Festival Tube Corals *Dendrophyllia gracilis* Milne Edwards & Haime, 1848 • Sponges and Lace Ascidians • ¾ life size • The Great Reef, Bailechesengel Island, Ngemelis Islands, Belau • 40 feet/12.2 meters • Day • 17 July 1973 • Similar: USNM No. 47223, 47229

Of the many divisions assigned to corals, one is based on the presence or absence of symbiotic algae within their tissues. If algae reside in a coral's flesh, scientists call the coral "hermatypic." Corals without zooxanthellae in their tissues are called "ahermatypic." Most often hermatypic corals have muted or predominantly brown to tan flesh, while brightly-rainbowed corals usually lack algal symbionts. Ahermatypic tube corals and similar species are smaller and grow more slowly than do hermatypics, often living under ledges in beautiful array, providing the underwater photographer with elegant tapestries of pattern and color.

9. Merlet Leather Coral *Sarcophyton glaucum* (Quoy & Gaimard, 1833) • Life size • Little Amédée Reef, New Caledonia • 15 feet/4.6 meters • Day • 4 February 1963 • No specimen.

I dedicated my first book, *The Hidden Sea*, to my friend Yves Merlet. From him I discovered the joy of sunbathing on the ocean with no need for a "nude beach" or organized nudist colony. Yves was a man of the sea, a French medical doctor living in New Caledonia. He willingly assisted Dr. and Mme. René Catala, collecting corals and other marine organisms for their unique displays at the Noumea Aquarium. He helped me trap my first chambered nautilus in 1965, and we motored to the Loyalty Islands on his little boat. Later we planned another trip around New Caledonia for 1967, but Yves ran out of air underwater. His life ended where he wanted to die, in the sea.

On February 4th, 1963, we spent the day together at Amédée Lighthouse Island, and dived at Little Amédée Reef. I remember the glare of the sun and its heat warm from the white, fragrant sand. Nearly 20 years later I still see the sky, blue as a postcard—deeper. I remember Yves' smile and pale eyes, on this day when I photographed this serpentine coral in an innocent sea.

10. Tree Coral *Dendronephthya* species Gorgonian and Fusiliers • Tree coral: 24 inches high • Southwest Wall, Cheleu Island, Ngemelis Islands, Belau • 70 feet/21.3 meters • Day • 24 August 1974 • No specimen

On a summer morning in Belau, the sun edges over the roof of the barrier reef wall. Silver linings descend over darkening terraces. One large, glassy tree coral glows in the sea's diamond-blue light. Above, fusiliers and other fishes feed upon countless plankton riding the tide home.

Class HYDROZOA
Order MILLEPORINA
Family MILLEPORIDAE Fleming, 1828

The family Milleporidae has two genera, one now extinct. *Millepora*, the surviving genus, dates to the upper Cretaceous, 70 to 100 million years ago. Millepores are related to stinging hydroids, the Man O' War, and the fresh water hydras. In keeping with their ominous name, fire corals have more powerful nematocysts than most anthozoans. Their polyps are hollow tubes without partitions. At a stage in the life history of fire corals, medusae are formed. These little jellyfish are retained within the colony or released into the water.

Fire corals inhabit Caribbean, Red Sea and Indo-Pacific waters. A few coral specialists believe that only one species of fire coral exists and any morphological variations are differences among widely separated populations. Other scientists believe morphological differences from isolation will eventually create divergence into taxonomic status. Conflicting scientific views arise from the difficulty of evaluating the taxonomic characters in fire corals. Dr. Bayer guesses that a number of "true species" do exist even though their characteristics are not easy to define with scientific certainty.

11. Staghorn Fire Coral *Millepora alcicornis* Linnaeus, 1758 • 1⅓ life size • Goat Cay Reef, Small Hope Bay, Andros Island, Bahamas • 40 feet/12.2 meters • Day • 19 July 1967 • No specimen

A young colony of Staghorn Fire Coral lives on the rim of a small ledge. Fire corals abound on many of Florida's shallower reefs and throughout the Caribbean. Unquestionably, thousands of skin and scuba divers have suffered intense burning and irritation from blundering into fire corals. In percentages, unpleasant encounters with fire corals reduce to virtually zero the infrequent hazards posed by actual shark attacks. The branches of this coral reveal tiny, hair-like polyps; the stinging nematocyst cells in them are the cause of our grief.

This young colony began as a single planula, settled and grew to approximately six inches by the time I photographed it. The colony is larger now, as this species grows to heights of three feet or more.

12. Red Sea Fire Coral *Millepora platyphylla* Hemprich & Ehrenberg, 1834 • Life size • The Creek, Red Sea, Obhor Kuraa, Saudi Arabia • 15 feet/4.6 meters • Day • 28 March 1965 • No specimen

The foliate or plate-like growth form of this coral renders it easily distinguishable from other fire corals. Another foliate fire coral lives in the Caribbean, but its plates are smoother and thinner than this species photographed in the Red Sea.

The wart-like bumps on the coral's surface are barnacles specialized for fire coral habitation. The barnacle's "shell" is nearly covered over by the coral's limestone deposits and flesh. A number of barnacle species are adapted to living with corals. They exist in a "minefield," and never seem to step on a nematocyst, the equivalent of a coral's personnel bomb.

13. Intricate Fire Coral *Millepora intricata* Milne Edwards, 1860 • Life size • East Reef, Macharchar Islands, Belau • 15 feet/4.6 meters • Day • 7 October 1967 • Similar: USNM No. 58592, 58593, 58594.

Only a small area of this two-meter-wide colony was photographed. Colonies of Intricate Fire Coral are abundant in Belau's shallower waters. Although these animals eat only tiny plankton they need their powerful nematocysts for defense. Realizing that parrotfishes and a host of smaller nibblers feed on polyps, this coral's "fire power" is certainly necessary.

Like many other corals, millepores have zooxanthellae in their tissues. Symbiotic algae give the hydrozoan corals a variety of beige colors. Without algae, fire corals would be snow-white, for their skeletons would be visible through transparent flesh no thicker than a sheet of writing paper.

Class   HYDROZOA
Order   STYLASTERINA
Family   STYLASTERIDAE Gray, 1847

This beautiful family of corals has 17 genera arranged in three subfamilies. Fossil lace corals date to the upper Cretaceous, but only 8 genera now survive. Most species inhabit shallow waters, but some live as deep as 837 feet. They inhabit all seas, including the Antarctic, the frigid North Atlantic, the Pacific and the tropics.

The stylasterids are closely related to fire corals, but unlike them, grow only a fraction as large and do not have powerful nematocysts. Lace coral colors contrast markedly with the unvarying tans of fire corals. Lace corals are pure white to rose, lavender to deep purple, gold to café au lait. Generally, lace corals live deeper than do the hermatypic fire corals.

Fire and lace corals have no septa or partitions in the columns of their polyps. Lace coral tentacles taper at the ends, in contrast to fire coral tentacles that end in little clubs. A basic morphological difference between lace and fire corals is a "style," a little calcareous column at the base of a lace coral's pores. Each lace and fire coral polyp resides in a pore, but fire corals have no column or pedestal in the pore, as do lace corals, for additional support.

14. Coffee Lace Coral, *Stylaster* species 1¾ life size • Mbere Reef, New Caledonia • 80 feet/24.4 meters • Day • 25 September 1965 • No specimen

The lace corals illustrated here inhabited cave-like areas or grew under ledges, typical habitats for these small, relatively delicate corals. Lace corals do not live deep within caves, but around the entrances or growing from the ceiling of ledges or undercut areas. The Coffee Lace Coral settled and grew on the upper surface of a rock, but its genetic inclination caused it to grow sideways and down.

Lace corals are easily mistaken for precious corals, but unlike them, a lace coral skeleton is too porous to take a high polish. Nonetheless, divers still collect these delicately-branched colonies for saltwater aquarium displays, or the pale, dried skeletons are propped on shelves where their empty pores catch the dusty air. A dried coral skeleton reminds me of Shakespeare's sonnet and the image of wintry tree branches—"Bare ruined choirs, where late the sweet birds sang."

15. Violet Lace Coral *Distichopora violacea* (Pallas, 1766) • 1½ life size • Southwest Wall, Ngcheangel Islands, Belau • 30 feet/9.2 meters • Day • 17 June 1973 • Similar: USNM No. 58505

Lace corals differ in the form of their branching, the distribution of polyps over their skeletons, and in the location of the ampullae, which are the reproductive structures housing modified medusae.

Lace corals generally branch along one plane, like sea fans, to better utilize the prevailing water currents. Most lace corals live quietly under reef ledges. Some inhabit tidepools along California's coast but only the quiet-water species grow elaborate, delicate branches.

The polyps of many lace corals encircle the branches or grow along their narrow edges. Each polyp is housed within a pore, but the Violet Lace Coral has a unique, continuous groove running along the narrow edge of each branch. The grooves are visible on the branches of the coral in the foreground. Hair-like polyps are aligned in a row along the length of a groove. The polyps do not build the grooves, which are constructed only by the adjacent tissue overlying the skeleton.

16. Snow White Lace Coral *Stylaster* cf. *S. echinatus* Broch, 1936 • Life Size • Ngerumekaol Pass, Ulong Island, Belau • 40 feet/12.2 meters • Day • 9 October 1967 • Similar: USNM No. 58504

Coloration in lace and precious corals results from pigment in the skeletons, not from flesh covering them. Lace coral flesh contains no zooxanthellae to modify the skeletal color.

Quite often a particular environment, more than any other, provides ideal conditions for a species' proliferation. Colonies populate one reef, attaining their most elaborate forms of growth and size. At these locations, I often photographed a species' most beautiful colonies. Moreover, a species may flourish in Papua New Guinea, but only live a modest existence in Guam, or not exist there at all. Corals have geographical centers of distribution, as well as those local reefs most favoring their needs.

Class   ANTHOZOA
Order   ANTIPATHARIA
Family   ANTIPATHIDAE Gray, 1840

Fire and lace corals are numbered among a class of animals known as hydrozoans but this family, Antipathidae, and all the remaining corals in the book are anthozoans. The anthozoans share at least one unifying characteristic: the body cavity of each polyp is divided radially with partitions of flesh.

Black corals are distinguished from other anthozoans by the tapered shape of their polyps and number of tentacles. Polyps have six, ten or twelve tentacles, depending on the species. All stony coral polyps have tapered tentacles but their skeletons are constructed from calcium carbonate. Unlike them, black coral skeletons are composed of protein rendered hard and strong by a tanning process, and have skeletal growth rings similar to the concentric rings of a tree. Approximately a hundred known species live in all seas from the shallows to 17,400 feet. The greatest numbers dwell 30 to 3,000 feet deep.

Black corals have not been reviewed world-wide for nearly a century, making their identification difficult. Originally, species were described from dried colonies. With today's technology and procedures, both old and new species of antipathids must be described to include the fleshy polyps as well as any other distinguishing characteristics that bear upon each coral's taxonomic position within the family.

17. Spiral Wire Coral *Cirrhipathes spiralis* (Linnaeus, 1958) • Life size • Southwest Wall, Uchelbeluu Reef, Belau • 60 feet/18.6 meters • Day • 11 August 1971 • No specimen

Wire corals generally grow on outer reef walls, living several feet beneath the surface down to several hundred feet. Young corals spiral outward from ledges and caves. Other wire coral species grow straight out or upright to lengths of 10 or 12 feet. A fellow diver told me he once saw an inch-thick, 50-foot colony living in a quiet lagoon.

It is evident from the photograph that this coral could have been named barbed wire coral, for its extended tentacles recall the wire barbs on a cattle ranch fence.

18. Nuba Black Coral *Antipathes bifaria* Brook, 1889 • ¾ life size • Beab Pass Reef, Beab Island, Belau • 90 feet/27.4 meters • Day • 28 October 1967 • No specimen

Black corals are not black for, when alive, their flesh is actually yellow, orange, brown or gray; the gray is a result of sediment on the coral's slippery flesh. The very dark brown, "black" skeleton is visible only after the animal's flesh is scrubbed off. With the flesh removed, one may feel the sand-papery surface of the skeleton, similar to the texture of a shark's skin. Dr. Bayer theorizes that this texture anchors the flesh more securely to the skeleton like any sanded surface holds a coat of paint better.

Many black corals thrive best below 150 feet. The largest ones are most abundant on outer reef walls, 200 feet and several thermoclines below the surface, where the water is cooler and sunlight is greatly reduced. In regions where there is less diving, one finds large colonies 10 feet high in only 60 to 70 feet of water. A New Zealand correspondent informed me that one black coral tree at Poor Knights Islands had grown 25 feet high. It has since disappeared.

19. Christmas Tree Black Coral *Antipathes* species • ¾ life size • Cousin's Rock, Santiago Island, Galápagos Islands, Ecuador • 50 feet/15.2 meters • Day • 2 May 1973 • No specimen

Most black corals favor cooler waters, amply provided by the currents bathing the Galápagos. Moreover, several species live at 18,000 feet. Members of the Challenger Expedition (1873 to 1876) dredged four species between 12,000 and 18,000 feet. Others, however, live attached to reef walls at much shallower depths, between 30 and 120 feet.

Black corals add a lovely forest-like mood to the reef. They have a high market value, but grow too slowly to be harvested from one reef or group of islands in any quantity without denuding the underwater landscape. Most harvesting is for the jewelry trade, sometimes under the guise of scientific research, particularly in Hawaii.

Irrespective of their market value, the vast majority of black or deep water precious corals become "junk jewelry." It pains me to see a street vendor at Waikiki's International Market peddling bins full of dime store necklaces made from familiar corals that were once so beautiful. Even jewelry store windows nearby display their overpriced items, the best of which is junk art compared to the intricate architecture of a living colony.

Class	ANTHOZOA
Subclass	OCTOCORALLIA
Order	STOLONIFERA
Family	CLAVULARIIDAE Hickson, 1894

Clavulariids inhabit Arctic and Antarctic waters, tolerating these dark, frigid realms, or live in the tropics, populating reefs a few feet down to 500 feet or deeper. No single species is this widely distributed, but family members have adapted to various extremes. *Clavularia* has no solid skeletons, but derives structural support from calcite spicules embedded in flesh.

20. Tree Fern Coral *Clavularia* • 1½ life size • The Cliff, Balanawang Harbor Entrance, Duke of York Islands, Papua New Guinea • 50 feet/15.2 meters • Day • 16 November 1976

Tree Fern Corals are common on reefs in certain geographical regions. They are small and live in clumps or are scattered. They favor recessed areas on reef walls. In Belau and Papua New Guinea a diver may look for them at 10 to 15 feet or deeper to 100 feet. In the Duke of York Islands Tree Fern Corals are abundant, living in masses several feet across. They glow pale green to emerald, deeper down the reef. However, the flash I used to make the photograph erased the intense green, leaving only a pale remnant on film.

Tree Fern Corals reproduce sexually, releasing eggs and sperm in the sea, but they insure their survival by reproducing asexually as well. Runners snake across the immediate substrate, budding new polyps, spreading the colony. Clustered Tree Fern Corals give one the impression of miniature rain forests. Spacing between the polyps enables them to expand and feed on plankton with a minimum of conflict. Colonies are male or female. Sexual reproduction occurs when sperm, released from a male colony, meets and fertilizes drifting eggs from a female colony. In this setting sexual reproduction is like a journeying space vehicle, transporting an egg and sperm, the union of two colonies. This new entity drifts in the current, possibly to colonize a new reef or Archipelago.

Class	ANTHOZOA
Subclass	OCTOCORALLIA
Order	STOLONIFERA
Family	TUBIPORIDAE Ehrenberg, 1828

The family, Tubiporidae, has but one genus and one species. Organ-pipe Coral is one of the most nondescript reef corals, having small, plain, grayish polyps that hug the bottom. A diver looking for the coral will miss it on the reef. Unfortunately, professional collectors, reef dredgers and dynamiters know what the live animal looks like. The fire-engine-red coral, with its tiny tubes held in place by horizontal platforms, is crated off to curio shops far from its birth place. Organ-pipe Coral has traveled the currents from the western Pacific and Indian Ocean to Africa, the Red Sea and the watery sliver of Aqaba, bounded by Egypt, Israel, Jordan and Saudi Arabia.

21. Organ Pipe Coral *Tubipora musica* Linnaeus, 1758 • 1⅓ life size • Mutremdiu Point, Uchelbeluu Reef, Belau • 70 feet/21.3 meters • Day • 27 July 1973 • Photographed: USNM No. 58496

Organ-pipe Corals, like Tree Fern Corals, reproduce asexually, sending out runners. In this instance, however, the runners are the transverse platforms of the colony. A platform supports the colony like the floor of a skyscraper, adding to its structural support. A new Organ-pipe Coral polyp builds its tube out of a transverse platform, the tube housing the polyp. To continue the analogy, organ-pipe tubes may be compared to the columns between floors in a building. Had Linnaeus been a contemporary resident of New York City, he would have noticed the resemblance of this coral to multi-storied buildings under construction, and perhaps named the coral differently.

Class	ANTHOZOA
Subclass	OCTOCORALLIA
Order	ALCYONACEA
Family	ALCYONIIDAE Lamouroux, 1812

Family members have one major characteristic in common: their polyps are interconnected by a mass of fleshy tissue with spicules embedded for support. Volume and density of flesh varies from species to species but the family wins polyps down when its flesh is weighed against that of any other coral family.

Its leathery appearance after the polyps contract has obviously inspired the common name. Leather corals are soft corals, but the flesh of some species is very compact, containing calcite spicules in such abundance that the flesh is firm to the touch. To tear or cut them is difficult. Some species are so densely packed with spicules that their remains make an appreciable contribution to limestone reef formation. The structural strength of these corals is precisely the purpose of their reinforcement, for many live on exposed reef flats and along the front of barrier reefs where wave action is severe during storms.

Fifteen genera live in all seas, mostly in shallow waters. *Sarcophyton* and *Lobophytum* are both exclusively tropical reef dwellers, but species of one genus live at 9000 feet.

22. Penis Coral *Bellonella indica* Thomson & Henderson, 1905 • 1¼ life size • The Great Reef, Bailechesengel Island, Ngemelis Islands, Belau • 15 feet/4.6 meters • Night • 6 August 1973 • Photographed: USNM No. 58497 and Similar: USNM No. 58498

About 12 to 15 penis coral species live in tropical to subtropical water from the Red Sea and the Indo-Pacific to the tropical Atlantic. The Atlantic member, no pun intended, is decorated white with red polyps, a Santa Claus Penis Coral. Colors range from brilliant orange to red or snow white, to a combination of these colors.

In Belau and other areas of the Pacific, penis corals are nocturnal. During the day they shrivel to inch-long nubs, but with the approach of darkness the colonies swell in length and diameter. The nub, which expands and from which the polyps extend, is known as the capitulum.

Generally, penis corals live attached to reef walls in depths between 10 and 50 feet, thriving best on roofs of ledges and in crevices and cave openings. This Orange Penis Coral is expanded six or seven inches, contrasting with the contracted colony above it.

23. Canyonlands Leather Coral *Lobophytum batarum* Moser, 1919?- • Life size • Ngeremdiu Reef, White Cliff, Ngeruktabel Island, Belau • 25 feet/7.6 meters • Day • 6 October 1970 • No specimen

Sometimes species are repeated in this book to show color variations and differences of form and behavior. On facing pages, the Canyonlands Leather Coral feeds while the other coral's polyps are contracted. The velvet appearance of the leather coral results from many thousands of polyps feeding. Leather corals trap plankton day and night on a running tide, but when it slackens the polyps contract and the coral turns bald. Their wind-sculptured look is reminiscent of a Utah landscape.

The up and down-hill terrain of a leather coral enlarges its surface area thereby increasing the colony's feeding and respiratory abilities.

Leather corals house zooxanthellae in their tissues, solving much of their food and waste disposal problems. Algae produce nutrients useful to the coral, simultaneously removing carbon dioxide from their host's flesh for their own use. Zooxanthellae release glycerol, alanine, glucose and oxygen into the coral's tissues, all of which the coral utilizes. Stony corals benefit from this rapid gas exchange because they can deposit calcium carbonate more efficiently, accelerating growth. Without zooxanthellae, corals metabolize and deposit calcium carbonate much more slowly.

24. Canyonlands Leather Coral *Lobophytum batarum* Moser, 1919? • Life size • Ngerumekaol Pass, Ulong Island, Belau • 45 feet/13.7 meters • Day • 23 October 1971 • No specimen

All coral colonies of one species, including leather corals, vary more or less from the average shape. A coral's genetic makeup and its immediate environment determine its particular size and form. Two corals of the same species living 30 feet apart may grow differently, because the current will favor one colony with more plankton, or buffet the other causing it to grow more compactly.

This leather coral and the previous one show differences between their mounds, the one having narrower ridges. The feeding leather coral lives on a fringing reef slope protected from strong currents but is subject, nonetheless, to waves and the surge of periodic storms. The non-feeding colony, pictured here, lives in the turbulent center of Ngerumekaol Pass, a constricted area of fast-flowing tidal currents. At slack tide the polyps ceased feeding and contracted into the capitulum.

25. Finger Leather Coral *Lobophytum batarum* Moser, 1919? • Life size • East Reef, Macharchar Islands, Belau • 25 feet/7.6 meters • Day • 4 August 1974 • No specimen

A quite different growth form of *Lobophytum batarum* is this coral, so named because its "fingers" resemble *Porites* finger corals.

The Egg Cowrie, a favorite of many shell collectors, is the bane of a leather coral's existence, for the white porcelain-shelled mollusk preys extensively on leather corals. Active day and night, a cowrie crawls across a leather coral's capitulum to eat its polyps and flesh. A mantle, flecked black and white, hides the cowrie's white shell underneath. When not feeding Egg Cowries often rest under the outer lip of the leather coral's capitulum.

26. Velvet Leather Coral *Sarcophyton trocheliophorum* Marenzeller, 1886 • 1¼ life size • The Great Reef, Bailechesengel Island, Ngemelis Islands, Belau • 30 feet/9.1 meters • Day • 13 September 1974 • Photographed: USNM No. 58499

Sarcophyton leather corals are easily distinguished by their columns or stalks rising from the reef substrate, mushrooming at the top, with convoluted surfaces. In a young colony the stalk is visible, but the capitulum of an adult overhangs its stalk, drooping to within inches of the bottom. The stalk of a large colony can be seen if one lifts the edge of the capitulum. Some colonies grow on the edge of a wall drop-off where the stalk can be glimpsed from below.

27. Velvet Leather Coral *Sarcophyton trocheliophorum* Marenzeller, 1886 • ¾ life size • Kesebekuu Pass Reef, Mekeald Lagoon, Ngeruktabel Island, Belau • 35 feet/10.7 meters • Day • 25 August 1969 • Similar: USNM No. 58499

Leather corals are well adapted to life in the lagoons. They inhabit Belau's inner coves and several marine lakes. Generally, leather corals live within 100 feet of the surface and most often within 40 feet. The zooxanthellae in their tissues thrive best in shallow water, contributing to large populations of leather corals on shallow reefs.

Coloration among different leather corals ranges from bluish gray to gray or yellow-tan to beige or golden brown, reflecting the varied colors of the yellow, brown, or yellowish brown zooxanthellae combined with pigments in the coral's flesh. A coral's color depends on the particular blend of zooxanthellae and pigments.

28. Velvet Leather Coral *Sarcophyton trocheliophorum* Marenzeller, 1886 • ⅔ life size • East Reef, Faulkner Island II, Belau • 10 feet/3 meters • Day • 23 September 1974 • Similar: USNM No. 58499

The facing photographs again show a feeding and non-feeding colony, one with a velvet surface of expanded polyps, the other with polyps contracted—a windswept austerity, sculptured by the elements. Tides and currents create the same effects in living flesh.

The smooth surface of this coral is dotted with little pinhead bumps, marking the places into which the polyps have receded. When the current slows, the polyps cease feeding and contract. Later, as the changing tide increases velocity, the polyps become stimulated and feed again. They bloom like the mist-awakened flowers of the Inca, flowers of the Loma, the yellow Amancai.

29. Daisy Leather Coral *Sarcophyton digitatum* Moser, 1919 • 1⅓ life size • Kuabsngas Point Reef, Teongel Pass, Ngeruktabel Island, Belau • 30 feet/9.1 meters • Day • 5 September 1969 • Similar: USNM No. 58500

The large polyps of the leather coral reminded me of daisies, hence their name. The scientific name, *S. digitatum*, calls attention to the finger shapes of the capitulum, formed like a mitt. This coral evokes a Picasso hand overgrown with wild flowers, petals snaring tiny crabs, shrimps, coral planulae—the sea's children.

30. Daisy Leather Coral *Sarcophyton digitatum* Moser, 1919 • 1⅓ life size • Kesebekuu Pass Reef, Mekeald Lagoon, Ngeruktabel Island, Belau • 40 feet/12.2 meters • Day • 19 October 1967 • Similar: USNM No. 58500

Leather corals have eight tentacles per polyp. This young colony's polyps are evenly spaced over the capitulum, making them easy to study. The white polyps contrast with the golden brown capitulum. Scientists have not determined why this color difference exists. Few or no zooxanthellae in a polyp's tissues would explain its lighter color, but no scientific study has been made to confirm this. A microscopical study of histological sections of a polyp would be a major requirement, for only in this manner would the investigating scientist discover the distribution of zooxanthellae in a polyp.

31. Belau Leather Coral *Sinularia polydactyla* (Ehrenberg, 1834) • 1¼ life size • Ngerumekaol Pass, Ulong Island, Belau • 50 feet/15.2 meters • Day • 23 October 1971 • Similar: USNM No. 58501

The polyps of the Belau Leather Coral are considerably smaller than those of the Daisy Leather Coral. This coral thrives in the strong currents of Ngerumekaol Pass. During new and full moon or equinox, unusually strong currents create whirlpools and churning waters as they speed through the pass. Due to "drag," the rushing tide is slowed considerably near the bottom around the corals. Nevertheless, having small polyps, flexibility and strength are valuable attributes in that region between lagoon and open sea.

Sinularia leather coral skeletons are very compact, containing many more spicules than their relatives, *Lobophytum*, and considerably more than *Sarcophyton*. *Sinularia* spicules are most dense in the stalk of the coral where the colony's structural support is vital.

32. Medusa Leather Coral *Sinularia flexibilis* (Quoy & Gaimard, 1833) • Life size • Ngerutechetachel Reef, Towachelmlengui Pass, Babeldaob Island, Belau • 15 feet/4.6 meters • Day • 21 August 1969 • Similar: USNM No. 58502

This Medusa Leather Coral is the epitome of flexibility, most appropriately named *S. flexibilis*. Its finger-like projections are reminiscent of staghorn coral branches, but there the similarity ends. Like the twisting snakes of Medusa's head, they evoke movement. Although the fingers are soft, its hard, spicule-packed stalk is comparable to other *Sinularia* stalks.

Sinularia range from the Red Sea, the Maldives, Papua New Guinea, Belau, Luzon, and Southeast to Tahiti.

Class	ANTHOZOA
Subclass	OCTOCORALLIA
Order	ALCYONACEA
Family	NEPHTHEIDAE Gray, 1862

Members of this family have their polyps clustered into tight groups rather than spaced over the colony's surface like other soft corals. The usual growth forms of this family resemble trees in spring before their leaves finally obscure the upper trunk and branches. Unlike trees, this coral's trunk and branches are translucent and sometimes transparent because a tree coral's skeleton is not very dense.

Tree corals take in sea water, expanding their bodies before feeding. The water gives form to their flesh in a manner similar to the propane heated air that fills a Hot Air Balloon. The water pressure inside a tree coral is not hot or great, but the lift required to expand the coral underwater is also not great. The surrounding water also supports the branches and trunk of the coral. The body wall of the colony is reinforced with calcite spicules. These spicules provide structural support and discourage predators, for they are glassy and spiked. Nephtheidae are worldwide in all seas, some species living at depths of 12,000 feet.

Dendronephythya colonizes the tropics and subtropics from the Red Sea to Tahiti. Several species live in New Zealand waters and north, at least, to Sagami Bay in Japan's Inland Sea.

33. Autumn Tree Coral *Dendronephthya* species • 1½ life size • Southwest Wall, Ngcheangel Islands, Belau • 45 feet/13.7 meters • Day • 10 September 1971 • Similar: USNM No. 58759

Tree corals are one of the most beautiful of all the corals. Visually, their transparent bodies are like water, sharing its magic, catching its light. Their colors and delicate branches evoke the golds of autumn and Spring's blossoms, pink dogwoods brightening the shadowy ledges of reef walls.

When the current flows, tree corals expand their bodies and feed. The polyps eat until the tide slackens; then they contract as the branches collapse like a circus tent when the children are gone and the tiger sleeps in his cage.

34. Salmon Tree Coral *Dendronephthya* • Life size • Southwest Wall, Cheleu Island, Ngemelis Islands, Belau • 70 feet/21.3 meters • Day • 5 July 1973 • No specimen

Tree corals, living on the reefs, grow within several feet of the surface downward to 250 feet. Two *Dendronephthya* species were dredged from 840 feet and may live deeper, but generally this genus favors shallow tropical waters, sometimes only a few degrees cooler than that which they are able to tolerate. If water discharged from a nuclear power plant raises the temperature on a reef only a few degrees, corals will die.

Tree corals live in several marine lakes, as well as coves, lagoons, passes and the outer reefs of Belau. They prefer a moderate current. Within the lagoons, they thrive on wrecks growing on the superstructure, especially the masts where living conditions become crowded as a result of the desirability/scarcity bind of oceanfront real estate. Tree corals can grow to heights of nearly three feet. Clustered on the superstructure of a wreck, they create floral arrangements six feet across.

35. Glassy Tree Coral *Dendronephthya* species • Life size • The Creek, Red Sea, Obhor Kuraa, Saudi Arabia • 40 feet/12.2 meters • Day • 9 March 1965 • No specimen

Tree corals are the most difficult of shallow water coral subjects to photograph for they branch outward in ways that interfere with my technique: to render the central area of the subject in sharp focus and allow the periphery to fall off. This creates depth and mood, infusing the image with strong composition. Foreground branches, out-of-focus, might make an effective photograph but, unavoidably so much is out of focus anyway, I prefer sharpness in the critical areas.

The Red Sea is home to tree corals. More seem to reside there than in any other region where I have dived. Typically, they attain, there, highly aesthetic states. The luminous pink trunk of this colony is flecked snow-white with spicules and polyps. With microscopic precision, a larger than life view clarifies the mystery of a soft coral's support, as if seeing for the first time the girdle under the dress.

Class	ANTHOZOA
Subclass	OCTOCORALLIA
Order	ALCYONACEA
Family	NIDALIIDAE Gray, 1869

Only five genera and less than 50 species comprise this family. *Siphonogorgia*, with forty species, is the dominant genus. Each family member shares the common characteristic of having very large spicules, densely packed in its flesh, rendering it brittle and easily broken.

The polyps of this family extend from projecting calices, prickly to the touch. *S. godeffroyi* is not quite as prickly because the ridges of its calices do not extend very far outward.

Only three known genera of the family exist. The Dandelion Coral of Belau closely resembles a relative from the Caribbean. The nidalias are club-shaped colonies, contrasted with the branching siphonogorgias. Both share subfamily status.

In all, the family is adapted to tropical and subtropical waters worldwide. Nidalias have been collected down to 1,000 feet. Siphonogorgias "do it deeper," as divers amusingly boast, managing depths to 2,000 feet.

36. Burning Bush Coral *Siphonogorgia* species • 1½ life size • Southwest Wall, Uchelbeluu Reef, Belau • 60 feet/18.3 meters • Day • 17 July 1971 • Similar: USNM No. 58506

Burning Bush Corals generally grow attached to the ceilings of outer reef ledges, and less often to the sheer reef walls. The colony pictured here was living in the mouth of an irregular cave. Others grow in tunnels bathed with flowing water—ideal for their needs.

37. Burning Bush Coral *Siphonogorgia* species • Life size • Mutremdiu Point, Uchelbeluu Reef, Belau • 60 feet/18.3 meters • Day • 27 July 1973 • Photographed: USNM No. 58507

The Burning Bush Corals are among those most vibrantly-colored. Their intense hues could be woven into Jacob's coat. The biblical name of the coral suggested itself by the colony's flame-like appearance, reminiscent of the burning bush.

This violet-colored colony hangs from the ceiling of a tunnel sixty feet from the ocean surface. The six-foot high tunnel runs parallel along the reef wall. Several dozen colonies live in the tunnel, collecting plankton from the passing current.

Many corals are host to other marine organisms: shrimps, crabs, fishes, sea urchins and sea stars. The Burning Bush Coral hosts small shrimps. Two or more shrimps coexist with the coral, their legs and claws specially modified to walk with ease along the coral's branches. The color of the shrimp matches the deep violet hue of the coral. Several of the little crustaceans were living with this *Siphonogorgia*, discovered only after I collected and brought the coral into my boat to preserve it for identification. The little shrimps never imagined that a predator might take away their world.

38. Burning Bush Coral *Siphonogorgia* species • ¾ life size • The Great Reef, Bailechesengel Island, Ngemelis Islands, Belau • 60 feet/18.3 meters • Day • 27 June 1973 • Photographed USNM No. 58508

From its base this coral's growth is directed outward. The reef is undercut, and the coral extends into the open water column to feed.

Corals are not greatly concerned with gravity for they displace water which supports them, both being nearly equal in weight.

39. Burning Bush Coral *Siphonogorgia* species • Life size • Mutremdiu Point, Uchelbeluu Reef, Belau • 60 feet/18.3 meters • Day • 24 July 1973 • Photographed: USNM No. 58509

Like most of the flexible-bodied corals, this one feeds day and night. Its crimson branches, festooned with white polyps, trap plankton gliding by on an incoming tide. Flexible-bodied corals are able to feed during the day, possibly because their small polyps have little fleshy substance and are armed with unpalatable spicules. Butterflyfishes and other finned coral polyp-nibblers probably avoid them for this reason. At night, when most of the coral nibblers are asleep, the larger-polyped nocturnal corals expand and feed in relative safety.

40. Burning Bush Coral *Siphonogorgia* species • Life size • Ngerutechetachel Reef, Towachelmlengui Pass, Babeldaob Island, Belau • 35 feet/10.7 meters • Day • 30 October 1967 • No specimen

At high tide in Towachelmlengui Pass, the polyps of this colony are partly contracted, rendering the spicules clearly visible. A coral colony contracts by releasing an excess of sea water from its system. If the branches were more contracted their texture would resemble a dried prune.

41. Cotton Candy Coral *Siphonogorgia godeffroyi* Kölliker, 1874 • 1¼ life size • Ngerumekaol Pass, Ulong Island, Belau • 35 feet/10.7 meters • Day • 6 October 1967 • Photographed: USNM No. 58581, 58582, 58583

Cotton Candy Corals inhabit Belau's passes. *Siphonogorgia* seem well suited to strong currents and swift tidal waters. Fluffy, white-polyped clusters sway from side to side as the branches of the colony vibrate in response to the speeding water.

At depth, Cotton Candy Coral has a grayish-purple coloration because water filters out the sun's red rays. The coral's crimson branches are only revealed by the flashbulb's momentary glare.

Cotton Candy Corals and other *Siphonogorgia* have no horny skeleton or internal "axis" as do the gorgonians. Siphonogorgias construct stems and branches of individual spicules bonded by a gelatinous substance, mesoglea. No animal cells hold the coral together but its nutrients, respiratory gases and wastes are transported in tiny tubular vessels through the mesoglea.

42. Candied Apple Coral *Siphonogorgia* species • 1⅓ life size • Kuabsngas Point Reef, Teongel Pass, Ngeruktabel Island, Belau • 30 feet/9.1 meters • Day • 29 May 1970 • Similar: USNM No. 58594, 58595, 58596

The Candied Apple Coral is distinguished from the Cotton Candy Coral by the pattern of polyp distribution on the main branches, the branch ends, and on the trunk. The clumped polyps of Cotton Candy Coral are like dandelions or the fuzzy-wuzzy eatkins of a pussywillow shrub.

Candied Apple Corals appear to be sprinkled with coconut shavings. Possibly in the past several million years, both species were one. The Cotton Candy Coral, judging from its abundance in the passes, may be better adapted to swifter currents. Candied Apple Corals seem best suited to less turbulent habitats. I took no census to verify my impressions.

43. Indian Summer Coral *Siphonogoria* species • 1¼ life size • Mutremdiu Point, Uchelbeluu Reef, Belau • 110 feet/33.5 meters • Day • 25 June 1973 • Photographed: USNM No. 58584, 58585

Living 110 feet down on the wall of Uchelbeluu Reef, the Indian Summer Coral has adapted to deeper water. The flexible-bodied colony has grown to three or more feet. Living 100 feet or deeper, this coral usually escapes the silt-laden water flowing out of the passes, or over the barrier reef flats on receding tides. Usually the water clarity on an outer reef is best from two hours before high tide until an hour afterwards. From the surface, visibility can be more than 150 feet or barely 30, determined by daily weather and tide fluctuations. Water clarity is a major factor in the quality of my underwater photography. I am acutely aware of it each day I dive.

44. **Dandelion Coral** *Nidalia lampas* (Thomson & Mackinnon, 1910) • 1½ life size • The Great Reef, Bailechesengel Island, Ngemelis Islands, Belau • 40 feet/12.2 meters • Night • 9 August 1973 • Photographed: USNM No. 58586

Seven species of *Nidalia* are known. Two inhabit the West Indies, five the Indo-West-Pacific region. *Nidalia lampas* was first collected at the Seychelles in 1905, but it soaked, unnamed in alcohol for five years before a description was published in the scientific literature.

Dandelion corals feed exclusively at night. As dawn approaches, the eight-tentacled polyps contract and the capitulum shrivels to a small knob on a short, leathery stalk. Inactivity begins. A diver would not notice them during the day, lost in the carnival and flash of colors on the reef wall.

Dandelion corals may live elsewhere around Belau but lagoon night life is unfamiliar to me. Nocturnal feeding activities of certain very large marine crocodiles render starlight explorations of the lagoons suicidal.

The taxonomic history of *Nidalia* shows how scientists keep their directory of scientific names current. *Nidalia* was first described as having a rounded capitulum. Later, a flat-headed *Nidalia*

was discovered. The officiating scientist concluded that the flat-headed corals were a new genus. Thus *Cactogorgia* was created. Recently, Professor Utinomi of Japan reviewed the corals and concluded that no generic distinction, based on the difference between a rounded and flat-headed capitulum, is valid in *Nidalia*. Dr. Utinomi rendered *Cactogorgia* defunct. Apparently the flat heads and round heads are "one nation, indivisible."

Taxonomists tend to fall within one of two groups, the "splitters" and the "lumpers." Lumpers seem to believe that evolution can be structured by scientific nomenclature. They are always happy when all the variations on a theme become just the many faces of Eve. Certainly it helps to consolidate as much taxonomy as possible. Even the splitters would agree. By reuniting round and flat-headed nidalias Dr. Utinomi scored a win for the lumpers, but life continues to slip past the border guards, Mexican style.

Class	ANTHOZOA
Subclass	OCTOCORALLIA
Order	GORGONACEA
Suborder	SCLERAXONIA
Family	BRIAREIDAE J.E. Gray, 1859

The Briareidae is a family of modest size. Two genera and less than a half-dozen species belong to it. Yet, Moss Corals are abundant on reefs they inhabit, sometimes blanketing 30 or more square feet of fringing reef slope.

They live in the Red Sea, the Indo-West Pacific and Caribbean waters. Atlantic and Pacific populations are so similar in appearance that only by knowing the collection site is a scientist able to determine the genus to which the specimen belongs.

Moss Corals are large-polyped with long pinnate tentacles. Their color varies from brown to greenish-yellow to brilliant lime, the colors of pigments, and their symbiotic algae partners.

Moss coral branches have taco-like projections of leathery flesh. The spicules embedded in them are many and colorful. Colorless or yellow spicules impregnate the outer layer of tissue. Reddish-to-deep-purple spicules serve to support the inner tissues.

In Belau the most prolific Moss Coral colonies live in 40 to 60 feet of water. Elsewhere, they are recorded from just below tide level down to 215 feet.

45. **Green Moss Coral** *Solenopodium stechei* Kükenthal, 1908 • 1½ life size • Bedulyaus Point Reef, Teongel Pass, Ngerchol Island, Belau • 20 feet/6.1 meters • Day • 31 May 1970 • Similar: USNM No. 58493

Moss Corals in Belau are usually gray-brown, more gray than brown. They spread carpet-like over large areas of reef slope often littered with dead coral skeletons.

The little white oral discs of each polyp are seen in this photograph. White as stars, they dot the green landscape. Each polyp's mouth is at the center of its oral disc. Flowing outward from the disc are luminous green tentacles. The coral's mossy appearance disappears when the polyps stop feeding and contract, and for a time they appear as lifeless as the stony rubble beneath them.

Class   ANTHOZOA
Subclass   OCTOCORALLIA
Order   GORGONACEA
Suborder   SCLERAXONIA
Family   SUBERGORGIIDAE Gray, 1859

Students of this family can claim only one known genus and less than a dozen species. The family is widely dispersed throughout shallow waters of the tropical Indo-West-Pacific.

46. Cork Sea Fan *Subergorgia suberosa* (Pallas, 1766) • 1¼ life size • Bedulyaus Point Reef, Teongel Pass, Ngerchol Island, Belau • 85 feet/25.9 meters • Day • 4 July 1973 • Photographed: USNM No. 58494

The Cork Sea Fan was photographed at the base of a reef fringing the large pass between Belau's south-western lagoon and Ngederrak Lagoon. The reef and its twin—north of the pass—are abundant with gorgonians, sea fans and siphonogorgias. Sea fans and other corals congregate here because the two limestone islands, in close proximity, constrict the current, causing it to increase speed through the 200-meter-wide pass.
    Cork Sea Fans extend their branches across the flow of the current. The sea fan is characterized by a skeleton composed of calcareous spicules and protein. Together the spicules and protein materials provide a strong, flexible skeleton. In the photograph of *Subergorgia*, the polyps are seen aligned in double rows along the branch edges. The flattened structure of the branches is visible. The coral resembles, in color and texture, wine bottle cork, hence its name.

Class   ANTHOZOA
Subclass   OCTOCORALLIA
Order   GORGONACEA
Suborder   SCLERAXONIA
Family   MELITHAEIDAE Gray, 1870

This colorful family has about five genera living in all warm seas, with the exception of the Mediterranean and Atlantic. About 60 species inhabit shallow water. A few live as deep as 2400 feet.
    A colony is not always fan-shaped; some species are bushy. The corals grow quite large—over three feet and wider across. The axial skeleton is composed of spicules fused together. Needed flexibility is attained by interruptions in the axis at regular intervals. The interruptions are actually nodes composed of spicules not fused together but joined by the horny substance which enables the nodes to swing like hinges, allowing the branches to bend. The fused skeleton becomes more brittle extending outward from the axial base, but flexibility is increased by the horny nodes. The coral polyps are small and embedded in a thin layer of tissue overlying the axial skeleton. Color among Melithaeidae is caused by pigment in the spicules—red, orange, yellow and purple. Occasionally, very rare, pure white colonies are found.

47. Gauguin Sea Fan *Melithaea squamata* (Nutting, 1911) • Life size • Ngerumekaol Pass, Ulong Island, Belau • 25 feet/7.6 meters • Day • 19 May 1970 • Similar: USNM No. 58587, 58588

The Gauguin Sea Fans were a living treasure, hidden from nearly everyone in Belau but me. For almost seven years, I visited them, imagining they would always be alive to see and photograph. Shortly after *This Living Reef* was published with a photograph and the location of this coral, a Belauan diver stripped Ngerumekaol Pass of its Gauguin Sea Fans to make jewelry. *Melithaea* abound along Belau's outer reefs, passes and lagoons, but in Ngerumekaol Pass, only remnants of these colorful corals remain.

48. Gauguin Sea Fan *Melithaea squamata* (Nutting, 1911) • Life size • Ngerumekaol Pass, Ulong Island, Belau • 45 feet/13.7 meters • Day • 18 May 1970 • Similar: USNM No. 58587, 58588

Sea fans feed day and night when the velocity of the current is forceful enough to stimulate the polyps to expand. This sea fan traps plankton from an ebbing tide as it flows out Ngerumekaol Pass. The tiny white polyps give the colony a velvet texture and soften the brilliant orange color of the bare branches, seen in the facing photograph, made when the polyps were contracted.
    For many years I photographed this same coral because it was beautiful and because I wanted to record its growth. These two photographs, made ten months apart, show some differences in growth and, most obviously, the colony's feeding and non-feeding appearance.

49. Gauguin Sea Fan *Melithaea squamata* (Nutting, 1911) • Life size • Ngerumekaol Pass, Ulong Island, Belau • 45 feet/13.7 meters • Day • 20 August 1969 • Similar: USNM No. 58587, 58588

The surface layer of spicules covering the sea fan's axial skeleton is revealed in great detail because the coral's polyps are contracted. Having retreated into their calices, the polyps become deep orange freckles dotting the colony's surface. Red spicules in the calices give the sea fan its rich color. The branches shimmer with a golden light reminiscent of Gauguin's work.

The trunk of this sea fan is quite strong and rigid. As the branches reach outward to their extremities they become more flexible, bending in strong currents and sometimes weathering violent storms. Nonetheless, they can be broken. In the name of science, I collected coral specimens, taking a few branches and the whole colony only if necessary. I collected a part or all of the colony I photographed, only when a surrogate was nowhere in sight, or when the coral was obviously a new species and Dr. Bayer needed more specimens for study. But my feelings were very strong for the corals. To destroy their beauty, never to see them alive again, seemed hardly worth trading for their identification.

This Gauguin Sea Fan no longer traps plankton, no longer exists except in fragments of my photographs and parts of earrings and necklaces. In 1975, I was diving in Ngerumekaol Pass and swam to the place where the coral lived.

A strange feeling pervaded the bare rock, recalling a time when I returned to my little house in Belau to find it empty. I stood in the doorway . . . the silence spoke of her departure. The dwelling had become a shell of wood and nails. The boulder, in Ngerumekaol Pass, never seemed devoid of life until I discovered the Gauguin Sea Fan was gone.

For many years I wanted to name a reef animal after Paul Gauguin. I found nothing appropriate, for Gauguin's art encompassed the tropics, predating our awareness of its pure colors. I found it difficult to associate him with any color or form and not have a dozen more crowd in upon me. Gauguin delighted in colors as much as I and he taught me how he saw them, not in isolation, but as part of life's fabric. The Gauguin Sea Fan evokes for me the essence of the artist and the man. It is dynamically structured, as any organism is always structured, but it sways in slow motion like the golden people populating his paintings. The sea fan is a world slowed down, living in easy harmony in a universe which is often not easy. Gauguin sensed it. A sad loneliness stares from the eyes of his women, despair in the faces of the aged. But Gauguin transcended sorrow reminding us of the beauty of our planet. Gauguin, one of her children, was "between worlds." He tried to erect a bridge in the mind: through his odyssey over water, his assault on rigid cultural barriers, through his adoration of colors and sunlight—in his quest for the essential innocence of life.

50. Scarlet Sea Fan *Melithaea* cf. *albitincta* (Ridley, 1884) ● Life size ● Beab Pass Reef, Beab Island, Belau ● 45 feet/13.7 meters ● Day ● 30 October 1967 ● Similar: USNM No. 58576, 58577, 58591

This sea fan's deep scarlet color results from a surface layer of spicules covering the axial skeleton, which is also red, but more pink in color. Gauguin Sea Fans are formed of yellow, orange and red spicules which, in various combinations, create impressionistic paintings of rust and gold.

The photograph of this Scarlet Sea Fan shows how the whole colony grows perpendicular to the current. Currents in Beab Pass are very swift during new and full moons when tidal fluctuations reach extremes. The nodes, raised joints along the branches, provide the needed flexibility to the coral.

Gauguin and Scarlet Sea Fan polyps are generally aligned along the edges of the flattened branches, a feature common to many sea fans.

51. Scarlet Sea Fan *Melithaea* cf. *albitincta* (Ridley, 1884) ● 1⅓ life size ● Three Rocks Reef, Ngeruktabel Island, Belau ● 20 feet/6.1 meters ● Day ● 29 August 1969 ● Similar: USNM No. 58576, 58577, 58591

The two *Melithaea* species in Belau inhabit outer reef slopes, passes and lagoons. Quite often one or the other exclusively colonizes a local reef. The Gauguin Sea Fans once thrived in Ngerumekaol Pass, the result of favorable environmental conditions.

52. Scarlet Sea Fan *Melithaea* cf. *albitincta* (Ridley, 1884) ● 1⅓ life size ● Sea Fan Reef, Faulkner Island, Belau ● 30 feet/9.1 meters ● Day ● 18 August 1969 ● Similar: USNM No. 58576, 58577, 58591

A small Scarlet Sea Fan population prompted me to name this area Sea Fan Reef in 1969. At that time, hardly another boat was to be seen on the water all day. The adjacent island (a modest piece of real estate too small for an oceanfront hotel) became Faulkner Island. It is not recorded in any registry, nor is it listed on any map. No tourist, Belauan or scientist will find this reef in my book. I vacated Faulkner Island years ago as growing debris from Belauan beer parties began to mar the breathless purity of its sand. Crystalline in sunlight, the beach slopes into turquoise shallows, a canopy of pine needles above and ancient rocks, weathered gray from the rain. I climb and sit upon them—staring out to sea.

53. Matisse Sea Fan *Melithaea* cf. *albitincta* (Ridley, 1884) ● Life size ● Bedulyaus Point Reef, Teongel Pass, Ngerchol Island, Belau ● 60 feet/18.3 meters ● Day ● 31 July 1973 ● Photographed: USNM No. 58577 Similar: USNM No. 58576, 58591

In all my years of diving in Belau, the sight of this lipstick pink sea fan was a unique experience. Dr. Bayer examined several specimens and decided the coral was similar to *Melithaea albitincta*, (designated in the data with cf., which means "compare with.")

When diving I have observed that a dying sea fan loses color, its branches turning white. This Matisse Sea Fan may be ailing. However, sea fans living in shallow water at the entrances to many of Belau's coves are pale red and have light pink-to-white branch endings.

Dr. Bayer is still uncertain about the correct identification of the Scarlet Sea Fan, and equally uncertain about the relationship between his Scarlet and Matisse specimens. Henri Matisse may or may not have a sea fan named after him, although scarlet was not alien to his palette. Whatever the outcome, the Matisse Sea Fan is dedicated to the idea that one beautiful color deserves another.

Class	ANTHOZOA
Subclass	OCTOCORALLIA
Order	GORGONACEA
Suborder	HOLAXONIA

The suborder HOLAXONIA includes gorgonian families in which member species have a horny axis. The axis of some species contains calcium deposits, others lack them. Of the ten known families four are represented here. Among the other six, three are deep-water inhabitants, with one having a poorly-known distribution in the central Pacific. The remaining two families are well documented in the Caribbean.

All ten are divided on the basis of the shape and arrangement of the spicules in their polyps, and on the bark-like tissue covering their axial skeletons. Moreover, each family is distinguished by the structure of the axis and the amount of calcareous deposits in it.

Family   ACANTHOGORGIIDAE Gray, 1859

The members of this family have no calcareous deposits in their horny axis. Moreover, their polyps have a strong armature of spindle-shaped spicules which in some species project glassy spines. The polyps of this family do not retract into the tissue of the branches, but fold the tentacles over their mouths and by the use of longitudinal muscles in their septa, shorten the body length.

Three known genera make up the family, which numbers 45 known species. They live at moderate depths down to 4200 feet. Of the three genera one lives in all seas, while the others are found only in the Indo-Pacific.

54. Belau Gorgonian *Acalycigorgia* species • 1⅓ life size • The Great Reef, Bailechesengel Island, Ngemelis Islands, Belau • 55 feet/16.8 meters • Day • 27 June 1973 • Photographed: USNM No. 58452

Because it is near the hub of the Indo-Pacific region, Belau is an exceedingly rich and varied marine environment. Dr. Bayer estimates that possibly 75 to 100 soft coral species and 100 gorgonians inhabit Belau's reefs. Of these, perhaps half will prove to be new species.

The Belau Gorgonian is most prolific along the outer reef walls, preferring slightly undercut terrain and a shadier environment. Underwater, this gorgonian is colored canary yellow which, Dr. Bayer

suggests, signifies the colony's ability to fluoresce. My flash obscured its fluorescent glow, recording only the coral's flesh color on film. Its yellow glow, emitted in response to the ultraviolet rays of the sun, results from the excitation of chemical substances within the coral's flesh. A particular color is determined by various chemical groups such as flavines, pterines and urobilines in the form of granules within each species.

These gorgonians have a strong, net-like weave of exceedingly flexible branches, but their skeletons do not gain appreciably in thickness at the base. Dr. Bayer commented that the skeletons can be rolled up like a sheet of paper, so flexible is the colony. Waves caused by the most severe storms probably would not destroy or adversely affect the coral in its usual habitat.

55. Maroon Gorgonian *Acalycigorgia* species • Life size • The Great Reef, Bailechesengel Island, Ngemelis Islands, Belau • 25 feet/7.6 meters • Day • 20 October 1971 • Photographed: USNM No. 58495

Belau and Maroon Gorgonians live up and down the outer reef walls which surround Belau. Generally these gorgonians grow between 25 and 120 feet from the surface. The Belau Gorgonians are most abundant below 100 feet. The Maroon Gorgonian lives in shallower water and although it is not uncommon on outer reefs, its most congenial environment is within lagoons where it grows atop stony coral boulders. The Belau and Maroon Gorgonians thrive best when not crowded among other corals that would eat the planula or obscure a young coral's growth.

Maroon Gorgonians also fluoresce, glowing deep purple in 30 to 70 feet of water. Their intense color is considerably more beautiful than the maroon coloring of their flesh, seen here. This is not unusual, for the purple color is altered by the flash and not necessarily rendered more beautiful.

Many of the gorgonians and stony corals expand their polyps even when not feeding to allow zooxanthellae optimum exposure to the sunlight for photosynthesis. Maroon Gorgonians are always feeding if their polyps are expanded, for their tissues contain no zooxanthellae that require daily sunbaths.

56. Lipstick Gorgonian *Acalycigorgia* species • 1⅓ life size • Bedulyaus Point Reef, Teongel Pass, Ngerchol Island, Belau • 70 feet/21.3 meters • Day • 31 May 1970 • Similar: USNM No. 58450

Possibly the Lipstick, Maroon and Belau Gorgonians are one and the same species. An examination of them by Dr. Bayer has revealed no appreciable morphological characteristics to separate them on a species level. In his office at the National Museum of Natural History, Dr. Bayer explained that it would be necessary to collect at least half a dozen specimens of each coral. It is difficult, sometimes impossible, to determine with scientific accuracy the morphological similarities or differences between two different specimens of the same genus. The specialist must have access to at least a modest coral population sampling for proper classification.

I have known about this need for specimens for some time. I have also known that reef areas are poisoned to acquire fish population samples. I know one person who eagerly returned home boasting of having collected 10,000 fishes in three weeks—not my ideal.

Science can be served also by underwater census rather than always by body count. I hope corals will not fare poorly for having been the subjects of our interest.

Class   ANTHOZOA
Subclass   OCTOCORALLIA
Order   GORGONACEA
Suborder   HOLAXONIA
Family   PARAMURICEIDAE Bayer, 1956

57. Stoplight Gorgonian *Swiftia exserta* (Ellis & Solander, 1786) • 1½ life size • The Wall, Stafford Creek, Andros Island, Bahamas • 180 feet/54.9 meters • 4 August 1968 • No specimen

An exotic world awaits the diver who has never descended deeper than 100 feet in the Caribbean, for many beautiful sea fans and gorgonians live at 175 feet and below. The few more shallow water gorgonians of Florida and the Bahamas only hint at the beauty of their Indo-Pacific relatives.

Ironically, the most brilliantly-colored Caribbean species live at depths beyond which the red and orange rays of the sun penetrate. Their electric colors can only be seen when illuminated with artificial light, flash bulbs, or strobe light.

The luminous red of the Stoplight Gorgonian derives from the red pigmentation in the coral's flesh. Its spicules are crystalline, neutralizing the coral's actual color, and rendering the colony translucent with a ruby-like glow.

Class   ANTHOZOA
Subclass   OCTOCORALLIA
Order   GORGONACEA
Suborder   HOLAXONIA
Family   ELLISELLIDAE Gray, 1859

Abundant deposits of calcium carbonate are inseparably mixed with the horny protein axis of Ellisellidae corals. Their skeletons are supple and springy when alive. After they are removed from the water and dried, they become very brittle.

"Members of this family are remarkable," says Dr. Bayer, "because of the uniform size and shape of the spicules filling their tissues. For the most part, the spicules look like tiny, warty dumb-bells about 0.1 mm long. It would take more than 250 of them placed end to end to equal one inch. They are mostly red or yellow, giving colonies their bright colors, which remain even after preservation."

The family contains roughly 45 known species grouped among six genera living in warm waters around the world. A few species live in deep water but most inhabit deep reefs from 250 to within 50 feet of the surface. Interestingly, several species live unattached, "footloose and fancy free," on sandy or muddy sea bottoms where no strong currents disturb them.

58. Halloween Gorgonian *Nicella goreaui* Bayer, 1973? • 1¼ life size • The Wall, Mastic Cay, Andros Island, Bahamas • 200 feet/61 meters • Day • 29 August 1968 • No specimen

The Halloween Gorgonian lives at depths between 150 and 300 feet on level bottom or attached to a drop-off wall. This colony was growing at 200 feet on the Andros Island wall, overlooking the Tongue of the Ocean. Though the coral lives deeper than most divers would care to venture, this gorgonian is considered a shallow-water form, for many family members live deeper than 5000 feet.

Six-thousand feet beneath this gorgonian, a sounding line would finally hit bottom. If all the ocean's water were removed for a moment, the Tongue of the Ocean escarpment would be considerably more impressive than the Grand Canyon. Shallow-water scuba explorers can only imagine what delicately-wrought gorgonians live in deep silence far removed from their world above.

59. Crimson Sea Whips *Junceella gemmacea* Milne Edwards & Haime, 1857 • 1⅓ life size • Ngerumekaol Pass, Ulong Island, Belau • 45 feet/13.7 meters • Day • 19 June 1957 • Similar: USNM No. 58492

In passes having swift currents sea whips are a common sight. They are best adapted to more turbulent conditions, perhaps more than any other coral. They are extremely flexible and bend horizontally with little or no structural stress. Corals in general, and also sea whips, can and do break at their holdfasts from the reef's surface. Sea whips evolved their structure in response to the rough-and-tumble, twist-and-turn existence between lagoon and sea. Passes are not a world of turmoil every hour of every day but, during those times when they are, only the well adapted survive.

Small fishes, like this wrasse, hover among the branches. Sea whips serve as way stations. The wrasse slips between the branches, lingering in the lee of the coral until the flow of the tide slackens.

60. Andros Sea Whips *Ellisella elongata* (Pallas, 1766)? • Life size • The Wall, Mastic Cay, Andros Island, Bahamas • 220 feet/67.1 meters • Day • 30 August 1968 • No specimen

The outer reef wall is a favored haunt for sea whips, which range from 40 or 50 down to 300 feet. According to Dr. Bayer, most live at moderate depths of less than 600 feet, though three species live at depths varying to 1400 feet.

The southwestern Pacific is ideal for sea fan and gorgonian sightseers because most of the very shallow water species live here. To see the beautiful Andros Sea Whips, one is required to dive 220 feet and deeper. Andros Sea Whips have been dredged from 246 feet to 720 feet, as recorded in the scientific literature. A specimen in the Smithsonian collection, however, was taken from a depth of only 80 feet. Andros Sea Whips grow to six feet, and the branches of at least one species grow nine to twelve feet in length.

Both sea fans and sea whips derive their colors from the outermost layer of spicules: bright red, orange-red, yellow or white.

Class	ANTHOZOA
Subclass	OCTOCORALLIA
Order	GORGONACEA
Suborder	HOLAXONIA
Family	CHRYSOGORGIIDAE Verrill, 1883

In Greek the name of this family means "gold gorgonian," for the strongly calcified axis is a brilliant iridescent gold in most species. Two species lack spicules; the others have thin slipper-shaped scales sparsely distributed in the tissue covering the axis and in the polyp's flesh. The coral's surface tissue is very thin, the golden axis showing through it.

Fifty known species divided among eight genera comprise the family. The genera are based on morphological differences in the way colonies arrange their branches. Of eight genera, only two, encompassing six species, live in shallow water accessible to a diver. All six species are delicate, feathery colonies branched along one plane like a sea fan. They live in the Philippines and tropical Pacific, South Africa and the Caribbean. The remaining species reside around the world in the deep sea to more than 11,000 feet. Most of the deep sea inhabitants have more elaborate, intricate growth forms than do their shallow water relatives. To quote Dr. Bayer, "The branches, either simple or dichotomous, arise in a spiral around the main stem, producing the most elegant of all gorgonian colonies."

61. Gold Leaf Gorgonian *Stephanogorgia faulkneri* (Bayer, 1974) • Life size • Mutremdiu Point, Uchelbeluu Reef, Belau • 60 feet/ 18.3 meters • Day • 3 August 1974 • Holotype: USNM No. 54035 and Paratypes: USNM No. 55552, 55553, 55554, 55555

Only three known species of *Stephanogorgia* exist, all living in the Western Pacific—in the Philippines, Belau and Fiji. They are the same color as this Gold Leaf Gorgonian. Their color derives from their skeleton or axis. Gold shows through the paper-thin flesh. The "gold-leafed" appearance is an optical effect created by very fine grooves in the surface of the axis. These grooves refract light, creating an iridescent, luminous color. The "gold-leaf" does not fade or discolor after the coral is removed from the water. Fortunately for its survival as a species, the very small sizes of its branches does not permit a jeweler to chop it up for necklaces. Certain things should be like the sun—to be touched by, never to be touched.

These Gold Leaf Gorgonians from the Philippines, Fiji and Belau seem to be home-bodies for other genera, inhabiting tropic and temperate regions, migrated to abyssal habitats.

To see them underwater is a memorable sight. In Belau they live between 50 and 80 feet below the surface where the temperature, water clarity, light, currents and minimal turbulence suits their needs. Gold Leaf Gorgonians grow downward from the ceilings of ledges and the mouths of caves along reef walls. Several reefs are inhabited by many colonies, others by only a few, which I attribute to their need for moderate environmental conditions, a ceiling from which to hang, and a picture-window with a view of the ocean. Like curtains overlapping, they peer outward in lacy silence.

Class	ANTHOZOA
Subclass	OCTOCORALLIA
Order	PENNATULACEA
Suborder	SUBSELLIFLORAE
Family	PENNATULIDAE Ehrenberg, 1828

Sea pens are the most highly organized order of octocorals. They have a fossil record estimated by some scientists to be more than 500 million years. Differing from all other octocorals, sea pens are not permanently attached to rocks or solid substrate but rather, are anchored in mud or sand by a muscular stalk. They can move up and down in the substrate and, in some cases, migrate to a more favorable location nearby. Instead of having one or two kinds of polyps like sea fans and soft corals, sea pens can boast three and even four kinds, each performing specialized functions for the colony. Although these feather-shaped colonies are soft and fleshy, in many species the tissues contain calcareous spicules shaped like glassy, three-flanged needles. A slender, calcified internal rod also supports the colony through most of its length.

Of the 14 sea pen families, only one is represented here from approximately 150 known species around the world. The animals live from the low tide mark to more than a mile down. Distribution among shallow-water species is restricted but many deep sea dwellers populate all the ocean basins.

62. Sunrise Sea Pen *Ptilosarcus gurneyi* Gray, 1860 • ½ life size • Dodd Narrows, Mudge Island, Vancouver Island, British Columbia, Canada • 20 feet/6.1 meters • Day • 22 November 1969 • No specimen

If placed alongside most of the shallow-water tropical species, the Orange Sea Pen would appear gigantic. A fully-expanded colony extends two feet or more above the sand, its fleshy anchor buried another 12 inches, or roughly half the length of the exposed colony. Orange Sea Pens inhabit the waters of Alaska to British Columbia, Puget Sound and farther south along the coasts of Washington and Oregon. A diving scientist who studied them in Puget Sound saw very dense populations crowding together on the bottom, like flowers in a greenhouse.

The Orange Sea Pens are not over-crowded around Vancouver Island, for at Dodd Narrows where I photographed this one, a scant dozen companions lived nearby. Possibly the senior citizen sea pens migrated south to Puget Sound, crowded together in blissful retirement.

Like most cold water marine animals, Vancouver Island's sea pens make the most of every 24 hours by feeding in daylight. Most tropical sea pens feed only at night. During the day, they burrow into the sand by expelling water from their bodies then collapsing them. In Papua New Guinea, I observed and photographed a sea pen oscillating its body in a manner similar to the way one would rock a shovel blade back and forth to displace the sand. The sea pen oscillated, and its body collapsed as the animal slowly expelled water. This going-home process resulted from the sudden shock it received as I photographed it, my flashbulbs igniting only a foot away.

Class	ANTHOZOA
Subclass	OCTOCORALLIA
Order	HELIOPORACEA
Family	HELIOPORIDAE Moseley, 1876

Octocorals of the order Helioporacea are unique for they produce massive skeletons of calcium carbonate in the form of aragonite instead of a spicular calcite skeleton.

Six genera are described from fossils, some dating from the Cretaceous. Two genera survive. The Blue Coral, *Heliopora coerulea*, is alone among octocorals because of its powder-blue skeleton. Blue Corals contribute significantly to the reefbuilding process by means of their skeletal mass.

63. Blue Coral *Heliopora coerulea* (Pallas, 1766) • 1¼ life size • Ulach Pass, Ngcheangel Islands, Belau • 15 feet/4.6 meters • Day • 2 August 1971 • No specimen

Blue Coral flourishes on reefs in the tropical Indo-Pacific from Seychelles eastward to Samoa. Fossils date from the Cretaceous of Japan and Taiwan. Through the Indian Ocean eastward to the Marshall Islands there is but one species, inhabiting very shallow water reefs just below the surface to depths of 60 feet. Blue Corals prefer a narrow range of warm Pacific water north and south along the equator.

The coral's blue skeleton is hidden by the brown-colored zooxanthellae residing in its flesh. Here, in a large mass, the colony bears a striking resemblance to the foliate form of the Caribbean Fire Coral. Convergent evolution may have occurred. Corals in similar shallow water habitats are confronted with many of the same environmental conditions. Also, the possibility for mimicry exists because the resemblance of Blue Coral to fire coral might well aid its survival. The shape may differ but generally the surface color and texture is quite deceptive, leading one to believe the Blue Coral is a fire coral.

Class	ANTHOZOA
Subclass	HEXACORALLIA
Order	SCLERACTINIA
Suborder	ASTROCOENIINA
Family	THAMNASTERIIDAE Vaughan & Wells, 1943

We are now entirely within the realm of stony corals. This family constitutes a major transition from the octocorals to hexacorals, characterized by polyps having six tentacles or multiples thereof. Hexacorals are the major reef building corals for their limestone skeletons accumulate, layer upon layer, over the centuries. In some measure, soft corals do contribute to a reef's growth, but not to the extent that hermatypic stony corals, mollusks, coralline algae and other organisms "build the reef."

Popular science writers have often over-inflated the importance of stony coral skeletal contributions to the reef, but obviously, their limestone remains have nowhere else to go. Stony corals do not construct their skeletons with reef growth as their goal. In part, a "coral reef" is the by-product or, more accurately, the waste product of coral growth and death. Corals alone would not make the reef what it is, for "coral reefs" are the net accumulations of all organisms large and small, with and without limestone skeletons and backbones.

When the supremacy of vertebrate existence begins to eclipse the sparkling sunlight of the invertebrate wonderland, I turn for solace to Tom Robbins' "Single Cell Preface" to his book, *Even Cowgirls Get the Blues*. Professor Robbins writes (with scientific accuracy, I trust), "Amoebae leave no fossils. They haven't any bones. (No teeth, no belt buckles, no wedding rings.) It is impossible, therefore, to determine how long amoebae have been on Earth.

"Quite possibly they have been here since the curtain opened. Amoebae may even have dominated the stage, early in the first act. On the other hand, they may have come into existence only three years—or three days or three minutes—before they were discovered by Anton van Leeuwenhoek in 1674. It can't be proven either way.

"One thing is certain, however: because amoebae reproduce by division, endlessly, passing everything on yet giving up nothing, the first amoebae that ever lived is still alive. Whether four billion years old or merely three hundred, he/she is with us today.

"Where?"

Everywhere, of course.

About two-thirds of the species of stony corals, including the species of Thamnasteriidae, are hermatypic, having algae in their tissues. The polyps and calices are small. Members of the family are colonial, with massive skeletons and growth forms covering many square yards.

Seven fossil genera have been described but to date only one living genus, having seven species, is recorded in the literature.

The family ranges from the Red Sea to Belau, Papua New Guinea, Queensland and Western Australia, the Solomon Islands, New Caledonia and Fiji, Tahiti, Tonga, Hawaii, the Galapagos and Panama.

64. Animal Crackers Coral *Psammocora digitata* Milne Edwards & Haime, 1851 • 1½ life size • Patch Reef, Mekeald Lagoon, Ngeruktabel Island, Belau • 30 feet/9.1 meters • Day • 8 September 1974 • Photographed: USNM No. 47043

Its scientific name draws attention to the coral's fingerlike growths. On first sight, I named it Knob Coral, which may be the best description for it since this colony may be the only one in the universe that would remind me of animal crackers—two camels—two childhood memories pulled from a little box half way down the grocery store aisle.

On this colony, one may see the small calice indentations across the surface of the columns. A closer look reveals the expanded polyps feeding. It is not unusual for columns to diverge or branch but the exaggerated branching of this colony is rare. The following two photographs show typical growth forms for *P. digitata*. Other species encrust dead coral substrate.

65. Animal Crackers Coral *Psammocora digitata* Milne Edwards & Haime, 1851 • Life size • Northeast Reef, Macharchar Island, Belau • 15 feet/4.6 meters • Day • 9 July 1973 • Photographed: USNM No. 47044

The previous colony was discovered living in a protected lagoon in Belau. This colony inhabited the shallows of a fringing reef, exposed to frequent storms. Its columns, or knobs, have grown to form closely-packed aggregations. Living flesh extends only part way down each column. Flesh ends and exposed skeleton begins somewhere near the base of the colony because here the polyps receive insufficient current and sunlight to sustain life.

The expanded polyps give the colony its velvety texture. Scientists have great difficulty identifying species from photographs because the expanded flesh and polyps of a coral obscure its skeleton, from which many of the taxonomic characters are determined. After five years of believing that these three photographs were of *P. exesa*,

Dr. Wells finally examined the collected specimens for taxonomic verification. The coral became *P. digitata*.

66. Animal Crackers Coral *Psammocora digitata* Milne Edwards & Haime, 1851 • Life size • East Cove Reef, Mekeald Lagoon, Ngeruktabel Island, Belau • 35 feet/10.7 meters • Day • 2 June 1970 • Similar: USNM No. 47045

Some lagoon areas are not suitable for coral growth because the bottom is deep or composed of sand or mud. By contrast, East Cove Reef is ideally suited to the growth of many different species. An oval of sandy bottom 30 feet beneath the surface is ringed with vast coral mounds, competing and interweaving with one another for sunshine and a place in the current. Smaller thickets are formed with more crowding. Animal Crackers Corals are not abundant here as on the outer fringing reefs. In ideal conditions a colony will dominate six or more square feet of reef. The skeleton is well suited to exposed reef conditions —a colony grows only a few feet above the bottom. The dense skeleton is solid, and not to be mistaken for an animal cracker. For then, Jawbreaker Coral would be a more appropriate common name.

Class	ANTHOZOA
Subclass	HEXOCORALLIA
Order	SCLERACTINIA
Suborder	ASTROCOENIINA
Family	POCILLOPORIDAE Gray, 1842

Members of this family live world-wide in tropical waters. Most are hermatypic and nearly all are branching forms, except *Madracis*, of which several species encrust the substrate. All Pocilliporidae have very dense, sometimes translucent skeletons. Their polyps are small, 1.5mm across, with calices containing six to 12 septa. The septa are composed of calcium carbonate ridges radiating from the center of each calice. Septa are most easily viewed on the Mushroom Coral, (Pate 101.) This solitary coral is a single, enlarged corallite with many septal ridges radiating from the central mouth of the calice. In the pocilliporids the calices and septa are very small. Through a microscope one sees that the calices rarely have more than two cycles of septa. The family ranges from low tide to 100 feet. *Madracis* lives as deep as 300 feet. Colony growth is by extratentacular budding, a common means of multiplication among stony corals. I queried Dr. Wells for a definition of extratentacular budding and received an abrupt, "Just put down extratentacular budding and don't try to explain it." I was persistent, however, and he finally remarked that an explanation would be a lengthy, four-hour lecture to students conversant with higher biology, involving very technical language. A half-hour explanation, he assured me, would be more confusing than none. So in capsule form, "Colony formation is by extratentacular budding."

67. Lady Finger Coral *Palauastrea ramosa* Yabe & Sugiyama, 1941 • 1¼ life size • East Cove Reef, Mekeald Lagoon, Ngeruktabel Island, Belau • 30 feet/9.1 meters • Day • 25 October 1970 • Similar: USNM Nos. 47047, 47048

This coral, named for Belau (Palau Islands), was described by two Japanese scientists working there before their country's war with the United States and her Allies. Japan had a modest marine biological station on the island of Oreor (Koror) with a view of Iwayama Bay. The Japanese scientists collected and studied marine organisms, among them corals. *Palao Tropical Biological Station Studies,* a journal published just before the war, was in part the result of their valuable work. In present-day Japan there is an informal group of scientists called "the old boys," who carried on field and research work in Belau. "The old boys" remember Belau with affection and nostalgia. Their dream has been to return as a group to visit the site of their former laboratory and be reunited, if only briefly, with the green land and blue sea of their memories.

This Ladyfinger Coral is a common inhabitant of the central lagoons around Belau. It is known from Australia's Great Barrier Reef, and must occur in Papua New Guinea and the western Solomons as well. *Palauastrea* is easily overlooked, the result of its very close resemblance to *Stylophora* and *Porites* finger corals.

68. Lady Finger Coral *Palauastrea ramosa* Yabe & Sugiyama, 1941 • 1½ life size • Patch Reef, Mekeald Lagoon, Ngeruktabel Island, Belau • 45 feet/13.7 meters • Day • 7 September 1974 • Photographed: USNM No. 47076

There is but one known species of *Palauastrea*. Among land animals, more are apt to be endemic or restricted to small geographical areas. Marine creatures are less apt to become endemic because ocean currents provide their larval forms broad avenues of dispersal across thousands of miles of ocean. Planktonic larvae colonize from island to island as they drift. Radiating from a population center, a species will maintain its numbers for a thousand miles in one direction, while a thousand miles in a different direction might fall beyond its range. Generally, species follow the equatorial zone, rapidly falling off north and south of it. *Palauastrea* would require a census to determine if it originated in Belau, Australia or somewhere in between.

69. False Finger Coral *Stylophora pistillata* (Esper) variety *mordax* (Dana, 1846) • 1½ life size • Lukes Reef, Oreor Island, Belau • 15 feet/4.6 meters • Day • 21 October 1970 • No specimen

The False Finger Corals are common to shallow fringing reefs and lagoon reef flats. A pleasing, compact form makes this coral an equally common sight to tourists along Florida's resort towns. Small white clumps are crowded together on glass shelves hung on tur-

quoise-painted pegboard walls, standard "Shell Shop" décor. The state of Florida has passed laws prohibiting commercial collecting of corals, but the Indo-Pacific continues to be an ever-increasing source for sought after corals and shells. Possibly the coral reef community will suffer less from the next ice age than from man's need to reconstruct a reef over his fireplace. In my youth I was party to this ritual, collecting shells and corals as well as reef fishes for sale to stores. My photographs are still a form of collecting. The instinct is not dead in me, but after many years of diving, my most satisfying experiences have come from seeing the creatures alive. At this moment, I am remembering two Skunk Clownfish dancing among the tentacles of a particular anemone. I recall reefs vibrant with activity, and not as collections of specimens, however elegantly displayed.

Stylophora is divided into four or five known species distributed from the Red Sea and Indo-Pacific, east to Tahiti and the Tuamotus. *Stylophora* has a dense skeleton and is hermatypic, traits common to all family members. This colony is one of several having similar growth forms. As this young coral grows, its finger-like branches will flatten and crease at their ends. Like folded playing cards, they slowly fill in the ever increasing spaces which occur as the branches grow apart.

70. Raspberry Coral *Pocillopora verrucosa* (Ellis & Solander, 1786) • Life size • The Creek, Red Sea, Obhor Kuraa, Saudi Arabia • 50 feet/15.2 meters • Day • 4 March 1965 • No specimen

Of Pocilliporidae, Dr. Wells wrote in 1972, "More than 40 species of this common Indo-Pacific coral have been named, but so great is intraspecific variation that it is doubtful whether 10 or 15 of these can be maintained." While researching my commentary at Cornell University in January 1979, Dr. Wells said there are 10 species of *Pocillopora*. The "lumpers" are obviously ahead. With 3000 stony corals—more or less—some editing is all to the good. Pocilliporids are the most wide-spread of all reef-building corals, "a very hardy bunch," adds Dr. Wells. Their range extends from the Red Sea to Ecuador and Panama, below the Equator to Pitcairn and Easter Island, or north as far as Midway.

Mostly shallow water corals, the family lives to 100 feet, rarely deeper. Most often they live atop the reef flat in mild to turbulent wave action. Their raspberry appearance results from wart-like bumps, groupings of six to 12 clustered polyps. A microscope reveals the clusters of tiny calices. I do not recall seeing this coral in the Pacific with pink coloration, but the species is said to vary from pink to yellow and light-to-dark brown.

71. Chocolate Raspberry Coral *Pocillopora eydouxi* Milne Edwards & Haime, 1860 • Life size • Southwest Wall, Cheleu Island, Ngemelis Islands, Belau • 10 feet/3.1 meters • Day • 20 September 1974 • Similar: USNM No. 47051

Chocolate Raspberry Corals grow to very large sizes, living in swift currents or where there is considerable wave action and surge. The coral's branches are very dense and hard to break, which is typical of stony corals living in or near the surge zones on exposed reefs.

Flesh covering the tips of its blunt branches is probably thin, containing few zooxanthellae, which allows the skeleton to show through. Corals, such as staghorns, also have white-tipped growing edges because the flesh covering them contains few or no algae. Even if the growing ends are not entirely white, their color is lighter than the more established areas of the colony.

Stony corals provide homes for other animals. The branches of this coral shelter several species of small crabs. To escape a predator or bothersome photographer, they quickly scurry around a branch.

72. Alabaster Coral *Pocillopora damicornis* (Linnaeus, 1758) • Life size • The Wreck, Bait Grounds Entrance, Ngeruktabel Island, Belau • 50 feet/15.2 meters • Day • 7 July 1973 • Photographed: USNM No. 47052

Alabaster Coral is the most prolific species in the genus, having migrated across the Indo-Pacific region east to Panama or west to the Red Sea, spanning 18,000 miles. It grows six to eight inches across and feeds day and night. The nearly-transparent flesh is yellowish-brown, covering an alabaster-like skeleton which has a beautiful translucency. The coral is one of several most commonly marketed to tourists.

Alabaster Corals live everywhere on shallow reefs down to 100 feet or more, or growing on vertical reef walls and on the hulls of wrecks, as seen in this photograph. Shallow reefs are its primary habitat, attested to by its abundance on them.

73. Caribbean Finger Coral *Madracis decactis* (Lyman, 1859) • Life size • Southeast Reef, Long Cay, Glover Reef, Belize • 100 feet/30.5 meters • Day • 24 January 1973 • No specimen

The Caribbean Finger Coral is one of the few Atlantic corals illustrated in this book. Many Caribbean shallow-reef corals are not aesthetically comparable to their Indo-Pacific relatives. The vast Pacific province has been a nursery to new species far longer than the Atlantic, which did not exist when Europe and Africa were still a part of North and South America.

This diminutive colony grows to five or six inches at most. The other half-dozen deep water species live in caves or down to 1000 feet, but the Caribbean Finger Coral rarely lives deeper than 100 feet. It is hermatypic, differing from the cave-dwelling deep-water species which are ahermatypic. In caves or at great depths, zooxanthellae would have little or no sunlight to live. *M. decactis* is golden-green with algae, its tiny expanded polyps feeding, giving the colony its fuzzy appearance.

Madracis inhabits the Mediterranean, the eastern Atlantic across to Bermuda, the Bahamas, Florida, West Indies, Belize, Honduras, Panama and elsewhere in the Caribbean. Several species have colonized the Pacific but are not common inhabitants.

Class	ANTHOZOA
Subclass	HEXACORALLIA
Order	SCLERACTINIA
Suborder	ASTROCOENIINA
Family	ACROPORIDAE Verrill, 1902

An example of how scientists communicate information among themselves in their own succinct shorthand may be seen in a description of a most prolific coral family, Acroporidae. I quote from the *Treatise:* "Massive or ramose colonies by extratentacular budding; hermatypic. Corallites small, synapticulothecate, pseudocostate, slightly differentiated from coenostheum. Septa nonexsert, in two cycles, formed by simple spiniform trabeculae projecting inward and upward from vertical mural trabeculae, commonly fusing to form laminae. Columella absent or trabecular and weak. Dissepiments thin and tabular when developed. Coenosteum extensive, light reticulate, flaky, generally spinose or striate on surface." Fortunately, after descending into the netherworld of *Acroporidae Simplified*, we are again deposited on terra firma. Rather than quote similar descriptions from the *Treatise,* I hope this appetizer will whet the tastebuds of emergent coral experts and language decoders everywhere.

Acroporidae encompasses more species than any other family of corals. Alone, *Acropora* has about 100 actual species. Scientists managed to give 300 names to them over the past two centuries but, as Dr. Wells explained, "They were led astray by the extremely varied growth forms of these corals."

All family members are hermatypic, shallow water inhabitants. Most are branched but some species grow solid, massive forms. Very porous skeletons are characteristic of the family. Their polyps are small, rarely more than 2 mm across.

In a reef zone from below the surface to 100 feet down this family encircles the globe. They abound in the Caribbean, Red Sea, Indian Ocean and across the Pacific north to Japan, east to Hawaii and south to the Tuamotus and Tahiti, Tonga, New Caledonia, the Great Barrier Reef, and all stops between.

The genus *Acropora* is distinguished from its other generic relatives by one important fact: the corallite structure at the very tip of each branch is longer than all other corallites on the branch. The lengthened tube-like corallite is the growing tip of each branch, similar to the uppermost growing tip of a christmas tree, where the star or angel is placed. Among acroporids only *Acropora* has this elongated corallite structure. No distinction of this nature exists in the other genera.

74. Staghorn Corals: [center] *Acropora robusta* (Dana, 1846)? • [foreground left] *Acropora surculosa* (Dana, 1846)? • *Acropora hyacinthus* (Dana, 1846)? • ⅓ life size • Mutremdiu Point, Uchelbeluu Reef, Belau • 15 feet/4.6 meters • Day • 16 June 1971 • Similar: USNM No. 47053 (*A. robusta*), USNM No. 47054 (*A. surculosa*) and USNM No. 47055 (*A. hyacinthus*)

Several different species of *Acropora* dominate the reef top at Mutremdiu Point, where they live 10 to 15 feet beneath the surface. The reef here has a south-to-southwest exposure and is somewhat sheltered by its eastward extension, permitting corals to grow closer to the surface. Only 300 feet away, the surf breaks—moreso between December and April when the northeast trade winds blow steadily, tumbling the waves against Belau's reefs.

   Staghorn corals number among the strongest and hardiest of *Acropora*. *A. robusta* grow three or more feet across. The whitetipped growing points of this staghorn coral easily distinguish them from the other genera. Although all the *Acropora* corals on this reef are constructed to withstand the force of surging seas, typhoons periodically destroy them. One five-day storm out of the southwest, followed by a typhoon passing over Belau during the winter of 1976, tumbled most of the staghorn corals on this reef. Nearly all the platter-shaped colonies were finally left upside down on the sand. Some colonies were beyond repair while others continued to grow new branches upwards from the edges of the overturned structures. The colony grows upon its own base, building from the overturned wreckage—reminiscent of an hourglass, which borrows time from itself.

75. Candle Staghorn Coral *Acropora splendida* Nemenzo, 1967 • ¾ life size • Kesebekuu Pass Reef, Mekeald Lagoon, Ngeruktabel Island, Belau • 25 feet/7.6 meters • Day • 17 May 1970 • No specimen

Candle Staghorn Corals proliferate in Belau's waters, especially within the lagoons, on its protected fringing reefs, and in the back waters of some passes where the current is less swift. Staghorns live between 15 and 50 feet beneath the surface.

   This candlestick-shaped colony is ideally branched to host a multitude of tiny fishes, including cardinal fishes, butterfly fishes, damselfishes and invertebrates. The candle-shaped branches arise from a five- or six-inch-thick pedestal to a massive under-network of branches that form the horizontal platform upon which the "candles" grow. One sees how the delicate branches curve upward from the elevated base, growing vertically six to eight inches or more.

76. Candle Staghorn Coral *Acropora splendida* Nemenzo, 1967 • ¾ life size • Ngerumekaol Pass, Ulong Island, Belau • 15 feet/4.6 meters • Day • 17 October 1967 • Photographed: USNM No. 47056

I vividly remember photographing this coral at Ngerumekaol Pass shortly after my first arrival in Belau in 1967. Unlike the typical undulating, weaving patterns of most corals, this formation was linear, although its vertical branches oscillated like a twinkling star. I have tried many times to record this same phenomenon using other colonies only to discover something missing. The colors were lacklustre, the magic gone. Over the years I never gave up trying to photograph the coral but I never fared as well as when I was gifted with beginner's luck. I photographed most of the corals in this book again and again, some with much improvement, but many never so clearly perceived as the first time. When it was necessary to collect the specimens, I returned to Ngerumekaol Pass where I knew the coral was growing on the terraced side of a 25-foot-high coral rock. The six-foot-across Candle Staghorn Coral was dying of old age, portions of its branches overgrown with algae. The following year the colony was barely alive, tilted at an angle, its base broken away from the coral rock. Moved by an undefined need and with much effort, I tipped over the skeleton. The rock beneath it seemed ready for new growth.

77. Lavender Staghorn Coral *Acropora formosa* (Dana, 1846) • Life size • East Reef, Ngeanges Island, Belau • 15 feet/4.6 meters • Day • 31 October 1967 • Similar: USNM No. 47057

Many corals achieve their most characteristic shape when they have good water cover and moderate currents that least disturb their branching patterns. Middle reef flats and leeward patch reefs are ideal places to investigate the norm of Staghorn Coral shapes. During underwater population surveys, a coral's color is a convenient indicator of the species. This coral's lavender hue is generally typical of the species in Belau. One thousand miles away, however, a field investigator may find the typical color of this coral to be brown.

   When looking for a Lavender Staghorn Coral, a diver may be disappointed, for the color revealed by the flash rarely exists except atop a reef flat in a few feet of water. Here the coral is closest to the sunlight and minimally filtered by the water. Its lavender color is most evident. Deeper down the reef slope, the water filters red from the sun's light, turning this coral a luminous purple. Like Maroon Gorgonians, its deep purple flesh is considerably more beautiful than the less intense color revealed by the flashbulb.

   This lavender-purple staghorn was photographed, living on a protected fringing reef at a depth deep enough to qualify as "normal." Moreover, no strong currents warped or frustrated the genetic unfolding of its branches other than the same tides which have been structuring it for millions of years. Scientists concern themselves greatly over these matters. If they didn't this book would be a random collection of photographs, like old snapshots in a shoebox. We rummage through them, noting the faces, aware only of personalities: a little girl on a horse, a man and woman standing in front of a vintage sports car, a boy in shorts, an older girl with a pageboy haircut standing behind him, her hands resting on his shoulders. A large print at the bottom of the box shows a group in front of a fireplace. Familiar faces reappear once more but now they are together for the first time as a family.

Lavender Staghorn Coral branches are similar to those of several other species. Consequently, no scientist will hazard a scientific name for this coral on the basis of my photograph. With 300 (mostly faulty) scientific names to rummage through in the family shoebox, one actual specimen—or more—for examination would assist greatly in matters of identity.

When a scientist revises a family of corals, he reexamines holotype specimens of all the species and paratypes, and as many other specimens in the family as he can visit, borrow or collect. Out of his shoebox collection, he synonymizes species, describes new ones, and generally orders relationships. The girl on the horse and the woman in front of the automobile become one person, though seen in separate photographs and at different ages. The horse and automobile are transferred to other kingdoms or different families. Everyone remaining in the family portrait is now properly identified, arranged, and ready to be hung over the sofa.

78. Platter Staghorn Coral *Acropora prostrata* (Dana, 1846) • 1⅓ life size • Bedulyaus Point Reef, Teongel Pass, Ngerchol Island, Belau • 12 feet/3.7 meters • Day • 4 July 1973 • Photographed: USNM No. 47058

In her scientific review of *Acropora*, Carden C. Wallace writes "All species which extend down the reef slope exhibit a gradual flattening out of shape with depth . . . a few species are characteristically flat but with a high radial to axial corrallite ratio, and do not extend into deep water." Although Wallace's experience was gained diving along the Great Barrier Reef, her observations are equally true for Platter Staghorn Corals and other similarly-shaped ones from Belau. Plate 74 confirms her observations. The flattening of a colony the deeper it lives is probably essential to compensate for decreasing sunlight with the increased depth. Flattening increases the colony's horizontal surface necessary for optimum photosynthesis.

Morphologically-flattened species in shallower waters result from adaptations to reef zones of strong water turbulence. One sees how flattening may be caused by two different environmental conditions or a combination of both. To a degree, both are genetically determined and are the result of conditions in the immediate environment.

Flattening due to increasing depth may not be of taxonomic importance but if a coral is adapted to a certain depth, its structure has certainly been modified to that habitat. The platter-shaped corals of the reef top have adapted on both levels.

Collectively, staghorn corals are limited to the top 100 feet of ocean. The large colonies result from the rapid metabolism of the coral in conjunction with its partners the zooxanthellae.

Genetics and environment are like a hermit crab in its shell: the crab finds a shell which fits his body, as if made for him. But, the hermit crab had to modify his tail and claws to fit the shell's interior. Imagine the environment as a sculptor's hands. What is molded when the sculptor molds the clay? The clay also presses against the sculptor's fingers, molding them. Each imprints the other, interwoven signatures that are the many shapes and modes of existence on this planet.

79. Bottlebrush Coral *Acropora subglabra* (Brook, 1891) • Life size • Kesebekuu Pass Reef, Mekeald Lagoon, Ngeruktabel Island, Belau • 35 feet/10.7 meters • Day • 24 August 1973 • Similar: USNM No. 47059

The Australians have given the name "Bottlebrush" to this coral because its branches are similar to test tube cleaners—bristles on a long wire for cleaning bottles. Bottlebrush corals range the Indo-Pacific from Singapore to the Philippines, Belau, Banda and the northern region of the Great Barrier Reef. Along Queensland's Great Barrier Reef, colonies vary in color from pale to pinkish brown. In Belau, their color ranges from tan to medium brown, grayish-tan to pink and blue-beige. The corals frequent depths from 25 to 50 feet in the shallower lagoons and reef slopes of Belau. Colors change with depth and, of course, do not photograph as they appear under water. Their pastel shades are much more luminous. This coral's branches are delicate when compared to other *Acropora* for they live in lagoons and along leeward reefs in deeper waters. The numerous tiny branches provide the colony with added structural support.

80. Pine Tree Coral *Acropora florida* (Dana, 1846)? • Life size • Jellyfish Cove I, Risong, Ngeruptachel Island, Belau • 15 feet/4.6 meters • Day • 30 July 1974 • No specimen

Another delicate *Acropora* is the Pine Tree Coral, living in one of Belau's innermost coves. Long ago, Jellyfish Cove I was a marine lake but the limestone roof of a tunnel connecting the cove with the lagoon eroded and collapsed. The tunnel is now a narrow pass which links the lagoon and the marine-lake-turned-cove. Water six feet deep flows slowly through the cove entrance. The cove is a quiet world, encircled by a high, jungle-covered wall of ancient limestone. The bottom of the cove is 60 feet down a sloping floor of sand. Around its shallow rim, in water 30 feet or less, there lives a collection of corals having a tolerance for silt. Jellyfish Cove I is fog-shrouded and removed from the mainstream of reef life.

Judged by their numbers, Pine Tree Corals seem most at home in the deeper lagoons and coves. In the shallows colonies build rounded, open structures. In deeper water the branches of this coral flatten horizontally. As depth increases, the interconnecting branches form a flat surface of lacework.

81. Christmas Tree Coral *Acropora procumbens* (Brook, 1893)? ● Life size ● Kesebekuu Pass Reef, Mekeald Lagoon, Ngeruktabel Island, Belau ● 50 feet/15.2 meters ● Day ● 28 June 1973 ● No specimen

Christmas Tree Corals are common to Belau's lagoons, particularly in Mekeald where they carpet large areas of the bottom. Their delicate branches appear to have collided in slow motion as they grew. The fringing and upper branches of the colony command a penthouse balcony "view of the city." In the cellar of the coral edifice, fishes and nocturnal invertebrates find shelter and a home. These catacombs were constructed by the ancestors of the polyps now having a penthouse view.

82. Green Forest Staghorn Coral *Acropora longicyathus* (Milne Edwards & Haime, 1860) ● Life size ● Bedulyaus Point Reef, Teongel Pass, Ngerchol Island, Belau ● 18 feet/5.5 meters ● Day ● 3 July 1973 ● Photographed: USNM No. 47060

Among Belau's lagoon-dwelling *Acropora* population, the Green Forest Staghorn Coral has the strongest and densest skeleton because it inhabits open ocean reefs as well. Carden Wallace found colonies living on reef slopes "from below the area of rough water surge to about 66 feet deep water reef flat areas, sandy floors of lagoons and leeward patch reefs . . ." of the Great Barrier Reef.

Much of Belau's outer reefs are inclined steeply. Consequently, these staghorn corals have found a more suitable environment along inner fringing reef slopes and the fringing and patch reefs of the central lagoons. The species lives on the Great Barrier Reef, around the islands of Papua New Guinea, Belau, the Philippines, Ousima and Samoa.

83. Rose Bush Coral *Acropora virgata* (Dana, 1846) ● 1¼ life size ● Center Cove Reef, Northeast Cove, Ngeruktabel Island, Belau ● 25 feet/7.6 meters ● Day ● 16 October 1971 ● Similar: USNM No. 47061, 47062

If some *Acropora* resemble bottle brushes, this Rose Bush Coral might pass for a pipe cleaner, though I would prefer not to be the pipe. The colony's elaborate branches have a delicate fragility despite their forbidding appearance. They may thwart hungry parrotfishes by offering them a mixed salad of flesh-covered "thorns." The blunt thorns would not deter parrotfishes but a stomach filled with them might give the predator indigestion. Parrotfishes feed mostly on rounded and stubby-branched colonies having relatively smooth surfaces. Parrotfishes scrape away a coral's

flesh and part of the limestone skeleton in one bite. A parrotfish is like the commuter who wolfs breakfast before catching the 8:15 train to New York. The coral's skeletal material enters the parrotfish's stomach just as it left the "plate." Fortunately for Rosebush Corals, their branches cannot be eaten and swallowed as unceremoniously as the corals having more solid, rounded surfaces. Therefore, branching may actually be a partial defense against the rasping bites of hurried commuters.

84. Van Gogh's Cypress Coral *Acropora echinata* (Dana, 1846) ● Life size ● Kesebekuu Pass Reef, Mekeald Lagoon, Ngeruktabel Island, Belau ● 45 feet/13.7 meters ● Day ● 10 September 1969 ● Similar: USNM No. 47063, 47064

The Cypress Tree Coral is one of four "bottlebrush" species having similar shapes. Radial corallites and coenosteal structures identify them. Van Gogh's images of cypresses come to mind when I see *Acropora echinata*. The long corallites of the colony evoke one of Van Gogh's mistral days.

Colonies usually grow on rubble, or the sand adjacent to rubble terrain. Species of algae overgrow the lower skeletons, crowding the living flesh of the coral.

Carden Wallace writes, "These species occur only in the sheltered, upper parts of reefs, where almost any *Acropora* species can survive. They appear to have poor differentiation of radial corallites from axials, and if this is accompanied by a similar lack of functional differentiation, it may account for their lack of colonizing success."

85. Purple-Polyped Plankton-Eater Coral *Montipora erythraea* von Marenzeller, 1906 ● Life size ● Fringing Reef, Macharchar Lagoon, Ngchelobel Island, Belau ● 20 feet/6.1 meters ● Day ● 4 August 1974 ● Photographed: USNM No. 47065

Next to *Acropora*, *Montipora* is "only number two" in numbers of species. Dr. Wells told me that about 100 species have been attributed to the genus, but in fact only half have valid names.

Montipora are quite varied in form: encrusting, branching chalice-shaped, leafy or foliate with big thin plates. The Purple-Polyped Plankton-Eater Coral is a case in point. Its most common form is the one illustrated here, but the facing page shows another colony with big, thin, foliated branches. This asymmetrical colony resembles an encrusting coral that managed to grow webbed feet and walk on water. The colony illustrated here is not foliate because its habitat is blessed with stronger currents.

86. Purple-Polyped Plankton-Eater Coral *Montipora erythraea* von Marenzeller, 1960 ● Life size ● East Cove Reef, Mekeald Lagoon, Ngeruktabel Island, Belau ● 30 feet/9.1 meters ● Day ● 2 June 1970 ● Similar: USNM No. 47066, 47067

A colony of this coral is usually a mixture of branched and foliated forms. The branches dominate the colony's base. The foliate branches are more centrally located, as in this coral which is growing sea-fan-shaped across the current's flow.

A very gentle current bathes this colony where it lives, in a small lagoon surrounded by islands. The coral's fan-shaped branches are rigid constructions of calcium carbonate, having little flexibility. All the colonies have a common characteristic—plum-purple polyps, the result of purple pigment, and not from zooxanthellae that would color the polyps beige to yellow. The yellowish-brown color of the colony's surface flesh strongly indicates the presence of zooxanthellae.

87. Chalice Coral *Montipora Foliosa* (Pallas, 1766) • ¾ life size • Northeast Reef, Macharchar Islands, Belau • 20 feet/6.1 meters • Day • 18 October 1967 • Similar: USNM No. 47070

The chalice shape and its many variations are common among reef corals because dish- or bowl-shaped corals expose more of their zooxanthellae to sunlight. I am reminded of the parabolic shapes of solar furnaces or radio telescopes: one reflecting and concentrating sunlight, the other intensifying radio waves.

In the case of the coral, the advantages of a chalice shape are somewhat offset by waste and silt disposal problems. Waste and silt accumulate in the bowl-shaped valley but the coral's continued growth keeps the colony alive and healthy.

This lovely chalice formation is part of a larger colony, belonging to an even larger Chalice Coral community. This species dominates one fringing reef several hundred yards east of Macharchar Island. Growing in large masses, colonies reach a width of six to eight feet across.

88. Chalice Coral *Montipora foliosa* (Pallas, 1766) • ⅔ life size • Patch Reef, Mekeald Lagoon, Ngeruktabel Island, Belau • 50 feet/15.2 meters • Day • 14 September 1974 • Similar: USNM No. 47071

A young colony begins life on Mekeald Lagoon's part-rubble bottom. The coral's calices are clearly visible, ringed in rows around the wall of its chaliced interior. Chalice Corals have very small polyps, rarely larger than 1 mm in diameter. Oriented upwards, they build tiers. Growth proceeds along the rim of the chalice where the coral's flesh color is nearly white from a lack of zooxanthellae in the tissues. The corallites of this colony seem larger than those on the facing page but this is an illusion, for the larger colony was photographed from the greater distance of twenty inches. The closer image, exposed twelve inches from the young colony, rendered the corallites disproportionately larger.

89. Ultraviolet Coral *Montipora cocosensis* Vaughan, 1918 • ¾ life size • Patch Reef, Mekeald Lagoon, Ngeruktabel Island, Belau • 25 feet/7.6 meters • Day • 11 September 1974 • Photographed: USNM No. 47074

An old branch of staghorn coral is like a sheep in wolf's clothing, having been consumed by this Ultraviolet Coral. The general shape is that of the *Acropora* branch but the detailed surface features are montiporian. The ultraviolet, discothèque color and "punk rock" electric-neon hair are characteristics of *Montipora* in a number of encrusting species. Encrusting is a natural way of life in environments where old skeletons abound by the acre amid coral metropolises.

Beside the Ultraviolet Coral, another young species is growing on the middens. These colonies construct their limestone edifices on old "window frames," "tumbled beams," "foundations," "fallen door frames," and the past's "abandoned stairwells."

90. Briar Coral *Anacropora spinosa* Rehberg, 1892 • 1½ life size • Patch Reef, Lagoon, Ngeruangel Atoll, Belau • 35 feet/10.7 meters • Day • 31 July 1971 • Similar: USNM No. 47075

Briar Coral is generally very uncommon in regions of the tropical Indo-Pacific. Four species are recognized, one is *A. spinosa*. Collectively they range from the Indian Ocean east to Fuji, New Caledonia, Belau and the Philippines, living to 100 feet, but more often 35-50 feet below the surface.

In Belau this Briar Coral frequently inhabits the rubble bottoms of the inner lagoons and coves where very little current and wave action exists. Even the larger lagoons, encircled by jungle-covered hills, provide the smaller coral colonies with relatively tranquil environments. Colonies dot the patch reef slopes and their bases, 50–60 feet down.

This coral's delicately colored flesh is caused by a scarcity of zooxanthellae in it. The flesh of some colonies is pale tan but at Ngeruangel Atoll, Briar Corals are snow white and grow elaborate colonies. The northern area of the lagoon is populated by foot-hills of Briar Coral 20 to 30 feet across, the greatest concentrations I have ever encountered. The pristine beauty of the snowy-white hills, shimmering in a sea of blue light, reawakened my memories of Alaska's high ice fields.

Class	ANTHOZOA
Subclass	HEXACORALLIA
Order	SCLERACTINIA
Suborder	FUNGIINA
Family	AGARICIIDAE Gray, 1847

This family of corals is circumtropical, ranging the Caribbean, the Red Sea and Indo-Pacific east to Panama. All family members are hermatypic and have dense skeletons, some growing 3 to 3½ feet high and across.

Outstanding family features are distinctive valleys, evident in *Pachyseris* and *Agaricia*. Moreover, very small, almost insignificant polyps are aligned in a row within each valley. The polyps are so closely connected with those fore and aft, they seem not to be feeding. In many species the tentacles are very small. One coral even lacks tentacles, yet seems not to be handicapped.

The family harbors six living genera; two are berthed in the tropical Atlantic and four securely moored in the Indo-Pacific. High sea voyages have not occurred between Atlantic and Indo-Pacific species. Most family members find secure anchorage in sheltered waters, some to 50 feet and several as deep as 200 feet.

91. Bark Cloth Coral *Pavona praetorta* Dana, 1846 • 1⅓ life size • Kekereltoi Cove, Ngeruktabel Island, Belau • 25 feet/7.6 meters • Day • 11 October 1971 • Similar: USNM No. 47076

Two young colonies of Bark Cloth Coral have established residence on a modest slope of limestone rock encrusted with algae and other organisms. Small coves, adjacent to the lagoons, offer many protected habitats for young corals. The colonies make ideal subjects for illustrating coral growth forms, surface details, overall colony shape, and juvenile characteristics. When the three views of this coral are compared, the reader will have a greater comprehension of the morphological changes that occur as a colony grows from infancy through adolescence to maturity.

92. Bark Cloth Coral *Pavona praetorta* Dana, 1846 • 1⅓ life size • Patch Reef, Mekeald Lagoon, Ngeruktabel Island, Belau • 35 feet/10.7 meters • Day • 14 September 1974 • Similar: USNM No. 47076

Numbered among the four Indo-Pacific genera, the Bark Cloth Coral is one of the most abundant species. The skeletal structure of Bark Cloth Coral is very thin and easily broken. Contrasted with a very young colony (Plate 91), the foliate "branches" of this adolescent colony are growing more leafy. The branches interweave and, with continued growth, will form a still tighter weave of sharp, razor-edged surfaces. The rows of irregular ridges and valleys landscaping the surfaces of this colony are evident but the seemingly invisible polyps living in the valleys are not easily glimpsed.

93. Bark Cloth Coral *Pavona praetorta* Dana, 1846 • Life size • East Cove Reef, Mekeald Lagoon, Ngeruktabel Island, Belau • 30 feet/9.1 meters • Day • 10 October 1971 • Similar: USNM No. 47077

Although reef corals dwell in the shallows and to depths of 100 feet or more, a species is probably at home and most productive within a fairly narrow depth range. The Bark Cloth Corals illustrated here were photographed at depths of 25, 35, and 30 feet. This coincidence may only reflect my predilection for structurally beautiful corals but, as previously stated, the most spectacular representatives of a particular species live in population centers having ideal conditions for their well-being and proliferation.

In part, beauty overflows from abundance. Sometimes I see corals, their branches raised, turned or contorted like the arms of a Balinese dancer. I remember her eyes, black and fearful, watching like a caged bird, waiting for her hands. In the still light of a flame I see her fingers dancing along the silence.

Large colonies of Bark Cloth Coral grow six to eight feet across, and multiply by dividing asexually, a new mouth forming beside the original one. All polyps of a colony originated from the first polyp which grew from a planula. Growth by division occurred over the entire surface of the colony, but most vigorously along its sharp growing edges. The flesh covering them contains few zooxanthellae. Beneath the flesh, the white calcium carbonate skeleton is revealed as surely as was the Emperor's nakedness when he wore "garments of gold," visible only to himself.

94. Castle Coral *Pachyseris rugosa* (Lamarck, 1816) • Life size • Center Cove Reef, Northeast Cove, Ngeruktabel Island, Belau • 15 feet/4.6 meters • Day • 16 October 1971 • Photographed: USNM No. 47080

Castle Corals range from the Red Sea through the Indo-Pacific to Tahiti, usually living within the uppermost 60 feet of water, the zone to which most hermatypic reef-building corals have best adapted. Castle Corals live in 15 to 40 feet of water. This particular colony is massive, measuring six to seven feet across, and five to six feet high. The skeleton is dense with accentuated surface ridges and valleys. The polyps live in the valleys in series. Scientists have been unable to locate tentacles on the polyps. They assume the polyps have no tentacles.

The "towers" and "turrets" of this coral remind me of King Ludwig's fabled castle, the mad King's original psychological equivalent to an atomic fallout shelter, held over at Disneyland by popular demand.

95. Platter Castle Coral *Pachyseris speciosa* (Dana, 1846) • ½ life size • Nature Reserve, Gulf of Aqaba, Eilat, Israel • 20 feet/6.1 meters • Day • 29 March 1965 • No specimen

The Castle Coral and this Platter Castle Coral graphically illustrate several taxonomic differences between two species of the same genus. The Castle Coral's flowing structure elevates it above actual comparison with a castle and the perpetual motion of the Platter

Castle Coral removes it from any resemblance to an everyday serving platter. Nonetheless, the Platter Castle Coral is essentially flattened, either platter-like or bowl-shaped. This species is quite delicate if compared to *P. rugosa*, for its leafy chalice-like constructions are not massive.

A Platter Castle Coral's ridges and valleys are aligned regularly in concentric rows. In contrast, a Castle Coral's ridges and valleys intersect one another. A comparison of both species, as they appear on facing pages, should clarify this difference.

This Platter Castle Coral, which was photographed in the Gulf of Aqaba, is the largest and most beautiful colony I have ever seen. It grew on the seaward face of a large coral boulder that was home to fishes, corals and other invertebrates. The colony decorated a 40-inch circle of underwater garden. The coral's curving ridges and valleys evoke the symmetrical patterns of raked pebbles in a Zen garden.

96. Castle Coral *Pachyseris rugosa* (Lamarck, 1816) • Life size • Ngerumekaol Pass, Ulong Island, Belau • 25 feet/7.6 meters • Day • 6 October 1967 • No specimen

This austerely-shaped Castle Coral is another image from my first trip to Belau. In the years following I have never encountered another like it. Located on a huge landmark boulder of coral in Ngerumekaol Pass, it was easy to find. The Candle Staghorn Coral lived less than ten feet away.

My first photograph began a long relationship with the Castle Coral. Over the years I documented its growth, and preserved the memory of it. Over a seven year period, the Castle Coral gained weight. Pockets of algae disfigured its lower surface and I watched it change in my photographs. The most dramatic changes occurred during the first three years of our relationship.

97. Castle Coral *Pachyseris rugosa* (Lamarck, 1816) • 1¼ Life size • Ngerumekaol Pass, Ulong Island, Belau • 25 feet/7.6 meters • Day • 13 October 1970 • No specimen

Castle Corals grow very slowly, only a few millimeters a year, but the rate of growth varies from one habitat to another. Those with more plankton and sunlight grow faster. Swift currents, sunlight and abundant plankton in Ngerumekaol Pass accelerate coral growth. If both photographs are scrutinized one discerns many of the same ridges and valleys but, as the colony grew, the terrain was layered over with new deposits of calcium carbonate.

This coral was first photographed a week before my 30th birthday, and again on my 33rd birthday, the 13th of October. The coral, unlike myself, had put on a few pounds.

98. Platter Castle Coral *Pachyseris speciosa* (Dana, 1846) • 1½ life size • Melo Pass Reef, Santa Cruz Island, Solomon Islands • 70 feet/21.3 meters • Day • 27 June 1977 • No specimen

Platter Castle Corals grow chalice- and bowl-shaped forms. This morphological difference enables scientists to differentiate *P. speciosa* from *P. rugosa*. Platter Castle Corals have flattened into leafy or bowl shapes, while castle-like towers are prominent in *P. rugosa*. The other distinguishing characteristic in *P. speciosa* is its circular ridges, like a tree's growth rings. New valleys and ridges are formed as the coral grows. This colony from the Solomon Islands shows one concentric pattern. The colony's small, transverse ridges extending up and over the larger ridges are the septa which lead from a calice in one valley floor to an adjacent calice in the next valley.

99. Caribbean Platter Coral *Agaricia grahamae* Wells, 1973? • Twice life size • Elkhorn Reef, Small Hope Bay, Andros Island, Bahamas • 45 feet/18.7 meters • Day • 11 July 1965 • No specimen

Among agariciids, this coral is the only Caribbean representative in the book. Its transverse septa extend from the calice centers in the valleys and are easily seen in the photograph. A twice-life-size reproduction of the colony magnifies the ridges and valleys, showing them in greater detail. The individual calices, with their mouths clearly evident, are aligned in the valleys.

This and other *Agaricia* live at depths from 50 to 160 feet along drop-off walls, but most often between 90 and 160 feet. Jamaica appears to be Mecca for this species. On some of this island's deep reefs, *Agaricia* colonies shingle the walls. Dr. Wells handed me a black and white photograph taken underwater by a diving scientist. The print depicted a population of Caribbean Platter Corals growing approximately 70 feet vertically by 200 feet horizontally on the sheer wall of a deep reef. Many more corals, evidenced by their "wall to wall" look in the photograph, probably extended along the reef in crowded abundance. Each colony must have been a yard across. The diver captured hundreds of them in his photograph.

Class	ANTHOZOA
Subclass	HEXACORALLIA
Order	SCLERACTINIA
Suborder	FUNGIINA
Family	FUNGIIDAE Dana, 1846

Precious coral, black coral and mushroom corals are the types most familiar to the general public. Mushroom corals fetch "dime a dozen" prices at the shell shops for an uncanny resemblance of some species to mushrooms has enchanted people. Little mushroom corals are piled in gift shop bins where tourists buy them for ten to twenty-five cents apiece, or packaged in plastic, "3 for $1."

Some fungiids are solitary, others colonial. Among 11 known

genera, eight are colonial and three solitary. The family presently claims 35 species. The colonial corals grow larger than do their solitary relatives, forming heavy domes or three-foot elongated forms similar to the "heros" or "submarines" prepared by Italian sandwich shops and delicatessens.

Fungiids are compact reef dwellers, equally common and widespread in the tropical Indo-Pacific, living mostly in 10 to 30 feet of water, though found to 100 feet. Fifty to 60-foot depths is their usual limit. Mushroom corals feed on plankton and trap detritus, including "fecal matter" expelled by fishes swimming above.

The family derived its name from the solitary members that look like topsy-turvy mushrooms, their septa resembling the gills of fungal forms.

All solitary mushroom corals are entities having but one polyp and calice of great size. The calice can be a flat disc 10 inches across. A *Fungia* calice, five inches across, may have as many as 700 septa with an equal complement of "costae" underneath the disc. The costae are the aboral skeletal ridges. Both septa and costae have very sharp, serrated edges, some spike-shaped, some triangular. The serrated septal ridges of several solitary mushroom corals are so sharp that picking them up with bare hands is equal to handling broken glass.

100. Violet Mushroom Coral *Fungia fungites* (Linnaeus, 1758) • 1⅓ life size • Ngederrak Reef, Ngederrak Lagoon, Belau • 10 feet/3.1 meters • Day • 5 October 1967 • Similar: USNM No. 47081, 47087

According to Dr. Wells, this mushroom coral's color is not unusual. Many species display patches of violet and green. *Fungia (Fungia) fungites* is more gaily colored than the other mushroom corals and more convex. A notch in the fore edge of the mushroom coral arose because it grew atop the branch of a deceased staghorn coral. The leading edge of the *Fungia* conformed to the terrain. When the coral relocated, as solitary corals are capable of doing, the skeletal notch no longer conformed to the substrate. Similar irregularities among mushroom corals are not uncommon because the reef surface is littered with skeletons.

101. Shark-toothed Mushroom Coral *Fungia (Ctenactis) echinata* (Pallas, 1766) • Life size • Ngeremdiu Reef, White Cliff, Ngeruktabel Island, Belau • 25 feet/7.6 meters • Day • 7 October 1970 • Similar: USNM No. 47083

Spiny mushroom corals are one of the most common family members, so named because they have saw-toothed septa. The coral forms oblong shapes, four inches wide by 12 in length. Relatively smooth terrain has resulted in its more regularly formed shape.

Dr. Wells has written of Fungiidae, "They are of special inter-est not only because of the generally rather large size of the polyps and their remarkable though not unique reproductive cycle, but also because they illustrate well an evolutionary trend common to most living and extinct zooantharian corals, that of a tendency toward colonial, or better, polystomatous (polycentric) forms from the basic monostomatous type, a trend that appears in the fungiids to be in full spate at the present day whereas in most scleractian (stony coral) groups it has already reached its full development." Which is to say: mushroom corals are just beginning to catch up to the other stony corals in making a transition from solitary to colonial status.

102. Frisbee Mushroom Coral *Fungia (Verrillofungia) repanda* Dana, 1846 • 1¼ life size • East Cove Reef, Mekeald Lagoon, Ngeruktabel Island, Belau • 30 feet/9.1 meters • Day • 25 October 1970 • Similar: USNM No. 47084, 47085, 47086

Originally, I referred to this species as Discus Mushroom Coral, but Dr. Wells suggested I call it Frisbee Mushroom Coral because its edge turns down like the rim of a frisbee.

Most *Fungia*, including this one, feed day and night. In this photograph two frisbees share the reef. The smaller one is alive and has polyps extended, softening its menacing septal ridges. The larger mushroom coral has died and is covered with encrusting algae. The sea does not store the dead for posterity or from sentiment but, like Jonah, life and death are swallowed by the sea and coughed forth again living.

103. Anemone Mushroom Coral *Heliofungia actiniformis* (Quoy & Gaimard, 1833) • Life size • East Cove Reef, Mekeald Lagoon, Ngeruktabel Island, Belau • 30 feet/9.1 meters • Day • 3 July 1973 • No specimen

Anemone Mushroom Corals are very common in the waters of Belau because the numerous lagoons, coves and marine lakes provide this unusually long-tentacled coral with tranquil habitats. The photograph shows the coral's white-tipped tentacles almost contracted, though beginning to expand. Several of the coral's numerous septa are visible, but the serrated ridges are softened by flesh. Compared with all other mushroom coral skeletons, this one is most beautifully structured, having delicate, high septal arches. Though they are commercially collected for sale, the average coral enthusiast cannot buy a *Heliofungia* undamaged. The coral's septa are very thin and easily broken, especially when shipped in sawdust, as are many corals. After undergoing "postage and handling," to borrow a phrase, the corals are ready for the insurance adjuster, but are merchandised nonetheless.

Dr. Wells explained that an Anemone Mushroom Coral's tentacles are only retracted at times during reproduction. One would assume this coral is reproducing early since it was photographed on July 3rd, and, according to a scientist writing in 1937, Anemone

Mushroom Corals in Belau are reported to reproduce between September and April. I suspect they must reproduce periodically all year or contract their tentacles for other needs as well. Reproduction among Anemone Mushroom Corals was explained years ago by Dr. Wells: "Like other scleractinians, the fungiids reproduce sexually with the release of free-swimming planulae and increase asexually by intra- and extratentacular budding. Planulation has been observed in only one fungiid, *F. (Heliofungia) actiniformis*, by Abe in 1937. According to him this form is hermaphroditic, the eggs developing in the gonads to the planula stage, with several hundred planulae being released daily for several days at the time of the new moon from September to April (in Palau). After two or three days the planulae settle on a substrate and within four days the first cycle of six septa has formed."

104. Anemone Mushroom Coral *Heliofungia actiniformis* (Quoy & Gaimard, 1833) • 1⅓ life size • Northeast Cove, Ngeruktabel Island, Belau • 45 feet/13.7 meters • Day • 14 August 1973 • No specimen

When a planula settles to the bottom and begins growth, it cements the first brick of its brand new skeleton to the rocky substrate. This young Anemone Mushroom Coral has relatively few tentacles and still remains attached to a rock. A mobile reef dweller may bump into the coral and snap off the "corallum," or the coral effects its own liberation by growing too large to balance on this remnant of its infancy. After the "umbilical cord" is severed, the coral is free to move about. If it is happy and healthy, it will stay put like a farmer rooted in the land. If unfavorable conditions exist, the coral expands its flesh and glides away like a cat, padding towards the desired rectangle of sunny floor beneath a window.

Interestingly, an Anemone Mushroom Coral cannot reproduce until its "corallum" is broken free from the substrate. Assuming no external force causes a premature break, this occurs some time during the coral's adolescence—the equivalent to that period in human development.

Heliofungia has a limited distribution, inhabiting only that circle of warm water encompassing Papua New Guinea, the Solomon Islands, eastern Indonesia, Borneo, the Philippines, Belau and western Micronesia. The above region is the evolutionary center for the entire family, of which *Heliofungia* is the youngest member. Anemone Mushroom Corals have not migrated beyond the family compound. In time currents will disperse the young, giving the species wider distribution.

Class ANTHOZOA
Subclass HEXACORALLIA
Order SCLERACTINIA
Suborder FUNGIINA
Family PORITIDAE Gray, 1840

Poritids are large in numbers of species, but few in genera and subgenera. Four living genera and their subgenera subdivide into 60 "valid" species, although the number of species is still under investigation. Like the acroporids, the poritids are difficult to describe taxonomically.

Of all the poritids, *Porites* has more species, the greatest populations, and is most widespread geographically. Scarcely a reef in the tropics escapes them. Of the four genera only *Porites* colonizes the Red Sea, the Indo-Pacific, the tropical Atlantic and Caribbean reefs. The three remaining genera exclusively inhabit the Indo-Pacific. *Porites* lives to 100 foot depths but species are most common on reef flats and to depths of 50 feet. *Porites* favor shallower depths with bright sunlight in quantity sufficient to satisfy the needs of their symbiotic partners, which in turn speeds the colony's growth. Their very porous skeletons also speed rapid growth. Vertical and horizontal rods, about one-half millimeter in size, form complex structures of considerable strength. The polyps deposit more calcium carbonate each day as growth proceeds. Strong, lightweight construction enables the polyps to build a collective skeleton more quickly than is possible for species with denser skeletons. Luckily, species of *Porites* grow rapidly—they are favorite fare among parrotfishes.

105. Sally Ann's Daisy Coral *Goniopora* "Solomon Is. 3" Bernard, 1903 • 1½ life size • The Wreck, Bait Grounds Entrance, Ngeruktabel Island, Belau • 80 feet/24.4 meters • Day • 7 July 1973 • Photographed: USNM No. 47093

The young Daisy Coral living on the wreck of a Japanese freighter is not numbered among *Porites* and *Alveopora* because 24 tentacles encircle each polyp's mouth. *Porites* and *Alveopora* polyps have only 12 tentacles.

This Daisy Coral inhabits the Red Sea, east to Fiji, and lives at depths of 100 feet or more. Adult colonies grow nearly a foot across. The elongated polyps of Sally Ann's Daisy Coral are considerably larger than the polyps of most corals. Oddly, the colony's skeletal base is roughly the size of a half dollar. The exact dimensions of the skeleton are accessible to researchers for the specimen is in the Smithsonian Collection. It saddens me to see my photograph and to be reminded by the data that I picked this sunny bouquet of daisies years ago.

106. Mountain Coral *Porites lutea* Milne Edwards & Haime, 1851 • Life size • West Reef, Kuabsngas Point, Ngeruktabel Island, Belau • 20 feet/6.1 meters • Day • 23 September 1971 • Similar: USNM No. 47094

Mountain Coral is easily one of the most common shallow water reef corals in the Red Sea and Indo-Pacific. They mature to very large masses weighing many tons, and their growth rate is measured at 1 cm or nearly ½ inch per year. Mountain corals do not grow as rapidly as others but their mass is impressive. Still more amazing, a colony ten feet across by ten feet high has at least 30,000,000 polyps and weighs several tons when dry.

Mountain Coral polyps are small compared to Daisy Coral polyps, though they have 12 tentacles. The tentacles are 2 cm in length when fully extended. All the polyps pictured here are contracted, revealing the position of every calice beneath the colony's salmon-colored flesh.

107. Mountain Coral *Porites lutea* Milne Edwards & Haime, 1851 • Life size • Northeast Reef, Macharchar Islands, Belau • 20 feet/6.1 meters • Day • 8 November 1967 • Photographed: USNM No. 47095 and Similar: USNM No. 47096

The unending carpet of polyps on this Mountain Coral is expanded, contrasting with the previous colony. Due to their zooxanthellae the polyps are distinctly yellow-hued compared to the base flesh color seen in the facing photograph. Coloration varies, colony to colony, from medium brown to rust red.

108. Mountain Coral *Porites lutea* Milne Edwards & Haime, 1851 • Life size • Bedulyaus Point Reef, Teongel Pass, Ngerchol Island, Belau • 20 feet/6.1 meters • Day • 31 May 1970 • Similar: USNM No. 47097

For aesthetic reasons, I photographed healthy corals and ones free of sediment accumulation, and, without even thinking, I dust any sediment off a coral with several waves of my gloved hand. Displaced water dislodges it from the valleys and crevices. After a minute or two the disturbed polyps assume their normal shape. Having straightened their collars and ties and, after dusting the "dandruff" from their shoulders, the studio photographer takes their portrait.

Mountain Corals and Chalice Corals attract the sea's "dandruff." Chalice Corals accumulate sediment on their inner floor. Mountain Corals "ritualize" sediment accumulation by forming mucous which traps and holds the detritus. The effect is like frost on leaves still lingering against the vaporizing warmth of the morning sun. Or the frail, billowing curtains, gossamer pieces of an Andrew Wyeth painting. Like a death veil, the sediment clings to the coral's surface until a windy, wet current blows it away. For a moment, the Mountain Coral is intensely colored like the hills after a rain. Mountain Corals living in very murky waters, due to dynamiting and dredging, are perpetually draped in sediment shrouds. Their ability to shed benefits them, but they must first accumulate mucous and sediment which blocks the sun's full rays, reducing photosynthesis. Feeding, respiration, metabolism and growth are equally impaired. If sedimentation (which I have documented in photographs) exceeds waste removal, the colony rapidly dies. A ragged-green carpet of alga then grows on the surfaces divested of polyps. As the weeks

pass—polyp by polyp—the colony is covered by sediment over the alga.

109. Mountain Coral *Porites lutea* Milne Edwards & Haime, 1851 • Life size • Nature Reserve, Gulf of Aqaba, Eilat, Israel • 20 feet/6.1 meters • Day • 9 April 1965 • No specimen

This lovely Mountain Coral, photographed in the Gulf of Aqaba, is probably dead, the result of dredging and increased industrial use of the harbor at Eilat. At the time I dived there 14 years ago, much harbor construction and dynamiting made visibility poor. The "Nature Reserve" at Eilat is, undoubtedly, passé due to "bigger and better reefs" on the southern Sinai; but this coral evokes old memories.

110. Witches' Finger Coral *Porites andrewsi* Vaughan, 1918 • 1¼ life size • Patch Reef, Lagoon, Ngcheangel Islands, Belau • 35 feet/10.7 meters • Day • 31 October 1970 • Similar: USNM No. 47099

The Witches' Finger Coral, growing in Belauan waters, has relatives in the Indo-Pacific and even relations in the Caribbean. One obvious difference between this species and others is its more gnarled, nearly crooked branches seen in this young colony. The coral inhabits lagoon shallows 30 feet deep or more, but has an optimum depth of 15 to 30 feet. Colonies grow very large and merge with their neighbors. The thickets might total 20 feet or more across. Some fringing reefs are dominated by 50- to 100-foot stretches of finger coral species.

111. Witches' Finger Coral *Porites andrewsi* Vaughan, 1918 • Life size • West Reef, Kuabsngas Point, Ngeruktabel Island, Belau • 15 feet/4.6 meters • Day • 30 September 1971 • Similar: USNM No. 47100

One small area of a large finger coral thicket shows the polyps nearly contracted (contrasted with the previous photograph of the younger colony with polyps expanded.) The polyps of many corals are usually white or lighter than the base color. Their effect makes lighter the color of the colony when the polyps are expanded. Finger coral polyps vary from brown to yellow.

Like staghorn corals, finger corals offer considerable protection to small fishes. Cardinals, squirrels, angels, butterflies, moray eels and a host of crabs, sea stars and mollusks consider the coral their home. These animals may assuredly be eaten sooner or later but, like most people, they prefer to be taken in the winter than in the spring of life.

112. Iwayama Coral *Porites (Synaraea) iwayamaensis* Eguchi, 1938 • Life size • Patch Reef, Lagoon, Ngeruangel atoll, Belau • 20 feet/6.1 meters • Day • 30 October 1970 • Similar: USNM No. 47098

Iwayama Coral is a rather uncharacteristic-looking form of *Porites*, lacking the smoother surface of finger and mountain corals. This very common coral in Belau's lagoons and coves forms clusters of knobby, lumpy columns. Spongy tissue separates the polyps from the corallites. Each polyp inhabits the corallite it built. Only the top part of a corallite is designated as the calice—the little cup wherein the polyp sits.

Though massive in size and seemingly strong, the colony's individual knobs are easily broken when careless divers kick against them with their swim fins. The skeleton is quite porous and therefore easily susceptible to damage. Delicately-branched corals deserve delicate treatment. Divers usually stand on large coral heads to rest or to survey the reef. The price may be the death of thousands of polyps and disfigurement of a beautiful colony. The temporary damage caused by a few divers on a remote reef is much less than that caused by a school of feeding parrotfish, but multiplied by thousands of divers, such as at John Pennekamp Park in the Florida Keys, and suddenly parrotfish damage becomes insignificant. Skin and scuba divers have the responsibility to remind themselves, until it becomes habit, that the reef is living and subject more to pain and destruction than the grass under one's feet. Vulnerable and tiny, coral polyps cannot endure the weight of someone millions of times their size.

113. Iwayama Coral *Porites (Synaraea) iwayamaensis* Eguchi, 1938 • ¾ life size • Bedulyaus Point Reef, Teongel Pass, Ngerchol Island, Belau • 12 feet/3.7 meters • Day • 27 May 1970 • No specimen

Comparing the Iwayama Corals, one sees at least two flesh-color variations. The flesh varies from pale pinkish brown to darker brown and tan to yellow. The only constant is the white skeleton beneath it.

When expanded, Iwayama polyps are comparable in size to the equally small polyps of *Porites lutea*. I have never observed Iwayama Coral polyps expanded during the day. Inasmuch as they and crocodiles feed at night, my eyes have never seen the polyps expanded.

Dr. Eguchi named this coral after Iwayama Bay, where he and his fellow Japanese scientists had their modest marine biology laboratory.

114. She Loves Me Not Daisy Coral *Alveopora allingi* Hoffmeister, 1925 • 1¼ life size • Patch Reef, Mekeald Lagoon, Ngeruktabel Island, Belau • 45 feet/13.7 meters • Day • 11 November 1970 • Similar: USNM No. 47102, 47103, 47104

The skeleton of this daisy coral is very delicate. If you could pluck her petaled tentacles she would remain inconstant in her love for you. If the first petal signifies that she loves you, the last will surely

decline, for each "daisy" has an even 12 tentacles. In this respect, even numbers are at odds.

115. She Loves Me Not Daisy Coral *Alveopora allingi* Hoffmeister, 1925 • 1¼ life size • Kesebekuu Pass Reef, Mekeald Lagoon, Ngeruktabel Island, Belau • 50 feet/15.2 meters • Day • 28 July 1971 • Similar: USNM No. 47105

The Daisy Coral colony grows across 15 to 20 feet. The polyps, when expanded, mask the skeleton's shape beneath, like daisies arrayed over rolling foothills. Crests occur where the large, blunt branches are present. Empty spaces between them are crowded with expanded polyps. This colony, divested of its polyps, is much less impressive and beautiful.

The coral's color contrasts nicely with that of the white-polyped colony on the facing page. Allowing for a color shift in printing, be advised that this coral is tan and white. The other coral, *in situ*, is entirely white. I have seen all white and partially white colonies. Knowing that algae give these corals their tan color, the periodic occurrence of white daisy corals is cause for speculation. The zooxanthellae may have vacated the coral's tissue. When the white color is localized, like a patch of snow lingering on a sodden field, the striking contrast suggests the obvious possibility that clusters of daisy coral polyps have lost their algal symbionts. Though unknown, the cause may be linked to reproductive, lunar or seasonal conditions.

116. She Loves Me Not Daisy Coral *Alveopora allingi* Hoffmeister, 1925 • Life size • Kesebekuu Pass Reef, Mekeald Lagoon, Ngeruktabel Island, Belau • 50 feet/15.2 meters • Day • 16 October 1967 • Similar: USNM No. 47102, 47103, 47104, 47105

A smooth knob of skeleton is capped with a bouquet of long-stemmed daisies. Mushroom coral septa are ridged; but this Daisy Coral's are spine-shaped. The interior of its calice is fashioned like a glass menagerie, a palace constructed of alabaster with elaborate chandeliers, arches and snow-frosted windows.

This was the fairyland Dr. Bernard glimpsed through his microscope. Each "palace" dazzled his senses until distinctions blurred. Each coral was unique. Bernard borrowed time by using the collection site of the coral as its temporary scientific designation. After 75 years, few adventurous scientists have taken arms against Dr. Bernard's sea of taxonomic troubles.

Daisy corals are basically lagoon inhabitants, living 35 to 60 feet beneath the surface. At this depth, surface disturbances and stronger currents do not disturb the formal arrangement of their flower-like polyps. Sunlight energizes the zooxanthellae in the polyps, which are active day and night, even when the algae are not photosynthesizing the sunlight.

117. Pillar Daisy Coral *Alveopora spongiosa* Dana, 1846 • Life size • Ngerumekaol Pass, Ulong Island, Belau • 25 feet/7.6 meters • Day • 20 October 1970 • Similar: USNM No. 47106

This small-polyped *Alveopora* lives where currents are usually strong, bathed in the clear waters of Ngerumekaol Pass. The colony was five feet wide—the only one I remember having seen in Belau. Dr. Wells mentioned that the coral is an uncommon species, recorded only from Samoa, Japan and now Belau.

The skeleton is quite dense when compared with other *Alveopora* corals, probably the result of more rigorous living conditions. The polyps feed during the day and probably at night on the tides. At slack tide, the polyps contract.

Class	ANTHOZOA
Subclass	HEXACORALLIA
Order	SCLERACTINIA
Suborder	FAVIINA
Family	FAVIIDAE Gregory, 1900

A very large family of stony corals, the faviids number 27 genera and 200 "actual" known species. Of the 31 families represented in *Living Corals*, faviids have more species than any other family. Looking over their species, one notices the extreme diversity of their growth forms. It seems difficult to comprehend that some genera are not families in themselves, their structures are so divergent. The taxonomic characteristics scientists have used to group these corals in one family are as follows. First, their skeletons are literally nonporous, which certainly separates them from the poritids. Secondly, the septa of faviids are dentate on their upper margins, coarse or nearly razor-edged. The colonies are hazardous to touch unless a diver wears rubberized work gloves, standard diving apparel in the tropics.

Some species grow three to six feet across. Conglomerate colonies carpet the bottom in some locales. Generally, faviid polyps are large, measuring ¼ to one inch across, having 24 or more tentacles. Polyps do not extend greatly above the calices but are wide and very fleshy.

Faviids span the tropics from the Red Sea to the Indo-Pacific and the Caribbean. Species populate Hawaii's reefs, and south to the Tuamotus, Society Islands and Tonga, west to Melanesia, including the Great Barrier Reef, and north to Micronesia.

118. Cat's Eye Coral *Caulastraea echinulata* Milne Edwards & Haime, 1848 • 1½ life size • Northeast Cove, Ngeruktabel Island, Belau • 10 feet/3.1 meters • Day • 7 July 1973 • Photographed: USNM No. 47116

This young Cat's Eye Coral illustrates well colony formation. In iso-lation a coral's growth is more readily observed. Each polyp reproduces by dividing. Here, branches are reproducing themselves. All corallites undergo the same process. It would be incorrect to say that one corallite was the parent from which the new one is dividing, for they are siblings of which the one has barely come into the world before dividing again.

As the young colony grows, the space between the corallites becomes more crowded, but additional space is created by the growing branches as they build outwards. In this genus, there are four or five species that grow very expansive colonies, forming a sea of tightly packed corallites. They look like a football crowd at the Rose Bowl on New Year's Day. If one looks closely the individuals are evident, but in actuality, only like dots coloring one another in a Seurat painting.

Cat's Eye Corals fluoresce yellow and green under ultraviolet light—their base flesh green, the polyps pale lime. This colony's polyps are contracted, but at night they expand to feed. Fluorescence in corals is more noticeable on overcast days because clouds do not filter out ultraviolet radiation. The visible rays of the sun are muted, thereby reducing the amount of light which drops even lower as it descends through the water. In sombre light the corals glow more brightly. In deep water, where fluorescent corals are common, the same effect occurs even on sunny days. A *Favia* coral, in the upper right area of the photograph, is fluorescing lime green.

119. Starry Night Fluorescent Coral *Favia pallida* (Dana, 1846) • 1¼ life size • Jellyfish Cove I, Risong, Ngeruptachel Island, Belau • 15 feet/4.6 meters • Day • 15 August 1973 • Similar: USNM No. 47107

The faviid in the preceding photograph, and the one pictured, are probably *Favia pallida*. In addition to each corallite's lime-green glow, surrounding violet areas probably fluoresce blue or purple. The darker blotches fluoresce red. I associate many corals with the works of my favorite painters. More than a few remind me of Van Gogh's world, for our visions harmonize well. His "Starry Night" and his other luminous night paintings conjure forth a universe of galaxies, whirling above me.

120. Moon Coral *Favia lizardensis* Veron & Pichon, 1977 • 1¼ life size • East Cove Reef, Mekeald Lagoon, Ngeruktabel Island, Belau • 25 feet/7.6 meters • Day • 4 August 1973 • Similar: USNM No. 47108

Like Starry Night Corals, this Moon Coral reproduces by intratentacular budding or fission. The polyps typically grow apart gradually, becoming two, four, eight, and so on. *Favia* corals are globe-shaped, "massive" colonies. Their elevated calices are circular or oval, growing closely together. The flesh covering the corallites obscures their shape. At the center of the photograph, the calices are sunk like moon craters, but as the surface curves around, the flash has accentuated the donut-shaped upper corallite walls. The septal ridges, extending upward from each calice interior, are also clearly delineated.

Favia are predominantly lagoon corals. They live where the light levels are reduced, either far enough below the lagoon surface or in shady coves. Greater concentrations of sediment do not adversely affect them. The mucous produced by the flesh simply slides the sediment slowly off the face of the moon-shaped colony.

121. Mosaic Coral *Favites flexuosa* (Dana, 1846) • 1½ life size • Northeast Cove Reef, Ngeruktabel Island, Belau • 25 feet/7.6 meters • Day • 12 September 1971 • Similar: USNM No. 47117

The calice walls of this coral are fitted like pieces of glass or tile in a mosaic. Each polygonal wall conforms to the shape of the adjacent corallite. The greenish polyps, seen at the center of each calice, are contracted. The calice walls are covered with darker flesh and surround the contracted polyps. This colony's browns and greens contrast nicely with the bluish grays and pinks of the Mosaic Coral, (photographed in the same cove several years later—facing page.) All corals have their own unique shape. Many illustrated in this book were selected to call attention to these distinctions.

Pairs of whitish parallel lines radiate from the center of each calice, marking the septal ridges which are thinly covered with flesh. Each polyp's contracted mouth is visible—a nipple-like bump at the center of a calice. Partially contracted tentacle tips encircle the mouth.

122. Mosaic Coral *Favites flexuosa* (Dana, 1846) • 1½ life size • Northeast Cove, Ngeruktabel Island, Belau • 20 feet/6.1 meters • Day • 7 July 1973 • Similar: USNM No. 47117

Mosiac Corals range the Indo-Pacific. In Belau they populate shallow lagoons and coves where the water is usually murky, certainly moreso than on the outer reefs, and where light levels are much reduced by surrounding tree-covered hills that cast the reef in shadow a part of each day.

Mosaic Corals feed at night and occasionally when it rains or when the sky becomes overcast. Often the polyps remain partly expanded, even when they are not feeding. I have stimulated them to expand by gently fanning water against the colony surface, for moving water reawakens the coral's hunger for plankton.

123. Lightning Brain Coral *Diploria strigosa* (Dana, 1846) • 1¼ life size • East Reef, Northeast Cay, Glover Reef, Belize • 65 feet/19.8 meters • Day • 16 January 1973 • No specimen

The Lightning Brain Coral has shallower, narrower valleys than the Andros Brain Coral. Both form massive colonies, globose or hemispherically-shaped, and live exclusively in the Caribbean.

The polyps of *Diplora* corals are closely connected in long, meandering series, and are demarcated only by the raised ridges of their adjoining septa. The polyps' electric green color is due to pigment in their flesh. Zooxanthellae are responsible for the dizzying, salmon-colored ridges that the reader sees swimming before his eyes. A colony can grow to be three feet in diameter. A relatively small area of the colony was photographed and enlarged in this book.

124. Labyrinth Brain Coral *Diplora labyrinthiformis* (Linnaeus, 1758) • Life size • Elkhorn Reef, Small Hope Bay, Andros Island, Bahamas • 50 feet/15.2 meters • Day • 13 July 1965 • No specimen

This young Labyrinth Brain Coral has valleys separated by wide, gradually inclined surfaces. The "labyrinth" is the calcicular "series" as it meanders across the colony surface. Polyps with partially contracted, translucent-white tentacles are glimpsed living in these deep cental grooves. This young colony is shown about life size. Less mature colonies are more irregularly shaped, having up-and-down-hill surfaces. The coral's shape becomes more regular as it matures. This eight-inch colony has reached the threshold of adulthood, if judged by its surface structure. With continued growth, its ridges will flatten still more. An inhabitant of the tropical Atlantic, Labyrinth Brain Corals are common to the Bahamas, the West Indies, and the reefs of the southernmost Florida Keys.

125. Belau Brain Coral *Oulophyllia crispa* (Lamarck, 1816) • 1½ life size • Ascidian Marine Lake, Mekeald Lagoon, Ngeruktabel Island, Belau • 20 feet/6.1 meters • Day • 11 November 1970 • Photographed: USNM No. 47118

The septa of this meandrine coral have ragged edges. Sharp ridges are evident beneath the brown flesh along boundaries where the calice walls meet one another. The pale-colored flesh denotes the polyps and the partially expanded tentacles. When fully expanded, the tentacles become a sea of white hiding the colony's undersurface.

Growth is by fission, unquote. The coral is restricted to the Red Sea and Indo-Pacific. In Belau, colonies favor shallow, sometimes brackish water often partially shaded. Belau Brain Corals thrive in the lagoons, coves, and in Belau's marine lakes having adequate water circulation. Ascidian Marine Lake connects to Mekeald Lagoon by several sea level tunnels, roughly 50 to 200 feet long, that pipe millions of gallons of ocean water in and out of the lake, bathing the corals around its shores. Among the dozen or two marine lakes nestled in Belau's limestone islands, Ascidian Marine Lake has the best water circulation and for this reason has the largest coral population. Other more isolated marine lakes having restricted water circulation support few or no corals.

126. Puzzle Brain Coral *Platygyra rustica* (Dana, 1846) • 1¼ life size • Northeast Reef, Macharchar Islands, Belau • 20 feet/6.1 meters • Day • 10 October 1970 • Similar: USNM No. 47109

Shaped considerably more like a maze than any of the other meandrine corals, this Puzzle Brain Coral has very narrow valleys, almost angular, bounded by tiny, relatively smooth surfaced ridges, scaled to test the intelligence of fleas more than mice. The coral's septa run up and over the "rounded" ridges and down into the adjacent valleys. According to Dr. Wells, the polyps are joined and run in a continuous series along the bottom of the valleys. Puzzle Brain Coral polyps, even when expanded, are very tiny. They feed at night, at which time the coral's skeletal surface is probably not obscured by the feeding tentacles.

Puzzle Brain Corals are common throughout the Indo-Pacific in shallow, open waters, favoring reef flats. Like *Porites lutea*, this faviid forms micro-atolls in response to low or minus tides.

127. Antler Coral *Hydnophora rigida* (Dana, 1846) • Life size • Kesebekuu Pass Reef, Mekeald Lagoon, Ngeruktabel Island, Belau • 40 feet/12.9 meters • Day • 21 June 1970 • Similar: USNM No. 47119

The Antler Coral only lives along a narrow equatorial band of ocean which encompasses the Caroline Islands. Apparently the Philippines are the northern limits to its driftings. Canton Island is recorded as the eastern extreme, while Tonga and Fiji mark its recorded southern limits.

Antler Corals tolerate murky, secluded waters prevalent in Belau's lagoons and coves and attain their most ornate growth forms in quiet solitude. Growing to 30 or 40 inches, the colony's fuzzy surface of partially expanded tentacles reminds one of the "velvet" cover on deer and elk antlers. The polyps run the length of each antler. When fully expanded, the illusion of velvet increases.

This photograph records a small area of an adult colony while the facing photograph shows the overall view of a young colony.

128. Antler Coral *Hydnophora rigida* (Dana, 1846) • Life size • Patch Reef, Mekeald Lagoon, Ngeruktabel Island, Belau • 35 feet/10.7 meters • Day • 4 September 1974 • Photographed: USNM No. 47120

The branching shape of this young Antler Coral superficially resembles that of several staghorn corals. However, its branches are smaller in diameter and are more closely spaced. Among staghorn corals the corallites encircle the branches. Confirmed by the photograph, the polyps run in roughly circular series, each interconnecting with those next to it. Serial form corals always reproduce by fission, or more romantically phrased, by intratentacular budding.

129. Antler Coral *Hydnophora rigida* (Dana, 1846) • 1¼ life size • Patch Reef, Mekeald Lagoon, Ngeruktabel Island, Belau • 30 feet/9.1 meters • Day • 6 September 1974 • Photographed: USNM No. 47121

This view of an adult Antler Coral shows in detail the interconnecting series and how each encircles a small hill or skeletal knob. The knobs are distinguished by their slightly darker coloration.

Antler Corals are closely related to Andros Brain Corals. At first glance, due to the differences in their respective shapes, they may seem worlds apart. Nevertheless, they are closely related by their common mode of reproduction and their serially aligned polyps. These and other characteristics link them taxonomically, even though they are not in the same genus.

Surprisingly, *Hydnophora* and *Colpophyllia* both have extremely lightweight skeletons. This is hardly surprising in the Antler Corals. Fortunately for Andros Brain Corals, a precedent for their "positive buoyancy" exists in the lightweight lava rock known as pumice. Gases form in the lava, displacing rock and reducing density. As a result the pumice may be observed "swimming" on the ocean, for it is, by volume, lighter than sea water. Similarly fragments of *Colpophyllia* brain corals are cast onto the beach where they join the other flotsam along the tide line. Later, they may be washed to sea on a full moon tide, to bob before the wind on the tug and the rise of the waves.

130. Andros Brain Coral *Colpophyllia natans* (Houttuyn, 1772) • 1¼ life size • The Wall, Small Hope Bay, Andros Island, Bahamas • 115 feet/35.1 meters • Day • 16 July 1967 • No specimen

Andros Brain Corals grow larger than their Caribbean twins, the Lightning Brain Corals, but *Colpophyllia natans* is a lightweight compared to *Diplora*. Though it floats when dry, its air spaces slowly take on water and it sinks again. Translated, the coral's specific name means swimming. When describing this coral more than 200 years ago in 1772, Houttuyn was obviously aware that *C. natans* could float. Evidently, in Houttuyn's era, swimming was synonymous with floating, while in our time swimming may be thought of in terms of diving to 100 feet or more.

The wide color variations among Andros Brain Corals are obvious, as seen in this book. Dr. Wells explained that their color is from pigment in their fleshy tissues. Different pigments cause different colors. If brain corals do not fluoresce their colors certainly glow.

131. Andros Brain Coral *Colpophyllia natans* (Houttuyn, 1772) • 1⅓ life size • Fresh Creek Channel, Andros Island, Bahamas • 110 feet/33.5 meters • Day • 17 July 1967 • No specimen

Andros Brain Corals may be thought of as "endemic" to Caribbean waters. The two colonies on facing pages have their polyps contracted, showing the wide, deep, meandrine series. In this colony the thin, flesh-colored septa are golden yellow. In the other colony, lime green septa have relatively smooth edges as they extend over a ridge and assume distinctly different patterns in their transition from the valleys to the brown ridges. Sometimes the ridges of Andros Brain Corals are mysteriously structured: both ridges and valleys straighten out, flowing evenly in parallel rows for a space of 12 to 16 inches square, in contrast to the frenetic convolutions more typical of the colony.

132. Andros Brain Coral *Colpophyllia natans* (Houttuyn, 1772) • 1⅓ life size • Stafford Creek Reef, Andros Island, Bahamas • 40 feet/12.2 meters • Day • 17 July 1967 • No specimen

I photographed nearly every day on my diving trips and I could find, in my files, photographs celebrating birthdays, holidays and a multitude of memories. These associations and coincidences play no part in the selection of photographs for my books but nevertheless come along as pleasant surprises and as welcome links to the past. The experience occurred 12 years ago yet I remember this dive with George Benjamin and his son, George Jr., at Fresh Creek Channel. It was a long descent of 110 feet to the reef below. Later in the day we explored a shallow, sunny elkhorn coral reef. This moment's discovery that these two images are twins, photographed on July 17th, revived in detail a carefree day with my friends. And apropos of nothing but my love for the sea, and especially Belau, I would leave for the Pacific in October to begin what is nearly complete.

133. Andros Brain Coral *Colpophyllia natans* (Houttuyn, 1772) • 1⅓ life size • Southeast Reef, Long Cay, Glover Reef, Belize • 65 feet/19.8 meters • Day • 17 January 1973 • No specimen

The dark ridges rising above the light colored valleys boldly reveal the dynamic surface structure of this brain coral. In this photograph a septa count is possible. Rows in the valleys are punctuated with pale, elongated mouths of polyps, spaced along a valley floor. At night when the polyps feed, expanded tentacles flood the valleys and overflow the hills, inundating the surface of the colony. Waiting tentacles snare planktonic capsules of new life.

134. Little Star Coral *Montastraea annularis* (Ellis & Solander, 1786) • Life size • Southeast Reef, Long Cay, Glover Reef, Belize • 35 feet/10.7 meters • Day • 20 January 1973 • No specimen

A "suspension of disbelief" is required if one, at first glance, is to bridge the taxonomic chasm between the meandrine corals and this Little Star Coral. If not for the Little Star Coral's larger, raised corallites, its lumpy, mountainous appearance is similar to Mountain Coral (*Porites lutea*.)

The Little Star Corals reproduce by extratentacular budding between the polyps, not by "fission." Each polyp is one-quarter to three or four millimeters across. A colony will grow three to six feet across and up to seven feet high.

Living in shallow water, colonies form rounded, lumpy edifices. Those growing in water 40 feet or deeper form irregular pillar shapes like the colony shown here. Still deeper to 100 feet, the colonies flatten on the bottom to best receive what sunlight there is, near the limits of hermatypic coral growth. The Little Star Corals are common throughout the Caribbean across the ocean to the Gulf of Guinea, where the tropical Atlantic nudges western Africa.

135. Caribbean Star Coral *Montastraea covernosa* (Linnaeus, 1767) • 1½ life size • Elkhorn Reef, Small Hope Bay, Andros Island, Bahamas • 40 feet/12.2 meters • Night • 15 July 1965 • No specimen

The Caribbean Star Coral quite unpoetically has been called Large Star Coral, because both calices and polyps are much larger than those of the Little Star Coral. (Turn back a page and the two views become self-explanatory.) Both star corals have dense, not-easily-broken skeletons.

This relatively young colony was photographed at night, its expanded polyps feeding. Its glassy, whitish tentacles are like starbursts. A polyp near the center has trapped food and is engulfing it. The mouths are easily seen as puckered slits, one at the center of each polyp. At dawn the polyps of this and other corals contract to rest. The night's catch digests and the zooxanthellae are warming to the glow of the reef as the sun rides higher above the sea.

136. Caribbean Star Coral *Montastraea cavernosa* (Linnaeus, 1767) • 1¼ life size • Stafford Creek Reef, Andros Island, Bahamas • 80 feet/24.4 meters • Day • 1 August 1968 • No specimen

Caribbean Star Corals, like the Little Stars, range from the western tropical Atlantic to the Gulf of Guinea. Very common in Caribbean waters, this coral grows to over six feet across at its base and roughly six feet high. The young colony, approximately lifesize when photographed 1 August 1968, weighed no more than 10 to 15 pounds. It has grown considerably since then. Beyond the year 2000, its height and width can be calculated in tons.

This photograph evokes many memories and feelings. Seemingly two dimensional, the image is nevertheless painfully alive. Without looking at the data information, I remember the day. It was my first day's dive on one of many trips to Andros. The following dive and those on succeeding days would be deep and still deeper. Eighty feet is a shallow dive, and seems not deep enough now, for I see this memory of a coral and wonder if it has survived the age of water sports. On a personal level, this commentary has necessitated a too-intimate reunion with many treasured friends. I turn the pages of this "family album" and wonder how they are.

Class	ANTHOZOA
Subclass	HEXACORALLIA
Order	SCLERACTINIA
Suborder	FAVIINA
Family	OCULINIDAE Gray, 1847

A small family of 10 genera and some 30 "valid" species, among them several ahermatypics, the oculinids are dispersed worldwide. Several species live as deep as 4000 feet.

Some oculinids grow rounded solid masses, others are branched. Their polyps are generally small, distinct, and reproduce by budding. The septa of several species are spike-shaped to an extreme, and have smooth septal margins. The "teeth" on the septa are best inspected through a microscope for they are extremely small and fine edged. A septa's overall spike shape more than compensates for its "baby teeth," somewhat the way a swordfish's bill overshadows whatever is or isn't inside its mouth.

137. Galaxea Coral *Galaxea fascicularis* (Linnaeus, 1767) • 1⅓ life size • The Great Reef, Bailechesengel Island, Ngemelis Islands, Belau • 40 feet/12.2 meters • Day • 1 October 1974 • Similar: USNM No. 47478

Four *Galaxea* species live in shallow water to depths of 60 feet in the Indo-Pacific east to Fiji. Several inhabit the China Sea, the Carolina Islands, the Great Barrier Reef, Seychelles, Aldabra, the Andaman Islands, Formosa, Bougainville, New Caledonia, the Philippines and Singapore.

All galaxeas are hermatypic, yet feed during the day. The spiked septa protect the polyps and general skeletal structure such as this platter-shaped young colony as well. Juvenile *Galaxea* Corals are characteristically flat but as they grow they form large mounds.

This coral lives on the undercut surface of the Great Reef Wall at Ngemelis. With increased age and size its base, which is insufficient to cement it to the reef surface, may break and the coral will tumble down the steep incline. Size and weight are common problems with many corals living on reef walls. This *Galaxea* might attain a span of three to six feet when "mature," but will never reach its potential. At some moment in time its future will be terminated on a ledge several hundred feet below. Sunlight will not fuel its zooxanthellae and life will run down for the colony. Development in corals, as among many marine organisms, is circumscribed by the environment whereon they alighted.

138. Galaxea Coral *Galaxea fascicularis* (Linnaeus, 1767) • Life size • East Reef, Ngeanges Island, Belau • 15 feet/4.6 meters • Day • 31 October 1967 • No specimen

Galaxea polyps sprout 12 tentacles and have 24 or more spiked septa. Beneath the polyps the base of the tubular corallites is connected by very fragile, cellular skeletal "tissue". This lovely adult colony is a rare sight. Many older galaxeas are damaged or deformed, possibly by grazing parrot fishes. Most grazers probably avoid eating the spiked septa, but a large parrot fish might only feel pain after colliding with the spikes. Galaxea Coral has a scarcity of continuous surface flesh not interrupted by patches of algae and other growth forms. The frame of my close-up lens includes roughly only an area 9 × 9 inches, yet I have avoided photographing this species many times because an area was blemished by a dead spot of grayish algae.

The Galaxea Coral's spiked septa remind me of the rose on Astroid B-612. She imagined herself protected from plant-eaters because her stem was endowed with several thorns. The Little Prince gratefully accepted a sheep sketched within the confines of a box. *Galaxea* might fare better if they or their predators were so confined. But the sea is more than a glass aquarium. It contains all, excludes none.

Spikes and polyps together give the surface of this colony a lovely texture. The colors of the coral vary from tan to gray-beige. Sometimes the polyps glow an ethereal blue opalescence, the effect of pigments.

During all the years I have dived in Belau I never again encountered a colony as beautiful.

139. Acrhelia Coral *Acrhelia horrescens* (Dana, 1846) • Life size • Cyclone Point Reef, Heron Island, Queensland, Australia • 35 feet/10.7 meters • Day • 11 October 1965 • No specimen

Branched rather than mound-formed, the corallites of Acrhelia Corals bear a strong resemblance to those of *Galaxea*. Different genera still resemble one another in this family.

Differences, however, exist. This coral's skeleton is smooth, almost polished, and its small, very delicate branches combine to form a colony three feet across and almost as high, the need of course being not so much for height, but a more flattened shape capable of receiving sunlight.

A corallite's septa are accentuated blades but are not spike-shaped as seen in this lifesize sectional view.

The coral's brown surface is caused by algae inhabiting the tissues. The polyps feed mainly at night. This *Acrhelia* coral lives in shallow, protected water just below the surface and to depths of between 30 and 50 feet where the largest ones live.

This *Acrhelia* is not particularly common. It has limited distribution within the extreme tropical Pacific region from Fiji and the Marshalls in the east, south to New Caledonia, north to the Philippines and slightly west along the mainland of Asia.

Class	ANTHOZOA
Subclass	HEXACORALLIA
Order	SCLERACTINIA
Suborder	FAVIINA
Family	MEANDRINIDAE Gray, 1847

Four of the five genera in this family inhabit Caribbean reefs including those around Bermuda, the Bahamas, Puerto Rico, Florida, Honduras, and Panama. The family is limited to the Caribbean because the *one* Indian Ocean representative was identified from only one coral and, to date, a mere half dozen specimens have been collected. Needless to say the coral is rare.

Meandrinids have very solid skeletons, and their septa smooth margins. True to their name, the valleys are meandrine or winding. Running down the center of each valley, a thin skeletal plate called the "lamellar columella" adds support to the polyps. Species are solitary or colonial with colony formation by intratentacular budding. In 1943 Vaughan and Wells rendered a more detailed definition of colony growth: "Colony formation by intratentacular polystomodaeal intramural budding." It must have been the title of the first X-rated movie to which no one between the ages of 99 seconds and 99 years was admitted unless accompanied by all great-grandparents, all with valid passports and dressed in proper tennis attire.

140. Quicksilver Coral *Meandrina maeandrites* (Linnaeus, 1758) • $1\frac{1}{3}$ life size • Southeast Reef, Long Cay, Glover Reef, Belize • 75 feet/22.9 meters • Day • 22 January 1973 • No specimen

Its liquid structure and silvery appearance reminded me of mercury, prompting my common name, Quicksilver Coral. Following all the brain corals and meandrine types, this species needed a new common name which will catch on or, perhaps, like quicksilver, slip-slide away. Dr. Wells called my attention to an old common name, Butter Print Coral. Ridges and valleys of this colony radiate from the hub. The "lamellar columella" discussed in the introduction to the family is easily seen among the surface features of the coral as ridges along the center of the valley floors. This coral's structure is fairly flattened. Colonies grow on steep reef slopes attached to ledges.

141. Pillar Coral *Dendrogyra cylindrus* Ehrenberg, 1834 • Life size • Southeast Reef, Long Cay, Glover Reef, Belize • 25 feet/7.6 meters • Day • 23 January 1973 • No specimen

Pillar Coral is a most dramatic Caribbean coral among several. It grows to seven feet high, a metropolis of skyscraper-like pillars that rise above a floor of coral rubble.

Pillar Coral is not as common as other Caribbean species but it is more abundant in the Florida Keys where it lives predominantly in 18 to 60 feet of water. A Pillar Coral's skeleton is very dense, and its surface features roughly similar to those of Pillar Brain Corals (Plate 143), although the two species are in separate families. Pillar Coral polyps are nearly always expanded, completely obscuring the coral's surface topography. The Australian relative's skeleton should satisfy the general curiosity while leaving undisturbed the long-tentacled polyps of the Pillar Coral. If one dives often enough, particularly at slack tides, sooner or later Pillar Coral polyps will be seen contracted, revealing the skeletal surface.

142. Pillar Coral *Dendrogyra cylindrus* Ehrenberg, 1834 • $\frac{2}{3}$ life size • Key Largo Dry Rocks, Upper Key Largo, Florida, U.S.A. • 20 feet/6.1 meters • Day • 25 April 1969 • No specimen

A teddy bear's softness is suggested by the small "pillars" at the colony's base but the skeleton beneath is like marble. The very sensuous tentacles vary in color from chocolate to golden brown, contrasted in the two photographs. The meandrine structure of Pillar Coral is modified by very thick septa which reduce the depth appearance of the valleys.

Probably the Caribbean's most spectacular stony coral is Elkhorn Coral, *Acropora palmata*. As a single entity it is the largest branching stony coral in the world. The Indo-Pacific has nothing to compare. Many corals weigh more and many proliferate over the bottom, but no other stony coral is quite so impressive in size and structure. Both the Elkhorn and Pillar Coral are unusual in this respect. Interestingly, they both favor level, dead coral terrain where growing space, the current, and shallow sunlit depths are optimum.

Class	ANTHOZOA
Subclass	HEXACORALLIA
Order	SCLERACTINIA
Suborder	FAVIINA
Family	MERULINIDAE Verrill, 1866

To date, scientists have recognized three living genera and among them six species. Fossil species also exist for every stony coral family has representatives from the fossil record, generally surpassing living species in their numbers.

Merulinid skeletons are thick or massive and dense. Characteristically, the septa are thick, too, with ragged dorsal margins. Characteristic of the family, corallite series are meandrine or nearly straight, but "straight" or not they grow by "intratentacular polystomodaeal budding."

143. Pillar Brain Coral *Scapophyllia cylindrica* Milne Edwards & Haime, 1848 • Life size • Cyclone Point Reef, Heron Island, Queensland, Australia • 40 feet/12.2 meters • Day • 9 October 1965 • No specimen

Pillar Brain Corals fill an ecological niche in the Indo-Pacific similar to the one occupied in the Caribbean by Pillar Corals. A Pillar Brain Coral's general structure varies from irregularly-shaped mounds to more formal pillar-shaped columns. This coral's surface ridges are angularly curved. The placement of Pillar Brain Coral in Merulinidae rather than in another family was based upon the very characteristic structure of the coral's septa. The septa are easily seen in this photograph as small transverse ridges aligned the length of the larger "brainy" ridges. At night the polyps expand upward from the valleys and a multitude of tentacles camouflage, or soften with flesh, the stone beneath. Scleractinian corals are dwellers in a hostile sea but their stony structure is "custom-made," a substrate of septa form-fitted to the contour of a polyp's posterior with the same precision as when making a denture, or when molding a couch to fit each astronaut's body—in essence, better to fit stone to captive flesh.

144. Cabbage Coral *Merulina ampliata* (Ellis & Solander, 1786) • Life size • Northeast Reef, Macharchar Islands, Belau • 18 feet/5.5 meters • Day • 18 October 1967 • Photographed: USNM No. 47122 and Similar: USNM No. 47123, 47125

Clear water with moderate wave action is favored by Cabbage Corals. Though ruffled and leafy in appearance, Cabbage Corals are strong and densely structured, enabling them to live on exposed reefs in intermediate to open-ocean conditions.

In terms of general structure, Cabbage Corals are undoubtedly one of the most beautiful stony corals, especially on the reef. They are impressive, growing 10 to 20 feet across and nearly three feet high. They follow the contour of the bottom. Most of the edifice is defunct for only the leafy branches at the surface of the colony are alive. Flesh no longer covers the skeleton below.

The coral reproduces, growing by intratentacular budding—"fission." The straight and forked valleys are easily seen in this photograph. The facing photographs show certain variations in their morphology, and in this respect Cabbage Corals are quite variable. In spite of the morphological divergence in the foliate branches, a close look at the surface details and the coral's correct taxonomy is not in doubt.

145. Cabbage Coral *Merulina ampliata* (Ellis & Solander, 1786) • Life size • Northeast Reef, Macharchar Island, Belau • 20 feet/6.1 meters • Day • 16 September 1969 • Similar: USNM No. 47123, 47125

Cabbage Coral is usually golden brown in color, but in Belau some are shaded pink to violet like this one. Its branches are more regular, at least within the small life-size area illustrated. Both colonies lived on the same reef at nearly the same depth, yet each is uniquely different.

Three known species comprise the genus *Merulina*, and all live in the tropical Indo-Pacific.

Class	ANTHOZOA
Subclass	HEXACORALLIA
Order	SCLERACTINIA
Suborder	FAVIINA
Family	MUSSIDAE Ortman, 1890

This prolific family has 12 genera of which seven inhabit the Indo-Pacific and five the tropical Atlantic. Both Atlantic and Pacific populations have solitary and colonial genera. Unfortunately, none of the solitary corals is illustrated in the book.

The mussids are characterized as having large, fleshy polyps three centimeters across. Colonies grow by intratentacular budding. A corallite's septal margin is very coarse, having serrated, sharp teeth. A diver should not kneel on these colonies for the serrated septa, hidden just below the surface flesh, pierce protective clothing and flesh.

Many mussids fluoresce, and favor shaded or deep water environments where fluorescence is common.

146. Bouquet Flower Coral *Lobophyllia corymbosa* (Forskål, 1775) • 1⅓ life size • East Cove Reef, Mekeald Lagoon, Ngeruktabel Island, Belau • 35 feet/10.7 meters • Day • 4 August 1973 • No specimen

Bouquet Flower Corals, such as this young colony, inhabit the lagoons, coves and several marine lakes. They prefer fairly shallow calm water among the "rock islands" where trees shade with eerie green the shoreline reefs. A soft fluorescent glow of scattered corals brightens the subdued reef like Christmas tree branches brightened by glowing lights.

A young colony in Mekeald Lagoon typifies the growth pattern for the species. Adults are still dome-shaped but the donut-shaped corallites grow much larger across and more irregular. A turn of the page to Plate 147 can be helpful when making comparisons between juvenile and adult corallites.

Corallites are quite interesting for each one is composed of three or more adjoining polyps with separate mouths spaced along the central valley. As the colony grows, polyps multiply, enlarging the corallites. The *Lobophyllia*, even when young, have still more elongated corallites evidenced in Plate 149. The longer corallites have more mouths to feed in the "nest."

147. Bouquet Flower Coral *Lobophyllia corymbosa* (Forskål, 1775) • 1¼ life size • Patch Reef, Mekeald Lagoon, Ngeruktabel Island, Belau • 25 feet/7.6 meters • Day • 10 June 1970 • No specimen

An unusual daytime photograph of this Bouquet Flower Coral captures the colony feeding. Normally *Lobophyllia* feed at night but do also feed on cloudy or rainy days. In comparing this coral with the younger colony, one understands how the polyps expand their tentacles to feed, which dramatically changes the surface appearance of the colony. The outline of the corallites is nonetheless discernible. This adult colony may have up to four polyps in each of the larger corallites.

148. Bouquet Flower Coral *Lobophyllia costata* (Dana, 1846) • 1¼ life size • Mouillage d'Améré, New Caledonia • 70 feet/21.3 meters • Day • 21 August 1965 • No specimen

Lobophyllia corymbosa has as many as four polyps per corallite. *Lobophyllia costata* will have up to a dozen, connected polyp to polyp the length of an irregular valley.

Viewing this coral here and on the reef, the flesh seems to cover a solid skeletal mass beneath. This is not the reality. When the polyps contract, a fleshy portion of each polyp remains expanded, closing the gaps between individual corallites. If irritated by the gentle movement of a finger over its flesh, a polyp contracts entirely, revealing an open space between it and its neighbor, and a view of the ravines below. From the colony base to the top of the convex growing surface, a coral may grow 12 to 20 inches.

149. Bouquet Flower Coral *Lobophyllia hemprichii* (Ehrenberg, 1834) • Honey Comb Coral *Favites abdita* (Ellis & Solander, 1786 • 1⅓ life size • Northeast Cove, Ngeruktabel Island, Belau • 25 feet 7.6 meters • Day • 27 September 1974 • No specimen

Very long corallite valleys differentiate this species of Bouquet Flower Coral from *L. corymbosa* and *L. costata*. The meandrine corallites are closely spaced edge to edge without actually touching. The very elongated, winding corallite configuration is characteristic of the species, most easily seen in this juvenile colony. Illustrated a little larger than life size, the young coral shares bottom space with *Favites*, a coral encrusting a staghorn coral skeleton. In time, the larger Bouquet Flower Coral may overgrow this *Favites*. The *Favites* may extend outward as it is crowded.

Needle-pointed teeth, barely concealed by the flesh covering the corallite ridges, are the serrated margins of the Bouquet Flower Coral's septa. These spiked serrations are sharp and capable of shredding a carelessly placed knee or hand. Protective covering is useless if a diver bangs hard into the coral. After many years of photographing these corals without mishap, I made this painful discovery by accidently banging my knee into a waiting "brace of kinsman." Like gentle Romeo, I learned by painful experience Shakespeare's awareness of the "other" in oneself.

150. Bouquet Flower Coral *Lobophyllia hemprichii* (Ehrenberg, 1834) • Life size • Hera's Cove, Ngelaol, Ngeruktabel Island, Belau • 25 feet 7.6 meters • Day • 9 June 1970 • Photographed: USNM N. 47111

Reproduced life-size, the crowded corallites near the center of the colony provide the viewer with an anatomical jigsaw puzzle. One may see small gaps between the different corallites and, in keeping with the continuation of the lines, the corallites can wistfully be lifted from the puzzle, like the cardboard pieces of a larger image. The whole colony may include an additional ten or more puzzles this size.

151. Bouquet Flower Coral *Lobophyllia hemprichii* (Ehrenberg, 1834) • Life size • Hera's Cove, Ngelaol, Ngeruktabel Island, Belau • 10 feet 3.1 meters • Day • 4 June 1970 • Photographed: USNM No. 47112

Between red and green, fluorescent greens photograph the easiest. With flash, red is impossible. Red fluorescent corals can only be photographed in aquariums by using artificial ultraviolet light, a tripod, filter and time exposures. It is possible to photograph fluorescent corals at night underwater using a generator-powered-water-proofed-UV-light, a filter, time exposures and a tripod. An incredibly fascinating, beautiful book could be assembled from an in-depth reportage of fluorescing corals. I offer this idea to a young diving photographer who should be prepared to devote 15 years of his/her spare time. If a book is not published entitled *Glowing Jewels of the Sea* by 1990, I plan to start work on it myself, for by then a tripod will be a prerequisite for all my work.

152. Symphony Coral *Symphyllia recta* (Dana, 1846) • Life size • Améré Island Reef, New Caledonia • 6 feet/1.8 meters • Day • 4 September 1965 • No specimen

Symphony Corals, though quite similar in appearance to the Bouquet Flower Corals, differ taxonomically. The skeleton is a solid surface like that of brain corals. No spaces or gaps exist between the corallites. Nevertheless, Symphony Corals are grouped with the *Lobophyllia* because they are related. Each corallite is large and its flesh is not connected to the flesh of a neighboring corallite. The corallites are like individual city buildings constructed to be self-contained dwellings, but erected with no space between the outer wall of one and the building next to it. Crowding on a reef is an important determinant of coral evolution. Morphologically, Symphony Corals may be closing ranks within the colony to increase "actual" or "real" living space for the polyps. Seen through the eyes of a developer, a "useless ravine" is filled to reclaim valuable real estate and to build "more homes for more people."

153. Symphony Coral *Symphyllia recta* (Dana, 1846) • 1¼ life size • Ngerumekaol Pass, Ulong Island, Belau • 40 feet/12.2 meters • Day • 27 October 1967 • Similar: USNM No. 47124

Symphony Corals effect optical patterns of frenetically orchestrated movements. Moods and rhythms are created by tricks of reversed depth perception. The viewer momentarily sees two-toned valleys plowed out of a seemingly flat plain, or as ridges rising above the narrow blue-gray valleys. Even when the truth is known, one's eyes dance between the two realities, tending to see one or the other dimension as the winding valley. Rarely is the actual ridge perceived as such.

154. Symphony Coral *Symphyllia recta* (Dana, 1846) • 1½ life size • Pass Reef, Ngeruangel Atoll, Belau • 40 feet/12.2 meters • Day • 3 November 1970 • Similar: USNM No. 47124

Cream-colored lines undulating along the middle of each ridge serve to demarcate corallite from corallite, one neighborhood of polyps from the next. Though seemingly their opposite, the white lines mark the highest elevations of the coral's contracted flesh.

My common name for this coral was inspired by the highly musical effect its surface evokes. The psychedelic concert of light on pattern is magical. Mesmerized by the pendulum tock of a metronome, I stare at a white mouse, pink nose twitching, scurrying along a cheese-white line. In a child's excitement, so runs a mouse in a hurrying groove.

155. Symphony Coral *Symphyllia recta* (Dana, 1846) • 1⅓ life size • Northeast Reef, Macharchar Islands, Belau • 20 feet/6.1 meters • Day • 8 November 1967 • Similar: USNM No. 47124

This colony's raised ridges are easier to perceive than those of any other species. The beige valleys are softened and the narrow line running the length of the ridges is clearly discernible. If uncertainty or confusion still lingers about the ridges and valleys, the following photograph of the Platter Brain Coral from the Caribbean should solve the problem. *Myctophyllia* is in a different genus but its radiating valleys and ridges are clearly seen. The grooved line is also seen atop each ridge. Together, the photographs should clarify the magical surface configuration of Symphony Corals. The similarities and differences between the two corals—representing closely related genera within the same family—are also evident.

156. Platter Brain Coral *Mycetophyllia lamarckiana* Milne Edwards & Haime, 1849 • Life size • Southwest Reef, Glover Reef, Belize • 60 feet/18.3 meters • Day • 21 January 1973 • No specimen

The Platter Brain Coral (seen life size) lives on the deeper reefs at 100 to 150 feet and occasionally fluoresces. The rust-brown ridges and margins usually fluoresce red. The red color "dies" when photographed with flash. The coral glows only in the soft reef light.

Platter Brain Corals are exclusively Caribbean, extending south to Panama. Fossil forms were discovered on Bermuda in the ancient limestone of upraised reefs. Platter Brain Corals grow cemented to the substrate, often under ledges. The coral's base extends outward to a flattened surface which has shallow circular plates and valleys radiating from the center. Toward the coral's margin or edge, the valleys split or divide and are separated by the ridges of septa. The transverse septa are thin and not closely spaced. The rust-brown flesh covering the septa does not aid the frustrated viewer who is prevented from seeing them by all the strengths "that flesh is heir to."

Class   ANTHOZOA
Subclass   HEXACORALLIA
Order   SCLERACTINIA
Suborder   FAVIINA
Family   PECTINIIDAE Vaughan & Wells, 1943

With collected specimens, scientists mapped pectiniids eastward through the Indo-Pacific to Tahiti, southern Japan, Tonga and New Caledonia as the known boundaries.

Twelve species among five genera comprise the family, which is characterized by spreading, foliate chalice forms. Colonies spread out, covering the substrate. Corallite centers are very distinct and are often widely separated, as in the Fluorescent Peacock Corals. The septa of this family "keep very low profiles," barely elevated above the surrounding corallite surface. They are irregularly toothed, which is perhaps why the septa keep low profiles.

Reproduction or colony formation in all the pectiniids is by intratentacular budding or the appearance of a new mouth inside the original polyp's circle of tentacles. By budding the one becomes two—"two partners" with the new mouth eventually separating from the original ring of tentacles.

157. Poppy Coral *Echinophyllia aspera* (Ellis & Solander, 1786) • 1¼ life size • Center Cove Reef, Northeast Cove, Ngeruktabel Island, Belau • 25 feet/7.6 meters • Day • 17 October 1971 • No specimen

Poppy Corals feed at night. The polyps are contracted in this daytime photograph, allowing the reader to view corallite "islands" in various stages of reproduction, budding, or caught in the process of multiplying. Each polyp, pale red in hue, is reminiscent of dried flowers. The red glows stronger in natural sunlight, indicating fluorescent capabilities.

Poppy Corals inhabit lagoons and cove waters where the environment is tranquil. This coral would be destroyed by strong currents and wave turbulence for it grows large, thin, leafy structures that encrust vertical and sloping lagoon surfaces.

Beneath the softening effects of the flesh the coral's skeleton is coarse, with the corallites rising like plateaus above a skeletal plain. The Poppy Coral's inner surface has grown nearly vertical, within which the corallites have oriented toward the light and a rain of food from above.

158. Ragged Chalice Coral *Oxypora lacera* (Verrill, 1864) • 1¼ life size • Northeast Cove, Ngeruktabel Island, Belau • 15 feet/4.6 meters • Day • 15 July 1973 • Similar: USNM No. 47126

"Ragged" and "chalice" aptly describe some of the characteristics of this coral. Though the precise form varies among colonies, a common form is the chalice among young colonies. Also characteristic of the coral is a rough-surfaced, unkempt appearance. The growing edge of the colony is smooth, like the surface of this coral's central "leaf." But as more and more calcium carbonate is deposited during growth, the deposits grow more lumpy and ragged. The colony grows by intratentacular budding.

The most distinguishing characteristic of the genus is a thin skeleton with irregularly-spaced slits in it. If a piece of skeleton is held up before a light, the slits are evident. Radiating from the central region of the coral's skeleton, they extend to the colony's thin, ragged edges. The slits resemble knife cuts in apple pie crust that permit easy escape of steam while the pie bakes.

159. Ragged Chalice Coral *Oxypora lacera* (Verrill, 1864) • Life size • Patch Reef, Lagoon, Ngeruangel Atoll, Belau • 20 feet/6.1 meters • Day • 27 October 1970 • Photographed: USNM No. 47113

A small area of a very large colony is illustrated here. Ragged Chalice Corals grow to massive dimensions, covering many square yards of reef surface. The young chalice grows more tortured as its growing edges encounter one another—"more violent in the return." This slow motion drama over living space is fixed in film like a fly in amber. Lifelike in its detail the image almost moves. Yet the living coral at Ngeruangel Atoll would no longer be recognizable from my photograph—a typographic map that no longer corresponds to the terrain.

160. Sun Dial Coral *Mycedium tenuicostatum* Verrill, 1902 • Life size • Mutremdiu Point, Uchelbeluu Reef, Belau • 60 feet/18.3 meters • Day • 21 August 1973 • Similar: USNM No. 47127, 47138

If the coral's overall shape looked less like an Aztec sundial I would name it Peanut Brittle or Crackerjacks Coral, for a view of the corallite surface seems to be of candy-coated popcorn. The more encompassing view of this dish-shaped coral, however, evokes a sun dial. Compared to more massive stony corals, the skeleton is thin but, nonetheless, considerably thicker than many other chalice-shaped species. The skeleton is thickest toward the hub of the colony.

161. Sun Dial Coral *Mycedium tenuicostatum* Verrill, 1902 • 1¼ life size • Mutremdiu Point, Uchelbeluu Reef, Belau • 60 feet/18.3 meters • Day • 13 July 1973 • Similar: USNM No. 47127, 47138

From both views, the coarse granularity of the skeletal structure is evident beneath the flesh. Dr. Wells describes this granulation as tooth-like structures. Its raised corallites incline towards the outer margin of the colony in rows that radiate from the hub.

Sun Dial Corals are hermatypic, living on outer reef walls in deeper water where light levels are reduced. Sunlight falling on a colony is reduced still more because its surface is oriented towards the sea, with only a nod towards the sun above. When the sun has gone, the "sun dial" transforms into a garden of night-feeding "flowers."

162. Fluorescent Peacock Coral *Mycedium elephantotus* (Pallas, 1766) • Life size • Jellyfish Cove I, Risong, Ngeruptachel Island, Belau • 15 feet/4.6 meters • Day • 2 July 1971 • Similar: USNM No. 47139, 47140

Another chalice form is this Fluorescent Peacock Coral. Relative to the Sun Dial Coral, the Peacock Coral's surface is smooth. Measured from rim to rim, colonies grow bowl-shaped structures three feet or more across. The skeleton of the coral is very thin and fragile, easily broken at its narrow base or caved in by a careless diver. This coral is certainly one of the most exotic and beautiful corals I have encountered. But to say "the most beautiful" wastes words. Why pick a wildflower for a vase on a glass table? Better to let them dance in the field.

163. Fluorescent Peacock Coral *Mycedium elephantotus* (Pallas, 1766) • Life size • Jellyfish Cove I, Risong, Ngeruptachel Island, Belau • 15 feet/4.6 meters • Day • 2 July 1971 • Similar: USNM No. 47139, 47140

Fluorescent Peacock Corals inhabit the more protected lagoons, coves, and a few of Belau's marine lakes, living in subdued sunlight on shaded reef walls, in deep water and on shaded reefs beneath cliffs and jungle foliage. Open shade is the favored environment of this coral, which ranges from the western Indian Ocean to Fiji, Samoa, and Tahiti, and to southern Japan.

164. Fluorescent Peacock Coral *Mycedium elephantotus* (Pallas, 1766)

A glance at the five views of *Mycedium elephantotus* provides a modest sampling of its colors. The pink/green color scheme was so unique I was able to locate and collect a piece of it for identification years after I made the photograph. The colony lives in Hera's Cove, on a fringing reef shaded at least half of each day by an ancient limestone reef upraised several hundred feet and now covered with jungle. The ridge shades the reef below until the sun creeps over the trees at noon. Until then the undersurface of the water glows a silvery green. This Fluorescent Peacock Coral, punctuated with pale pink polka dots, also glows green.

At night the crocodiles are awake and about in the cove, hunting fishes and crabs while Peacock Corals feed. Luminous halos flow around the swimming reptiles and the twinkling of plankton ignites on contact with the sting of carnivorous flowers. At dawn the sun's light erases one by one the stars below and across the sky.

165. Fluorescent Peacock Coral *Mycedium elephantotus* (Pallas, 1766) • ⅔ life size • Northeast Reef, Macharchar Islands, Belau • 20 feet/6.1 meters • Day • 14 September 1969 • Photographed: USNM No. 47137

The fluorescent flesh of this coral flows like a rolling white-capped sea, a wind-drift of stars corresponding to skeletal contours. The corallites orient (left) toward the outer rim of a colony living on the recessed surface of a large coral boulder. The boulder sits atop a fringing reef which faces seaward, although a barrier reef protects it. The Peacock Coral lives a far less sheltered life here than in some quiet lagoon or cove. As a result, the coral encrusts the surface of the boulder instead of growing its characteristic chalice structure.

166. Fluorescent Peacock Coral *Mycedium elephantotus* (Pallas, 1766) • 1¼ life size • Fringing Reef, West Point, Ngermechaech Island, Belau • 65 feet/19.8 meters • Day • 14 October 1971 • No specimen

Among those illustrated, this Peacock Coral most resembles a peacock's tail feathers. Originally I gave the species another common name until I photographed this colony. When Pallas gave the coral its name over 200 years ago in 1766, he had not the advantage of scuba equipment. Our underwater capabilities today would be his science fiction. Pallas' orientation and associations were based far more on his impressions of coral skeletons than on the animals that built them. In a sense his observation of more than two centuries ago is valid and still useful to scientists and laymen. The coral's large, thin skeletal structure reminded Pallas of an elephant's ear.

167. Maze Coral *Pectinia lactuca* (Pallas, 1766) • Life size • Hera's Cove, Ngelaol, Ngeruktabel Island, Belau • 5 feet/1.5 meters • Day • 16 August 1973 • Photographed: USNM No. 47128

Some corals have beautiful skeletons reminiscent of snowflake geometry or the grandeur of architecture at its finest. The Maze Coral is one of extreme visual interest and beauty. Its intricate skeletal pattern is fascinating when viewed under a microscope. Merely stripped of flesh, the skeleton is forlornly naked for having lost the thin layer of life. Certainly flesh becomes them more than their skeletons become a museum shelf.

168. Maze Coral *Pectinia lactuca* (Pallas, 1766) • 1⅓ life size • Patch Reef, Mekeald Lagoon, Ngeruktabel Island, Belau • 70 feet/21.3 meters • Day • 5 November 1967 • Similar: USNM No. 47129

Maze Corals are characterized by high ridges and deep valleys. The corallite centers are at the bottom of the valleys where the polyps run along them in series. From the valley center septa run in parallel rows up the ridges, stopping at the summit. Each polyp series lives within its own valley. The rows of septa (seen on this coral) do not continue over the summit of the ridges and into adjacent valleys as occurs in other species. This *Pectinia lactuca* would be considered a "flat" growth form of the species, while the previous colony is "foliate."

169. Maze Coral *Pectinia lactuca* (Pallas, 1766) • Life size • Mutremdiu Point, Uchelbeluu Reef, Belau • 60 feet/18.3 meters • Day • 3 August 1974 • Photographed: USNM No. 47129

This Maze Coral is intermediate between a foliate and flat form. Foliate colonies are common to protected coves where they live to within a few feet of the surface at low tide. In waters 60 feet or deeper a colony flattens, maximizing the available sunlight for its zooxanthellae garden.

Maze Coral polyps feed at night and like many stony corals, puff out their flesh a little during the day. The actual surface contour of the coral's skeleton lies hidden precisely because its flesh is partly expanded. The septa are more defined at times when the flesh is contracted.

170. Rice Terrace Maze Coral *Pectinia lactuca* (Pallas, 1766) • Life size • Patch Reef, Lagoon, Ngeruangel Reef, Belau • 45 feet/13.7 meters • Day • 2 November 1970 • Photographed: USNM No. 47115

This Rice Terrace Maze Coral is the same species as those previous but in Ngerungel Lagoon the colony has formed a distinct terraced look. The coral (four feet high when photographed) was the most compact, yet largest Maze Coral I ever encountered. Many corals thrive to excess in the clear oceanic waters of Ngerungel Reef. The oval barrier shelters more delicate corals within the deep, 45-foot end of the swimming pool. The pulsing tide of oceanic water bathes and exits the lagoon by way of a large, deep pass in the northeastern reef.

Maze Corals are very cosmopolitan for they range between marine lakes, coves and lagoons, and through passes to the outer reefs. They seem equally at home in calm or murky, even brackish habitats with subdued light or in sunny, clear ocean waters. For many years this coral appeared to be a new species. Recently Dr. Wells examined a piece of the skeleton collected years before.

I have kept my common name to call attention to the coral's peculiar growth form. A Maze Coral, however, by any other name is still a *Pectinia lactuca* (Pallas, 1766). In this colony one may see the more clearly defined septa running from valley floors to the ridge peaks. This view of the septa is made possible by the coral's fully-contracted flesh. The flesh of the Spired Maze Coral (facing page) is considerably more expanded. The coral's skeletal features are only hinted at in the contoured striations.

171. Spired Maze Coral *Pectinia alcicornis* (Saville-Kent, 1871) • 1⅓ life size • Northeast Cove, Ngeruktabel Island, Belau • 15 feet/4.6 meters • Day • 7 July 1973 • Photographed: USNM No. 47130 and Similar: USNM No. 47131

No one would confuse a Spired Maze Coral with Maze Corals, for its "spires" are not a part of *P. lactuca* architecture. In Belau its habitat is considerably restricted: smaller lagoons and secluded coves, where colonies live on shallow fringing reefs at the base of the islands.

Its distinctive spires are the equivalent of the walls or ridges in *P. lactuca* but in the Spired Maze Coral the walls between valleys are much reduced, rising only here and there as horn-like projections. This Maze Coral fluoresces green with yellow polyps. One never sees their glow when the polyps are expanded, for at night the sun's ultraviolet rays are blocked by the planet. Unlike bioluminescence, which is generated by the organism, fluorescence requires an external stimulant to emit "light." The calices are easily distinguished because a yellowish glow sets them apart from the long radiating septa that are "all in green."

Spired Maze Corals are comparatively rare in Belau, and are known also from the Solomon Islands and the Great Barrier Reef. Spired Maze Corals have been collected in very few locations, so their distribution is largely unknown. This lovely coral was the only colony that fluoresced. Others I saw were always brown or grayish-brown.

Class	ANTHOZOA
Subclass	HEXACORALLI
Order	SCLERACTINIA
Suborder	CARYOPHYLLIINA
Family	EUSMILIIDAE Milne Edwards & Haime, 1857

Of six known genera, the Caribbean claims one, the Indo-Pacific five. The family has very few species considering that only ten species are grouped among the half dozen genera.

Several characteristics distinguish the family. Its members have very large polyps, either single or meandrine. Thin septa rise high above the rim of the calices; the septal margins are perfectly smooth.

Only colonial, hermatypic corals number among the eusmiliids. Colony formation is by "intratentacular intramural di-to-poly-stomodaeal budding." Thats right: "di-to." Artoo-Detoo? R-2 D-2? Look it up in the *Treatise*.

172. Tom Robbins Weenie Coral *Euphyllia fimbriata* (Spengler, 1799) • 1¼ life size • Patch Reef, Mekeald Lagoon, Ngeruktabel Island, Belau • 50 feet/15.2 meters • Day • 2 October 1971 • Photographed: USNM No. 47132

Tom Robbins Weenie Coral is characterized by long meandrine corallites separated by deep ravines. The corallites diverge and merge with one another. The kidney-or weenie-shaped mass of flesh is the coral's typical daytime attire. Each "weenie" is the fleshy knob on the end of a tentacle. Rarely do *Euphyllia fimbriata* polyps contract entirely. Protection and exposure of zooxanthellae to the sun are probably the daytime functions of these tentacular knobs. At night when the polyps are fully expanded and feeding, the "weenies" are submerged in a sea of flesh.

This photograph caught the weenies "dozing" because, when fully expanded, they normally overhang the crevice between corallites meeting those from across the way like a canopy of leaves overhanging a tree-lined street.

In Belau at least, this pale bluish-white colony is a rarity. Most colonies are lime green, brownish or brownish-pink. The green variation is published in *The Hidden Sea* and *Dwellers in the Sea*, previous books. If there is a periodic loss of zooxanthellae from the flesh of Daisy Coral polyps, the same temporary loss may occur in the Tom Robbins Weenie Coral. Interestingly enough, the Daisy Coral (Plate 114) and Tom's Weenie Coral were photographed within 1500 feet from one another at nearly the same depth and time of year in Mekeald Lagoon. Undoubtedly, Tom Robbins, the inventor of belt-buckle-less-amoeba, should be delighted to learn that his fossil-prone weenie coral could be investigated to determine if, and if yes ... why are the colony's zooxanthellae not buckled down?

173. Opal Bubble Coral *Plerogyra sinuosa* (Dana, 1846) • Life size

- The Wreck, Bait Grounds Entrance, Ngeruktabel Islands, Belau • 80 feet/24.4 meters • Day • 7 May 1971 • Similar: USNM No. 47133, 47134

Opal Bubble Corals have even more exotic "knobs" or bubbles on their tentacles than does the Tom Robbins Weenie Coral. This very young colony has few tentacles and, perhaps, only a single corallite. The bubbles and tiny tentacle tips are clearly seen. When the tentacles expand to feed at night the size of the bubbles decreases. Water ingested through a polyp's mouth, or the mouths of many polyps, is channeled into the tentacles. When the contracted part of the tentacles expands to feed at night, water is probably transferred to them from the bubbles. An excess of water would be expelled through the coral's many mouths.

One might question the function of the bubbles. Dr. Wells said, "No one really knows"—a safe response until, by experiment or observation, the answers are found. Facts rarely fall in one's lap if one's attention is directed elsewhere, and not on the subject. Like a sky filled with stars, so many are around us, that only a mind endowed with many previous observations and association, is able to percieve those facts most meaningful to the understanding of a subject. Charles Darwin meticulously documented evolution as he perceived it, more to convince the scientific community and those among the public who might criticize his theories. This documentation made a bulwark against cultures wrapped in their antiquated beliefs, religious or secular. Darwin knew his theories would be violently opposed, for he lived in the same cultural world *The Origin of Species* would overturn. His solid documentation strengthened his own belief in what he undertook, but the core of the theory was self evident 20 years before *Origin* was published.

In contrast to Darwin's massive documentation, what follows is a possible core for some other researcher to confirm, expand upon, or disprove. If I were to provide an explanation for the oversize bubbles of this coral, several possibilities suggest themselves. The bubbles do contain zooxanthellae that are "farmed" more efficiently in greater quantity if the surface area of bubble coral flesh is exposed to increased sunlight. Because bubble corals usually live in murky or deeper water, their expanded bubbles may be a vital requirement to survival. Taking into consideration the high-ridged septa, the bubbles may offer much better protection than a flattened layer of contracted polyps. Coral grazers, such as parrotfishes and the smaller nibblers, would find the water-filled bubbles inedible or too large and smooth to nibble on. The septa and contracted polyps should be relatively secure.

174. Opal Bubble Coral *Plerogyra sinuosa* (Dana, 1846) • 1¼ life size • Ulach Pass, Ngcheangel Islands, Belau • 65 feet/19.8 meters • Day • 5 August 1971 • Similar: USNM No. 47133, 47134

The bubbles of two young corals in this photograph are nearly contracted. Those of the smaller coral are a little more inflated. The entirely contracted flesh of a bubble fits a thin septa like a surgical glove fits a doctor's hand. The bubbles and septa correspond because the septa are constructed to support the tentacles, "one to a customer."

A comparison of this coral with the colony on the facing page demonstrates what I call the "Wizard of Oz Life Style." The reader may recall that, when confronted with the sound and the fury and a castle full of smoke, Dorothy and her friends immediately assumed the Wizard to be far larger than life. Perhaps this Bubble Coral, at a tender age, is eager to play the Wizard to a passing parrotfish. Furthermore, neighboring plants and animals on the ledge are not garden decorations, but rather compete with the bubble coral for living space. Seen in this light, one may understand every Wizard's need for a little sound and fury.

175. Opal Bubble Coral *Plerogyra sinuosa* (Dana, 1846) • 1⅓ life size • Fringing Reef, Rock Islands, Iwayama Bay, Belau • 40 feet/12.2 meters • Day • 10 October 1971 • Photographed: USNM No. 47136 and Similar: USNM No. 47135

Bubble Corals grow or increase by intratentacular budding, forming meandrine-shaped skeletons. At this stage of the colony's development one recognizes certain morphological similarities between Bubble Corals and the Tom Robbins Weenie Coral. Adult Bubble Coral polyps are joined, forming winding rows atop meandrine corallites, and are supported internally with high thin septa that extend from the valley to the corallite rim.

Adult colonies grow to four feet or more across and 15 to 20 inches high. The skeleton is dense and strong, in part the result of its meandrine structure. Adult bubbles, when expanded, are not as large as a juvenile's. Individual bubble size may no longer be critical in adults or they may have a space problem as a result of crowding. Moreover, each polyp is a part of the whole, contributing to and sharing in the colony's abundance. Multitudes of bubbles protect more effectively the delicate corallite surfaces from parrotfishes and other coral grazers. The bubbles, in far larger masses, still sun their zooxanthellae.

176. Opal Bubble Coral *Plerogyra sinuosa* (Dana, 1846) • 1½ life size • Cape Roussin Reef, Maré, Loyalty Islands • 45 feet/13.7 meters • Day • 25 August 1965 • No specimen

Opal Bubble Corals live in the tropical western Pacific. Colonies are quite common in Belau's lagoons, especially in the murky waters of Iwayama Bay. Bubble Corals accumulate sediment which is discarded after any edible matter is transferred to each polyp's mouth and consumed. The waste is expelled from the mouth and the sediment slides off the bubbles on a "magic carpet" of slime. All stony corals are slippery or slimy to touch because an outer layer of mucous protects the flesh.

This colony, photographed north of New Caledonia in the Loyalty Islands, has fully expanded bubbles more than the colony from Belau (Plate 175). To borrow from Tom Robbins, it is a "Jellybean Bonanza." But when night returns the "jellybeans" are consumed. As the bubbles contract, a carpet of tentacles covers the surface of the colony.

177. Stinging Bubble Coral *Physogyra lichtensteini* Milne Edwards & Haime, 1851? • 1⅓ life size • Patch Reef, Mekeald Lagoon, Ngeruktabel Island, Belau • 40 feet/12.2 meters • Day • 10 November 1970 • Similar: USNM No. 47141

Several differences exist between Stinging Bubble Coral and Opal Bubble Corals. As the name implies, Stinging Bubble Coral has nematocysts powerful enough to sting a diver. As flesh touches flesh, a diver suffers immediate irritation which grows more painful by the minute. In the tropics skin rashes persist, often becoming infected and difficult to cure.

Another difference between the two species is the smaller bubbles of this stinging coral. Perhaps more powerful weaponry reduces the need for larger bubbles. The nematocysts of *Plerogyra sinuosa* are not as powerful.

In this photograph the stinging bubbles are shown contracted, revealing the coral's skeletal surface features. Spaces between the meandrine corallite series in *Plerogyra* do not exist in the genus *Physogyra*. Instead, the short meandrine series are fused together, corallite to corallite, a layer of flesh covering the skeletal surface between the calices. Notable are the much smaller septa of this coral. Each septal-ringed calice shows the shrunken bubbles covering the septal "blades". Stinging Bubble Corals expand and contract their bubbles more often than either *Euphyllia* or *Plerogyra*. From my observations the coral appears to expand and contract in tidal cycles, its bubbles possibly feeding on plankton. At night, the primary tentacles still expand to feed. Some other cycle may govern bubble expansion for this coral expands and contracts with much more regularity than the other genera. Most often, I was alert to colonies with contracted bubbles for the surface of this coral was more interesting and aesthetically pleasing than its bubbles. I have photographed many Stinging Bubble Corals in coves, lagoons, passes and along outer reefs but, normally, the small grayish-brown bubbles of *Physogyra* would trap more plankton than "shutter-bugs" unless one alighted on a colony.

178. Flower Coral *Eusmilia fastigiata* (Pallas, 1766) • Life size • Southeast Reef, Long Cay, Glover Reef, Belize • 60 feet/18.3 meters • Day • 22 January 1973 • No specimen

This Flower Coral is the only Caribbean representative of the eusmiliids. The family name, Eusmiliidae, and the genus name, *Eusmilia*, reveal a little of the genealogy of scientific names. Pallas originally described the Flower Coral as *Madrepora fastigiata* in 1766, but Milne Edwards & Haime relocated this *"Madrepora"* to *Eusmilia* when they described the new genus in 1848. When, nine years later in 1875, the same two scientists published their description of Eusmiliidae, *Eusmilia* was the source for the family name. Since most of the family members are Indo-Pacific, and vary radically from *Eusmilia*, one wonders why.

Unlike other family members, Flower Corals are distinctly branched with a single polyp carried atop each corallite branch. The corallites are not fused or meandrine, nor are the septa as high as those belonging to Bubble and Weenie Corals. Flower Coral septa are quite prominent during the day for there are no inflatables to hide them. Flower Coral polyps expand only at night to feed. A colony can grow to 12 inches across, living just below the surface to 100 feet and deeper. It does not live in Bermuda; nonetheless, it ranges the Caribbean south to Panama and east to the Windward Islands.

Class   ANTHOZOA
Subclass   HEXACORALLIA
Order   SCLERACTINIA
Suborder   DENDROPHYLLIINA
Family   DENDROPHYLLIIDAE Gray, 1847

Although the book is concluded with dendrophylliids, many more families have gone unrepresented, among them the deep water precious corals, solitary corals, and fossil families which follow in taxonomic arrangement. The blank spaces are unfortunate, but a "definitive work" on anything seems a bit indulgent on anyone's behalf. In the process of making the book, I learned much, and my perceptions will be more accurate when I see the corals again. As a lover of the abstract I could not wish for a more colorful array of subjects as a finale to the book.

With 18 genera and 74 known species, dendrophylliids rank as one of the largest families. Members live worldwide, and to depths of 7500 feet. Most species are not restricted to shallow sunlit reefs. Of the 18 genera, only two are hermatypic reef inhabitants. By contrast, the 16 ahermatypic genera live beneath ledges attached to shaded reef walls or inhabit cold water environments unfavorable to most reef corals. As one would expect, the two hermatypic genera are shallow reef dwellers.

179. Festival Tube Corals *Dendrophyllia gracilis* Milne Edwards & Haime, 1848 • Sponges and Tunicates • 1⅓ life size • The Great Reef, Bailechesengel Island, Ngemelis Islands, Belau • 75 feet/22.9 meters • Day • 7 November 1970 • Similar: USNM No. 47224

The *Dendrophyllia* number some 30 species and, Arctic and Antarctic excluded, they inhabit the oceans worldwide. Species live from just below the surface to 4500 feet deep. The genus dates from the Eocene with several species recorded from fossil finds of that period. The pattern of branching varies in *Dendrophyllia*. In the near future the genus will probably be divided among several genera or subgenera on the basis of their branching patterns. The typical form of branching is dendroid, exhibited by *Dendrophyllia gracilis*. Other growth forms are phaceloid, clumped or irregularly branched.

The most abundant ahermatypic tube coral in Belau is *Dendrophyllia gracilis*. On The Great Reef at Ngemelis Islands it grows to within three feet of the surface to 130 or more. Between 20 and 80 feet the tube corals are at home.

180. Festival Tube Corals *Dendrophyllia gracilis* Milne Edwards & Haime, 1848 ● 1⅓ life size ● The Great Reef, Bailechesengel Island, Ngemelis Islands, Belau ● 50 feet/15.2 meters ● Day ● 22

At the time I collected Festival Tube Coral specimens for Dr. Wells, the orange corals appeared to be a species distinct from the Monet Tube Corals which are pink. Color among tube corals is usually not of taxonomic importance because their colors vary. Dr. Wells noted that the structure of the calices seemed to differ. Later, he made more extensive comparisons using larger numbers of specimens and concluded they were all *Dendrophyllia gracilis*. The Festival Tube Corals, once *Dendrophyllia elegans*, are now synonymous with *D. gracilis*, which is the older of the two names describing the same species.

181. Festival Tube Corals *Dendrophyllia gracilis* Milne Edwards & Haime, 1848 ● 1⅓ life size ● The Great Reef, Bailechesengel Island, Ngemelis Islands, Belau ● 45 feet/13.7 meters ● Day ● 21 May 1971 ● Similar: USNM No. 47227

Festival Tube Corals are characteristic of many which grow under the ledges of Belau's outer reef walls. A continual competition exists between them and their rivals for living space; other tube coral colonies, black or yellow encrusting sponges, ascidians, various algal forms, boring bivalved mollusks and numerous reef inhabitants.

What was a single tube coral colony has become an assemblage of individual corallites surrounded by yellow sponge. In many instances sponges grow around the base of tube corals, isolating the corallites from one another. This "island-forming" process is more evident in several other photographs. Both sponge and coral continue to grow outward. If the corallites remain above the engulfing sponge, they will survive, though living a quicksand existence.

182. Monet Tube Corals & Festival Tube Corals *Dendrophyllia gracilis* Milne Edwards & Haime, 1848 ● 1¼ life size ● The Great Reef, Bailechesengel Island, Ngemelis Islands, Belau ● 60 feet/18.3 meters ● Day ● 30 July 1974 ● Similar: USNM No. 47229

Monet Tube Corals and Festival Tube Corals are one and the same The Monet Corals (upper center) bulge from a bluish sponge and are possibly losing the battle. A crimson encrusting sponge is to the left. Crustose coralline algae is above the corals. Clusters of little Pink Lace Ascidians are sprinkled across a roughly eight-by-eight-inch square of reef.

Assuming that the Monet and Festival Tube Corals are one species, it is certainly interesting to speculate just why corals living within a few inches of one another would acquire different colors. The tube corals must have cause to be so arrayed.

183. Monet Tube Corals *Dendrophyllia gracilis* Milne Edwards & Haime, 1848 ● White Lace Ascidians, Red, Yellow and Blue Sponges ● Life size ● The Great Reef, Bailechesengel Island, Ngemelis Islands, Belau ● 70 feet/21.3 meters ● Day ● 30 July 1974 ● Similar: USNM No. 47229

On matters of color, Monet Tube Corals are only pink when photographed with corrected artificial light, either strobe or flashbulbs. Otherwise, 30 to 40 feet underwater the flesh color is a light pastel green. Either way both pastels are lovely, equally reminiscent of Monet's lily pond.

The orange-pigmented Festival Tube Corals do not grow lovelier the deeper they live. Immersed in the sea's sapphire-blue light, the orange corallites are muted at best. As a diver descends the face of the reef the Festival Tube Corals turn brown like Autumn leaves. Having no zooxanthellae in their tissues, tube corals, like sea fans and gorgonians, are colored by pigments.

184. Monet Tube Corals *Dendrophyllia gracilis* Milne Edwards & Haime, 1848 ● 1¼ life size ● The Great Reef, Bailechesengel Island, Ngemelis Islands, Belau ● 45 feet/13.7 meters ● Day ● 30 July 1973 ● Similar: USNM No. 47223, 47229

These *Dendrophyllia* and millions of others actually live on the wall of one reef. Turn the pages back and forth to gain an awareness of only a few of the "squares" of reef, each endowed with its own atmosphere. Each photograph reveals a unique arrangement of colors, a distinct mix of life forms. The tube corals are everpresent but their interplay with neighbors is unique. They are a little like period paintings, each the work of a different painter, yet obviously the creations of an age.

185. Monet Tube Corals *Dendrophyllia gracilis* Milne Edwards & Haime, 1848 ● 1¼ life size ● The Great Reef, Bailechesengel Island, Ngemelis Islands, Belau ● 30 feet/9.1 meters ● Day ● 11 August 1973 ● Similar: USNM No. 47223, 47229

These Monet Tube Corals and those on previous plates were not photographed at night. A distinct visual change occurs when the polyps expand. The landscape becomes more diffuse, almost anti-abstract. Structural lines are blurred and existing details are cluttered (Plate 188). Here, the corals wait for night. Both Festival and Monet Tube Coral polyps are orange. Only the pigment color of the flesh covering the corallite surface is different.

186. Monet Tube Corals *Dendrophyllia gracilis* Milne Edwards & Haime, 1848 • 1⅓ life size • The Great Reef, Bailechesengel Island, Ngemelis Islands, Belau • 60 feet/18.3 meters • Day • 10 July 1973 • Similar: USNM No. 47223, 47229

These facing photographs show *Dendrophyllia gracilis* during the day and at night. The pink Monet Tube Corals are inactive but the orange Festival Tube Corals are feeding. That these animals can make this transformation each night is quite amazing. The mouths of a few Monet polyps are seen situated in the center of the calices with flesh-softened septa radiating from them.

Several small fishes populate the reef wall in this photograph. The reef is host to many smaller fishes, within or on its surface in holes in the rock, in sponges and among the corals. The fishes feed on plankton, snatched as it passes in the current. A tiny world is revealed but, if one were to explore this tapestry through a microscope's "eye," the weave would be wondrous and strange as some far and alien planet in the universe.

187. Festival Tube Corals *Dendrophyllia gracilis* Milne Edwards & Haime, 1848 • 1½ life size • The Great Reef, Bailechesengel Island, Ngemelis Islands, Belau • 40 feet/12.2 meters • Night • 9 August 1973 • Similar: USNM No. 47223, 47229, 47230

Festival Tube Coral polyps vary in color, some nearly transparent-white. Others, such as the nearby Monet Tube Corals, are orange. Tube corals are extremely sensitive to light. The flashlights held by my Belauan friend Singer Kochi and myself have already caused several polyps to contract. When I made the photograph the flash of intense light caused the polyps to contract entirely. After one exposure we swam on to other corals not yet disturbed by our disruptive behavior. Tube corals trap drifting plankton that collide with their tentacles. Each tentacle is armed with numerous nematocysts that fire off tiny venomous harpoons. A polyp continuously traps plankton and transfers those caught to its mouth. When successful, a tentacle bends toward the central mouth until both make contact. When the meal is transferred from the tentacle to the mouth, the tentacle bends outward again to await its next midnight traveller. Tiny white stinging nematocysts aline the length of a tentacle to the tips. With this weaponry a polyp subdues plankton, wards off a nibbling reef inhabitant, or, in some corals, kills a fish or serves notice to a diver. Certainly tube coral tentacles are designed for night feeding. I believe many corals, including most tube corals, feed at night to avoid daytime encounters with angelfish that love to . . . "nibble

on they tiny feet," succulent tentacles, nematocysts and all. Many corals expand to feed at night when butterfly and angelfishes sleep nestled in their branches.

188. Monet and Festival Tube Corals *Dendrophyllia gracilis* Milne Edwards & Haime, 1848 • Twice life size • The Great Reef, Bailechesengel Island, Ngemelis Islands, Belau • 40 feet/12.2 meters • Night • 9 August 1973 • Similar: USNM No. 47223, 47229

The color differences and similarities of clusters of nightfeeding tube corals are revealed by their expanded polyps. Monet Tube Corals are distinguished by their pink mouths surrounded by orange tentacles. Festival Tube Coral polyps are uniformly orange with more pigmented flesh covering the corallites than the tentacles.

This larger-than-life-size view shows the tiny orange nematocysts along the largest tentacles. The tube-shaped corallites are spaced with minimal over-lapping of tentacles. The structure of the corallite clumps and competition provides "clearings" between colonies and between the corallites.

189. Monet Tube Coral *Dendrophyllia gracilis* Milne Edwards & Haime, 1848 • Robin Hood Tube Coral *Tubastraea micrantha* (Ehrenberg, 1834) • Twice life size • The Great Reef, Bailechesengel Island, Ngemelis Islands, Belau • 30 feet/9.1 meters • Night • 27 August 1974 • Similar: USNM No. 47225, 47228, 47229 (*D. gracilis*) and Similar: USNM No. 47142, 47143 (*T. micrantha*)

They have not been formally introduced, but this nighttime portrait of Monet Tube Corals clustered on the greenish branches of a Robin Hood Tube Coral is an appropriate beginning. Robin Hood Tube Corals are ahermatypic, yet grow as large and larger than many hermatypic species. The photograph does not adequately illustrate the Robin Hood Tube Coral but the following illustrations are more helpful. Momentarily my interest and my camera were focused on the feeding Monet corals. Had I included both colonies in the photograph, the orange-polyped partner would have appeared like a kitten atop a tiger. Both species' polyps are comparable in size, favoring Robin Hood only a little, but the branches of the nearly black-green coral are large enough to provide sleeping quarters for butterfly fishes who would probably eat the "mattress" were the polyps expanded during the day.

190. Robin Hood Tube Coral *Tubastraea micrantha* (Ehrenberg, 1834) • Life size • The Great Reef, Bailechesengel Island, Ngemelis Islands, Belau • 35 feet/10.7 meters • Day • 22 June 1973 • Photographed: USNM No. 47143

The calcium carbonate skeletons of all the dendrophylliids are quite porous. The smaller and more delicate tube corals break easily. Though porous, the massive base of the Robin Hood Tube Coral is very strong. The *Tubastraea* corallites are aligned in spacious rows along the trunk. Their diameter is similar in width to the Monet and Festival corallites. However, at the base of this Robin Hood Coral, the "tubes" do not greatly extend above the trunk's surface. On the facing page, this species' less massive branching ends are festooned with taller, more closely spaced corallites. Perhaps real estate was less expensive in the earlier days of the colony, permitting more spacious lawns. Actually, the corallites along the base and trunk of the colony acquired their "wealth" with age.

191. Robin Hood Tube Coral *Tubastraea micrantha* (Ehrenberg, 1834) • Life size • Ngerumekaol Pass, Ulong Island, Belau • 14 feet/4.3 meters • Day • 6 October 1967 • Photographed: USNM No. 47142

Branching and corallite formation of a young colony is similar to the outer branches of this adult colony. However, the branches of the young are not as large or crowded. Generally, a juvenile colony sprouts a few sparse branches as it grows outward from a recessed area of the reef wall. Robin Hood Tube Corals live in passes and lagoon areas with sufficient water circulation. Their favorite habitats are the outer reefs and passes where they are the most abundant and grow to impressive sizes.

Both colonies were photographed during the day. At night they feed. Interestingly, the polyps of this tube coral are much less sensitive to the beam of a flashlight and even to the glare of a flashbulb. They seem slow to contract and react only after two or three flashes. Their deep-green pigmented flesh color is nearly non-reflective, requiring two f-stops more exposure than is necessary for other shallow water corals. If a copy of my book *This Living Reef* is available, refer to the Robin Hood ("Green Tube Coral" Plate 46.) The photograph depicts this coral feeding, capturing the ballet-like beauty of its star-tipped tentacles.

Dendrophyllia gracilis lives in the Red Sea through the Indo-Pacific to the Galápagos. *Tubastraea micrantha* also lives in the Red Sea and was collected from Sagami Bay, Japan, Amakura Islands, Micronesia, New Caledonia, the Korean Strait, Bohol, Fiji and Australia's Great Barrier Reef. It is delaying a trip to Waikiki Beach until the Pacific Plate slides the Hawaiian Islands farther westward, or until retirement, whichever occurs first. Other members of the genus live in waters off Panama, the Galápagos, the Gulf of Guinea and the West Indies.

There are about five known species of *Tubastraea* living from just below the surface to 300 feet. Three to 300 feet is the known range of Robin Hood Tube Corals.

192. Belau Tube Coral *Tubastraea* new species • ⅔ life size • The Great Reef, Bailechesengel Island, Ngemelis Islands, Belau • 25 feet/7.6 meters • Day • 10 July 1973 • Holotype: USNM No. 47145 (a similar specimen which was collected near the corals illustrated)

Belau Tube Corals resemble the base branches and corallites of the Robin Hood Tube Coral. Their similarity is not surprising because both are *Tubastraea*. The Belau Tube Coral fills much the same niche as its more delicate *Dendrophyllia* neighbors. It does not grow into large-branched colonies like the Robin Hood Tube Corals.

The Belau Tube Coral is a new unidentified species. On July 10, 1973, I collected a specimen for Dr. Wells who is a world authority on tube corals. When I think about Dr. Wells I remember something Robert Frost once said during a lecture I attended at the University of Miami. Frost explained that every new book he purchased or received as a gift was placed on a shelf where he contemplated its spine for a year, or perhaps many years, until it was a familiar face. When finally at home with the title and sufficiently motivated, Frost removed the book from the shelf and they continued their conversation.

To think that this coral still has no scientific name is frustrating. To realize that another Belau Tube Coral was pried off the reef and dropped in Clorox, to provide a proper corpse, is frustrating. The spine is still being read. But as frustrating as it may be, there is great value in letting a "work in progress" progress unhurried. The child grows and departs the house soon enough.

The Belau Tube Coral is new and rare. Only a handful of clumped colonies were living on the reef. Their salmon-pink color is a pigment, not zooxanthellae, for the coral is ahermatypic like its other relatives. The porous skeleton is comparable to that of the Robin Hood Tube Coral, both having a thicker mass than the Monet and Festival skeletons. Although the polyps feed at night they do not seem to contract entirely during daylight hours. Tentacles of orange flesh are visible at the bottom of some calices.

193. Galápagos Tube Corals *Tubastraea* new species • ¾ life size • Tagus Cove, Isla Isabela, Galápagos, Ecuador • 25 feet/7.6 meters • Day • 27 March 1974 • Holotype: USNM No. 46977 and Paratype: USNM No. 46978, 46979

The Galápagos Tube Coral is an odd find considering the number of scientists who must have followed Darwin to The Enchanted Isles before I collected it from Tagus Cove on March 27, 1974. Immediately several Galápagos Tube Corals found their way to Dr. Wells who examined and described them for future publication. A Holotype and two Paratype specimens are now stored in the Smithsonian collection.

This coral is exceedingly beautiful as seen in the center colony. Almost-transparent flesh barely covers the skeleton. Dr. Wells characterized the corallites as "short and clumped," reminiscent of a pin cushion. He adds that the skeleton is porous and colony formation is by extratentacular budding, typical of the tube corals. Like other related species, Galápagos Tube Corals are ahermatypic. Reddish-orange polyps, the tentacles of which are expanded, contrast with the pale yellow-pigmented flesh covering the corallites.

The rocks and steep hillsides surrounding Tagus Cove have become a difficult-to-erase blackboard for the government of Ecuador. The rocky walls of this amphitheater are painted with the names of many seafarers and their yachts. After some public criticism the name "SEARCHER" was spraypainted with brown paint, converting "E" into "F" and "R" to "P" and so on. Rather than spray all the white letters brown, a new adaptation of protective coloration was employed. However, the novel paint job hardly mattered for above sea level Tagus Cove still looked like a panoramic nautical billboard. High above the crowd, someone had risked life and limb to paint in huge white letters, "CHICKEN OF THE SEA."

Ten feet below sea level, along the cove wall, a galaxy of exotic corals lives and multiplies. To collect, to photograph and to name them expresses man's need to leave one's own mark like any dog, or sea dog. Photography mars the rock least, unless it lures others to the spot.

194. Velvet Chalice Coral *Turbinaria peltata* (Esper, 1794) • 1⅓ life size • North Cove Reef, Macharchar Lagoon, Macharchar Islands, Belau • 70 feet/21.3 meters • Day • 21 June 1971 • Similar: USNM No. 47144

Unlike preceding genera, the Velvet Chalice Coral is hermatypic and a shallow-water reef-builder. The color is that of its zooxanthellae. *Turbinaria peltata* is a common coral, the most common member of the genus having roughly 25 species. The coral inhabits the Great Barrier Reef north to Papua New Guinea, east through the Solomon Islands, and to New Caledonia, Fiji, Micronesia, the Philippines and Malaysia.

In Belau and Papua New Guinea, Velvet Chalice Corals live on seaward reef slopes or in shallow lagoons having relatively clear water. A colony grows to massive proportions, either chalice or foliate. The polyps feed during the day as tidal conditions bring food. The inner surface area of this adult, chalice-shaped colony is many times the size of this illustration. The coral's outer wall lacks polyps but it is covered with flesh. Amazingly, the inner polyps support the whole. The mouths of all the polyps tilt upward, reminding me of baby birds, hungrily awaiting food from the sea.

ACKNOWLEDGMENTS

A book of this nature encompasses many years of my life, enriched by a multitude of friends. The exclusion of any seems neglectful. Some held underwater flashlights while I photographed at night. Others generously took me diving when I had no boat, dived with me to 270 feet, prepared hot meals, provided a roof and bed. Some assisted with proofing, typed, made color prints with great care, edited and copy-edited. My willing publisher supported the book with 50 to 95% infinite patience, spare change and a year's supply of tranquilizers.

If judged a white elephant, the pachyderm is nonetheless, a festive one. I envisioned a row of stained-glass windows smiling through the walls of a cathedral. Their colors stand in sunlight. As I write, Keith Jarrett makes love to his piano. The ivory keys fly like wind-chimes in a gale. You say, "Keep in mind the Board of Directors". Considering the odds, and with nothing to lose, I would like instead, to introduce the 185 major shareholders:

Emiliano Adelbai • Haruo Adelbai • Taro Alexander • Ernest Anderson • Cesare and Ann Antoniacci • Kikutaro Baba • Isaac Bai • Edward Barnard • Arthur Barnett • Frederick Bayer • George Benjamin • George Benjamin Jr. • Jim Bennett • Uldekel and Ermang Besebs • Dick and Rosie Birch • Tewid Boisek • Patrick Bryan • Michelle Burgess • Stephen Cairns • Roman Calces • Cornell and Edith Capa • Joseph Carraha • Edward Castillo • Rene Catala and Ida Catala-Stucki • Fenner Chase • Richard and Freddy Chesher • Drayton and Ann Cochran • John Cochran • Gail Cohen • Barbara Coleman • Vernon Cooper • E.E. Cummings • Thomas Dawson • David Dickerson • Yecheluu Dimas • Nina Dlutaoch • Maureen Downey • Nancy Dukek • Loren and Mabel Eiseley • Walter and Berry Eitel • Lucius Eldredge • Robert Endean • Thomas Ermang • Louis Eschembrenner • Timothy Fagan • Laura Faulkner • Sally Faulkner • Seymour and Alice Faulkner • Sharon Faulkner • Archie Forfar • Martin Forscher • Richard Foster • Ira Friedlander • Carl Gage • Thomas Gibson • Charles and Julianne Golding • Jerry and Idaz Greenberg • Ward and Maryke Griffioen • Ann Guilfoyle • Ernst Haas • Dennis Hanson • Tony Hazlewood • Will Hopkins • Richard Hoar • Frederick Horbert • Harvey Horowitz • Jack Houssian • James Jacob • Richard Janaro • Keith Jarrett • Robert and Chris Johannes • Leonard Jossel • Andre Kertesz • Idesmang Kitalong • Hirao Kloulchad • Singer Kochi • Nina Kowaloff • Yvonne Lefter • Milton Liberty • Kenneth and Gisha Lieberman • Anna Lincoln • Les Line • Isadore and Mary Lipson • Becky Madraisau • Tom Martin • Michael and Maria McCoy • Peter McKinnon • Heath and Judy McLendon • Robert and Nancy McManus • James McVey • Philip Mendez • Yves and Germaine Merlet • Blanche Montgomery • Carl and Ellen Montgomery • Carl Montgomery Jr. • Francisco Morei • Sakie Morriss • John Moylan • Katherine Muzik • Elliot and Phyllis Nagelberg • Sylvain Napoleon • Fred Nathan • George Ngirarsaol • Erica Ngirausui • Yaoch Ngirmang • Mary O'Grady • Dennis Opresko • Demei Otobed • Robert and Hera Owen • Brian Parkinson • Toshiro Paulis • David Pawson • Frank Pecca • Annemarie Philippi • Michel Pichon • Joanne Porinno • Arnold Post • Seymour Post • Richard Randall • Sidney Rapoport • Kenneth and Jane Read • Reg and Shirley Rice • Tom Robbins • Charles Roberts • Ronn Ronch • Robert Ross • Belhaim and Margo Sakuma • Sandra Sharp • Norman Snyder • David Sousa • Walter and Janice Starck II • Chase and Susanne Stevens • Karen Straus • Yosiharu Sungino • Takeshi Suzuki • Mitsuhiro Tada • Ted and Mac Tansy • Suzanne Ternes • Takasi Tokioka • Brian Turner • Yosinao Ubedei • Huzio Utinomi • David Vitarelli • Janice Vitarelli • Sandy Vitarelli • William and Henrietta Vitarelli • Allen Vogel • John and Pie Wells • Jane West • Peter and Ann Wilson • Robert Woodward • Joseph Yockel • Leonard Zoref

CONCEIVED & DESIGNED
BY
DOUGLAS FAULKNER

TYPOGRAPHIC & JACKET DESIGN
BY
JIM BENNETT

EDITORIAL & TECHNICAL ASSISTANCE
BY
KAREN STRAUS FAULKNER

TEXT & COMMENTARY COMPOSITION
BY
PUBLISHERS PHOTOTYPE INC.
CARLSTADT, NEW JERSEY

TITLE PAGES & POETRY & THE FAMILIES
BY
PHOTO LETTERING, INC.
NEW YORK

COLOR SEPARATION & PRINTING & BINDING
BY
TOPPAN PRINTING CO. LTD.
TOKYO